PARTNERSHIP
WITH PARENTS IN
EARLY CHILDHOOD
Today

Sara Miller McCune founded SAGE Publishing in 1965 to support the dissemination of usable knowledge and educate a global community. SAGE publishes more than 1,000 journals and over 800 new books each year, spanning a wide range of subject areas. Our growing selection of library products includes archives, data, case studies and video. SAGE remains majority owned by our founder and after her lifetime will become owned by a charitable trust that secures the company's continued independence.

Los Angeles | London | New Delhi | Singapore | Washington DC | Melbourne

PHILIPPA THOMPSON
HELEN SIMMONS

PARTNERSHIP WITH PARENTS IN EARLY CHILDHOOD

Today

Learning Matters,
A SAGE Publishing Company
1 Oliver's Yard
55 City Road
London EC1Y 1SP

SAGE Publications Inc.
2455 Teller Road
Thousand Oaks, California 91320

SAGE Publications India Pvt Ltd
B 1/I 1 Mohan Cooperative Industrial Area
Mathura Road
New Delhi 110 044

SAGE Publications Asia-Pacific Pte Ltd
3 Church Street
#10-04 Samsung Hub
Singapore 049483

Library of Congress Control Number: 2022948438

British Library Cataloguing in Publication Data

A catalogue record for this book is available from the British Library

Editor: Amy Thornton
Senior project editor: Chris Marke
Project management: TNQ Technologies
Marketing manager: Lorna Patkai
Cover design: Wendy Scott
Typeset by: TNQ Technologies
Printed in the UK

ISBN: 978-1-5296-0590-7
ISBN: 978-1-5296-0589-1 (pbk)

At SAGE we take sustainability seriously. Most of our products are printed in the UK using responsibly sourced papers and boards. When we print overseas we ensure sustainable papers are used as measured by the PREPS grading system. We undertake an annual audit to monitor our sustainability.

CONTENTS

ACKNOWLEDGEMENTS

We would like to thank the support of all contributing authors who have been so enthusiastic in the development of this book. Their wide-ranging experience and knowledge have provided a timely resource when both practitioners and parents are still recovering post pandemic. We hope that this book challenges thinking and generates discussion to acknowledge how truly working together can have benefits for everyone. As parents and practitioners, we have both experienced a range of approaches that stimulated our thinking and wondering how we could address some of the policy and practice stereotypes that can be so damaging to relationships and ultimately the child at the centre of this.

I would like to thank my son Tom, husband Neil, childminder Wendy and the pastoral/medical care (Deborah and Pauline) at Meadowhead School Academy Trust. Through our shared experience of anaphylaxis, this showed how true partnership can make such a difference to everyone's lives. You inspired this book to show how marginalised families need greater understanding and support. Thank you, Philippa.

I would like to thank my husband Jon, and my children Liv and Jack for their endless love and support. I would also like to thank all of the parents that contributed to the research explored within this book. Your stories highlight the need for meaningful partnerships that centre on individualised and respectful support for parents. Thank you for sharing your reflections with us, Helen.

ABOUT THE EDITORS AND CONTRIBUTORS

About the editors

Helen Simmons is a Senior Lecturer in Education (Childhood, Youth and Families) at the University of Northampton, Vice Chair for Policy, Lobbying and Advocacy for the Early Childhood Studies Degrees Network (ECSDN) and a Doctor of Education. Her teaching, research and publications centre on the discipline of early childhood studies, with a particular focus on the sociology of childhood, the social and cultural pressures in modern motherhood and support for a critically reflective early childhood workforce.

Philippa Thompson is a Principal Lecturer in Early Childhood Studies at Sheffield Hallam University and Co-Chair of the ECSDN. Her research interests in early childhood include play, participation, co-production, outdoor learning and parents/children living with anaphylaxis. She has a strong practice background of 20 years across a broad range of settings in the United Kingdom and internationally. Philippa advocates regularly for changes to policy and practice and recognition for the sector and a graduate workforce.

About the contributors

Professor Tony Bertram has honorary academic posts at Birmingham and Wolverhampton Universities and currently is a Visiting Professor at Birmingham City University. He is a Director of the Centre for Research in Early Childhood (CREC) and a Director of Amber Publications & Training Ltd (APT). He is the Co-Founder and Trustee of the European Early Childhood Education Research Association (EECERA) and is currently the Coordinating Editor of the European Early Childhood Education Research Journal (EECERJ).

Jenny Boldrin is a Senior Lecturer for the BA (Hons) Early Childhood Studies degree at the University of Derby and the Academic Lead for the BA (Hons) Early Childhood Studies Online Top Up. She has a particular research interest in the early experiences of previously looked-after children and the ways in which professionals can work to support them and their adoptive families.

Penny Borkett retired as a Senior Lecturer in Early Years and Early Childhood Studies from Sheffield Hallam University. During her working life, she worked as a Teaching Assistant, Portage Worker, Special Educational Needs Co-ordinator and Integrated Services Co-ordinator in two Sure Start Children's Centre before joining academia and working within it for 14 years. She has always been passionate about inclusion, especially when focussing on children with Special Educational Needs and Disabilities and is pleased to have written in this book, which seeks to focus on the importance of working in partnership with parents in a democratic and supportive way.

Aaron Bradbury is a Principal Lecturer in Early Childhood at Nottingham Trent University with a specialism in Early Help, Child Development and Child Protection. He is currently a member of the Executive Committee of the ECSDN and is the Co-Founder of the Early Years Academy. He has an online platform for practitioners and all Early Years professionals, Early Years Reviews by Aaron, which can be accessed on the web or via his app.

Hattie Campbell is a Senior Lecturer at the University of East London in the School of Education and Communities. Her research interests focus on positions of power and micropolitical constructs in diverse educational contexts

Dr Valerie Daniel is a qualified teacher with over 30 years' experience with the last 15 years as a Maintained Nursery School head teacher and more recently an executive head teacher over two schools. Valerie has a deep interest in the dynamics of the current Early Years Sector and received her Doctorate in Education from the University of Birmingham on her thesis titled 'The Perceptions of a Leadership Crisis in the Early Years Sector (EYS)'.

Dr Katarzyna Fleming is a Senior Lecturer and Researcher in the Sheffield Institute of Education at Sheffield Hallam University. Previously a special needs teacher, Katarzyna currently focusses on research within the areas of co-production, parent–practitioner partnership, critical pedagogies and the community of philosophical inquiry.

Donna Gaywood was a doctoral student at Birmingham City University and CREC. Her studies were supervised by Professor Tony Bertram, Professor Chris Pascal and Dr Jane O'Connor. Donna is now a Senior Lecturer at the University of Gloucestershire teaching on the Children, Young People and Families course, in the School of Health and Social Care.

Davis Alexander Gisuka (Advance Diploma in Social Work) is an Early Childhood Development and Education Specialist at Children in Crossfire, Tanzania, and Accredited Science of Early Childhood Development (SECD) Regional Facilitator by Aga Khan University. He has supported teachers and parents to support and improve children's literacy and numeracy through the implementation of Tanzania Pre-Primary Curriculum and day care centres. He is a Global Leader for Young Children in Africa.

Wendy Kettleborough is an avid advocate for children, parents, professionals and lifelong learning. Her focus and application of developmental psychology, applied neuroscience and brain health has positively impacted on hundreds of parents and children across the Education, Social and PVI sectors. Her longitudinal study of 'Children and Schemas' and the subsequent development and delivery of 'Parents Are Experts' have resulted in the publication of four children's books

Martin Needham is an Associate Head of School of Childhood, Youth and Education Studies at Manchester Metropolitan University. He initially worked as an early years teacher, and then in developing Early Years services, before taking up an academic role that has focussed on workforce development, especially engaging with parents to support early learning.

Dr Kay Owen is a Chartered Psychologist and Senior Lecturer in Education and Childhood at the University of Derby. Her research interests mainly centre around the role of play, creativity and relationships.

Professor Chris Pascal (OBE) is an Honorary Professor at Birmingham City University and Co-Director of the charitable CREC. Pascal has served as a UK Ministerial Advisor and as an Early Years Specialist Adviser to the UK House of Commons Select Committee on Education. She founded, and is now President of, the EECERA and the Co-Editor of the EECERJ.

Mwajuma Davina Rwebangila (MA, Development Studies) is a Tanzanian Executive Director for Tanzania Early Childhood Development Network (TECDEN) and the Co-Chair for Tanzania National Early Childhood Development (ECD) Stakeholders Group, National Multisectoral Early Childhood Development Technical Working Group and Secretariat Group. She provides strategic leadership and technical guidance to Tanzania ECD Network to ensure ECD stakeholders effectively support the Government of Tanzania in promoting early childhood programmes. She is a Global Leader for Young Children in Africa.

INTRODUCTION

Engagement with parents has long been at the forefront of early childhood practice and policy. However, there appears to have been an overall acceptance that parents are a homogenous group and that if they follow the processes set out by the early childhood setting, then their child will settle and achieve successfully as a result (McWayne et al., 2022). This book seeks to challenge this thinking and asks the reader to consider the perspectives of those who may currently be marginalised by this approach. It is accepted that not all marginalised groups can be represented in one book but that this will provoke thinking about how settings can become more inclusive in their practice and more welcoming to all families and consider the starting point at the home rather than the setting. With insight into real-life issues explored within the different chapters, readers can reflect on how they can develop their practice and provide meaningful support for children and families. The combination of critical approaches and theoretical perspectives, applied to professional practice, will provide a useful resource for lecturers, students and practitioners alike. The book is accessible to a range of readers (including parents) whilst providing suggestions for lecturers for their teaching alongside supporting practitioners to question their own practice. The book deconstructs the current rhetoric around parent–practitioner partnership from a policy and practice perspective whilst sharing experiences of parents and considering how those working in early childhood can really make a difference.

Why this book is needed

Support for early childhood has never been more important than in the current political climate. Coming out of a world pandemic and entering a cost-of-living crisis has had a significant impact on children and families. Young children and their families need significant support across all realms of health, social care and education. Cattan et al. (2022) report on the impact of the huge inequalities in home environments for young children and how this has a marked impact on both socioemotional and cognitive development. It is crucial that early childhood practitioners in the United Kingdom get relationships right and are encouraged to think across education, health and social care when working with families.

The term 'parents' is clearly defined at the beginning of each chapter, along with practitioner. It is important for all those who have parental responsibility AND those who have caring responsibilities are acknowledged under this definition. Young children are often cared for by a wide range of adults, and these come together under the umbrella term of 'parents' as having equal importance for this book. The chapters all refer to parents who have perhaps not been included in previous writing and certainly are not acknowledged significantly in current policy. This book confronts the reader at times, yet allow them to reflect and think about their own unconscious bias and the current practice they may have observed. It hopes to create opportunities for discussions and change.

Early childhood practitioners are also defined to include not only educational settings but also professionals who work across all sectors with children aged 0–8 years old. The term 'early childhood' is chosen carefully. It reflects the use of the term used globally and acknowledges early childhood studies an academic discipline. Whilst Early Years is a common term in practice in the United Kingdom, it can be interpreted as an educational term as well as political and focusses on children aged 0–5 years.

Each chapter of this book considers how to truly listen to all parents who know their children best; the importance of respecting and valuing equality, diversity and inclusion; how leaders must provide clear leadership and review practice whilst listening to the voice of parents. Meaningful engagement with families will also be explored throughout. This will include, as highlighted through Birth to Five Matters (Early Years Coalition, 2021, pp. 28–29) reflections on how and why families engage, and approaches that support each family on an individual basis. With the proposal of 'Best Start for Life' (DHSC, 2021), including recommendations for Family Hubs really taking shape, it is a crucial time for all practitioners in early childhood, across all sectors, to reflect on and reconsider ways of working.

What it will cover

This book considers and critiques current practice more widely and challenges the true roles of parents and practitioners across early childhood. It asks, how can we do more? Policy documents and research are currently confusing for early childhood practitioners, and they are charged with working with a wide range of parents often without training or further advice. Unconscious bias also needs to be challenged sensitively by leaders who themselves may need further development. The book centres on important aspects of contemporary parenting and explores social, cultural and structural pressures within modern parenting.

Each chapter considers a group of families that may be labelled as 'hard to reach' or struggle with having their voices heard or are positioned as a 'group' and become no longer seen as having individual needs. It challenges the negative concepts of language such as 'hard to reach' to consider that the problem lies in policy and practice rather than with families. The book brings experts together to suggest practical advice whilst raising the key issues faced, critiquing the source of these issues and some of the wider questions that need to be considered.

The book challenges assumptions and asks current and future practitioners to reflect and challenge their current practice and ask themselves 'Do I *really* work in partnership with parents?' Some of this reading may be uncomfortable, but it is time for these conversations to be had if early childhood is to be truly inclusive.

Key points and themes in this book

- Themes centre on silences within modern parenting and how, via a label of 'hard to reach', parents are oppressed and their voices not heard.

- This is a practical book with a focus on the individual needs of parents, often grouped under the banner of 'inclusion'.

- Chapters will deconstruct these experiences and consider respectful, co-productive ways for students and early childhood practitioners, across the sectors, to celebrate and empower parents.

- This book encourages insight into myth busting, challenging misconceptions and encouraging a relational approach to support and recognising the importance of whole family and extended family support that values generational insight and cultural history.

- It explores strategies for meaningful support from early childhood practitioners, through the critique of current policy and practice, exploring the importance of critical reflection regarding positionality, power and professional identity.

Book chapters in detail

Chapter 1: The politics of parenting

Chapter 1 is written by Helen Simmons and explores the rise in structural attention on parenting that has developed in recent years, along with a focus on early intervention. The spotlight on parenting has increased as neuroscientific research has developed and highlighted the importance of the 0–3 age range for all aspects of development. Early childhood experts have called for this research to be seen as evidence for a highly qualified and well-valued early childhood workforce, but increasingly, what can be seen instead is the use of neuroscientific research embedded into parenting intervention policy and agenda.

Chapter 2: The potential of co-production

Chapter 2 is written by Katarzyna Fleming and Penny Borkett, and it explores the potential of co-production in enabling inclusive partnerships with parents and carers of children categorised as having Special Educational Needs and Disability (SEND) within the context of early childhood and beyond. While the focus here is predominantly on the lived experiences of families with children with SEND, this chapter argues that the discussed potential of co-productive partnerships can also aid relationships with families in all settings from conception through to the age of 25.

Chapter 3: Understanding food allergies and anaphylaxis

Chapter 3 is written by Philippa Thompson, and it explores the experiences and related literature of children and families living with anaphylaxis as a result of food allergies. Anaphylaxis and food allergies are explained and the context is set initially in terms of global statistics. The impact on parents liaising with a wide range of practitioners and in social situations is explored from both an autoethnographic position and that of current research. The well-being of parents is emphasised, and the chapter encourages students and practitioners to reflect on their own practice and potential unconscious bias through reflective practice exercises. Also acknowledged and explored are the ways in which both practitioners and parents are positioned in policy and how this can have a significant impact on developing co-productive relationships. The chapter takes the position that in current practice these parents are marginalised and through a deeper understanding relationships can significantly improve children's outcomes in both health and education.

Chapter 4: Race and inequality in early childhood health

Chapter 4 is written by Valerie Daniel, and it explores child health equity and what it would mean for every child in the United Kingdom to have what they need to be as healthy as possible. In the United Kingdom, it would seem entirely feasible that all children should have access to basic health determinants like clean water, sanitation and adequate nutrition, so why would there be irrefutable evidence of vast health inequities in early childhood? The simple answer to this question is that social and economic factors also play a major role in shaping children's health outcomes. Early childhood development is a critical element in health equity: the earliest years of a child's life provide a window that can either determine lifelong vulnerability or create opportunities for children to thrive and grow.

Chapter 5: Understanding and supporting adoptive families

Chapter 5 is written by Jenny Boldrin, and it explores the fundamental principle that adoption represents a process, rather than a single event. In viewing adoption through this lens, professionals can begin to acknowledge the individual narratives which provide the threads of the process, casting a broader net in understanding the journey the family is on. The point at which the narratives of parents and children become intertwined through adoption must not be viewed as the beginning of the process, rather a single point on a much more complex and nuanced journey for all involved.

Chapter 6: Working with LGBT+ parent-led families

Chapter 6 is written by Aaron Bradbury, and it explores many aspects of working with parents and carers who identify as lesbian, gay, bisexual and transgender within the early childhood sector. It considers aspects of working with parents who are under-represented in society, thinking about ways in which children and parents can be supported and practice can be enhanced. Families come in all shapes and sizes, and it is a common misconception that they should all be treated the same. It is of course a myth that LGBT+ families do in fact need to be treated differently. Being treated differently is not the answer, but treating them so that they are represented is. This chapter goes onto further look at many aspects of the role of an early childhood practitioner and what is needed to ensure that LGBT+ parent-led families are given the space to be represented.

Chapter 7: Perspectives on multilingualism

Chapter 7 is written by Martin Needham, and it explores the advantages and challenges of supporting the home language or languages that children have access to. The chapter explores evidence that English as dominant language may displace and weaken fluency in the home language. The author argues that there are many potential short- and long-term advantages of maintaining bilingualism in early childhood and explores some of the strategies that settings and families might adopt to support multilingualism.

Chapter 8: Cultural approaches to parenting

Chapter 8 is written by Hattie Campbell, and it explores the importance of culture, constructed through interaction with others and associated with social groups. However, no two individuals within a group share the same cultural characteristics. The chapter draws attention to the competing definitions of parenting culture. Forging meaningful relations with parents is the subject of much debate, with inclusion and diversity at the heart of early childhood practice. While legislation and policy are solid indicators for inclusion and diversity, there is still confusion about how practitioners move beyond and into meaningful territory with parents. Indeed, while early childhood settings celebrate diversity, practitioners experience discomfort talking with parents about cultural differences, except in the context of shared events where early childhood professionals can unwittingly sweep individuality aside.

Chapter 9: Supporting refugee families

Chapter 9 is written by Donna Gaywood, Tony Bertram and Chris Pascal, and it explores research which looked at the lived experiences of refugee children in early childhood education and care. The children and their parents in the research had very conflicted feelings about the Early Years practitioners and their settings. Staff all expressed compassion towards the families and recognised their pre- and peri-migration experiences but were largely ignorant of their daily challenges. Practitioners seemed to be unknowingly influenced by wider narratives about refugees, which negatively impacted the parents. They followed *taken-for-granted* practice norms which tended to marginalise the parents. This chapter will outline how the way we think about refugees impacts relationship building with parents and how unquestioned practice norms can be unhelpful.

Chapter 10: Student mothers in higher education

Chapter 10 is written by Kay Owen and Helen Simmons, and it explores experiences of student mothers, shared through a recent research project. During the 'second wave' of the coronavirus pandemic, research participants were drawn from undergraduate and postgraduate programmes within the discipline of Education and Childhood, in a UK university. The research was initiated in response to the strains and pressures academic staff had noted amongst student mothers. The chapter explores a range of issues that student mothers shared, resultant from their perceived need to excel in both roles, reflecting the internalisation of societal pressures that can be associated with intensive parenting ideologies. This chapter explores the reflections of participants regarding pressures and important sources of support for student mothers, paying close attention to the role of the early childhood practitioner.

Chapter 11: Practice perspective: Parents as experts

Chapter 11 is written by Wendy Kettleborough, and it explores strategies that encourage the positioning of parents *as experts* in relation to their children. This is an innovative project developed by the author who has a passion for truly listening to parents and taking time to understand how best to work together. The chapter takes the reader through how a programme has developed in Sheffield that gives parents the lead to truly work together to build relationships in the interest of the whole family. It encourages the recognition that 'perception' and 'mindset' drive how individuals act, react and interact with others. Connection and positive interactions have a significant impact on the self-efficacy and emotional well-being of all practitioners, parents and children, and this chapter explores some of the ways, along with the challenges, in ensuring that children, parents and practitioners feel seen, heard and valued.

Chapter 12: Practice perspective: Learning from Tanzania

Chapter 12 is written by Mwajuma Kibwana, Davis Gisuka and Philippa Thompson. The three authors met at the World Forum in 2022 where Mwajuma and Davis presented about this project. This chapter explains the influence of sensitive parental engagement on learning at home and in school environments during the pandemic. It challenges the reader to consider the high reliance on digital communication in the United Kingdom and that during the COVID-19 pandemic our approach meant many families were isolated due to lack of Internet access or the devices required. This project shows how a true understanding of the needs of families during difficult times can also have unexpected benefits. Relationships and regular communication were key to this project and are at the heart of all quality early childhood practice.

References

Cattan, S., Fitzsimons, E., Goodman, A., Phimister, A., Ploubidis, G., & Wertz, J. (2022). *Early childhood inequalities* (vol. 1). Institute for Fiscal Studies.

Department for Health and Social Care (DHSC). (2021) *The best start for life, a vision for the first 1001 critical days: The early years healthy development review report.* Retrieved from: https://assets.publishing. service.gov.uk/government/uploads/system/uploads/attachment_data/file/973112/The_best_start_for_life_a_ vision_for_the_1_001_critical_days.pdf (Accessed 16th September 2022).

Early Years Coalition. (2021). *Birth to five matters: Non-statutory guidance for the early years foundation stage.* Early Education.

McWayne, C., Hyun, S., Diez, V., & **Mistry, J.** (2022) 'We feel connected … and like we belong": A parent-led, staff-supported model of family engagement in early childhood. *Early Childhood Education Journal, 50,* 445–457. Retrieved from: https://doi.org/10.1007/s10643-021-01160-x

1 THE POLITICS OF PARENTING

HELEN SIMMONS

CHAPTER OBJECTIVES

By the end of this chapter, you will be able to:

- Consider the rise in political attention on parenting
- Reflect on the messages embedded into current parenting intervention and the potential impact
- Explore strategies to ensure the inclusion of parental, family and community voices in future provision
- Consider the role of the early childhood practitioner in supporting parents

KEY DEFINITIONS

Parents

Any person who has parental responsibility or has care of a young child during early childhood (from conception to eight years of age).

Parenting culture

Ideas, behaviours and social norms associated with parenting.

Parenting intervention

Government directives and formal strategies that aim to support children and families.

Practitioner

A person who is qualified to work with children (from conception to 8 years old) across health, education and social care.

(Continued)

(Continued)

Problematisation

The process of regarding something as a problem, in need of a solution.

Professionalisation

The process of acquiring qualities, status and/or qualifications for those within a specific role.

Neuroscientific research

Research that centres on the study of the brain and links to behaviour and cognitive development.

Introduction

This chapter will explore the rise in structural attention on parenting that has developed since the Allen report (2011, p. xiv) highlighted the 'right kind of parenting' and the importance of early intervention. The spotlight on parenting has increased as **neuroscientific research** has developed and highlighted the importance of the 0–3 age range for all aspects of development. Early childhood experts have called for this research to be seen as evidence for a highly qualified and well-valued early childhood workforce, but increasingly, what can be seen instead is the use or misuse of neuroscientific research embedded into political agenda 'with a focus on deficit parents' (Vandenbroek et al., 2017, p. 13).

This focus on **parenting intervention** was echoed in the Autumn 2021 Spending Review as government ministers allocated funding across England with an aim for 'Start for Life services, perinatal mental health support, breastfeeding services, and parenting programmes' (foundationyears.org, 2022). Whilst it is heartening to see a focus on early childhood and support for new parents, it is also important to consider embedded political narratives that consistently use parents, and particularly mothers, as a 'scapegoat' to 'negate state responsibility' (Burman, 2008, p. 154). This chapter will explore some of these dominant narratives within current parenting support and consider the implications of political intervention and surveillance (Simmons, 2020) in relation to the provision of support for new parents.

The spotlight on parenting

The development of our understanding of brain development since the early 2000s (e.g. Gerhadt, 2004) brought with it an increased focus on the critical period of early childhood. Government initiatives and directives began to include recommendations regarding the fundamental importance of strong attachment and secured early relationships and how these aspects of development link directly to the foundations for learning, the building of sustained relationships and the meeting outcomes in later childhood and into adulthood.

Some examples of reports and governmental directives that have included a focus on parenting are as follows:

Allen. (2011). *Early intervention: The next steps. An independent report to her Majesty's Government* by Graham Allen MP. The Stationery Office: highlighted the 'right kind of parenting' (2011, p. xiv) and the importance of early intervention.

All Party Parliamentary Group (APPG). (2015). *Conception to age 2: First 1001 days. Perinatal inquiry – Evidence sessions on first 1001 days.* UK: focussed on support for babies and infants, with neuroscientific research and attention on parenting intervention linking to positive outcomes for children and families.

Clarke et al. (2017). *Helping parents to parent.* London: Social Mobility Commission: recommended an increase in universal parenting programmes and suggested that they 'are shown to enhance parental knowledge about child development, equip them with knowledge of the most effective parenting strategies' (2017, p. 30) with parenting described as a 'public health issue' (2017, p. 5).

Most recently, we have seen the 'Best Start for Life' strategy (DHSC, 2021) which centres on the importance of the first 1001 days as a critical period. This initiative focusses on six key action areas:

1 Seamless support for families: a coherent joined up Start for Life offer available to all families.

2 A welcoming hub for families: Family Hubs as a place for families to access Start for Life services.

3 The information families need when they need it: designing digital, virtual and telephone offers around the needs of the family.

4 An empowered Start for Life workforce: developing a modern skilled workforce to meet the changing needs of families.

5 Continually improving the Start for Life offer: improving data, education, outcomes, and proportionate inspection.

6 Leadership for change: ensuring local and national accountability and building the economic case.

Best Start for Life (DHSC, 2021, p. 8)

Current initiatives include important messages regarding support for infant feeding, professional development within the workforce and a recognition of the need to support families from diverse social and cultural contexts. Principles for designing the Best Start for Life offer explore the importance of collaboration, a relational approach with continuity of care and consistency of messages. Support for parents and recognition of the importance of early childhood is essential. It is encouraging to see a commitment to provision that supports this age range, along with their families, such as those highlighted above.

Some questions do remain though, particularly regarding how support will take shape and how it will consider the voice of new parents and the voice of the early childhood workforce. As we see throughout this book, true partnership working with parents is holistic, respectful and empowering, and anything other than this may add to isolation for parents and limited engagement with support and initiatives. Narratives that suggest a one-size-fits-all philosophy to parenting support should continue to be questioned by a critically reflective and politically engaged workforce.

As highlighted at the start of this chapter, Autumn 2021 saw the government set out its Early Years Spending Review, outlining the strategies to support the sector, post COVID-19. An example of how, as a critically reflective workforce, we can work together to raise our questions can be seen in the response from the Early Childhood Studies Degrees Network (ECSDN) below.

REFLECTION

ECSDN Spending Review Response

Early Years Funding: Autumn Spending Review 2021

On 27th October, the Chancellor outlined the 2021 spending review, with further early childhood related detail from Children and Families Minister following on from this.

The key announcements are:

- Government is investing additional funding for the early years entitlements worth £160m in 2022–23, £180m in 2023–24 and £170m in 2024–25. This is for local authorities to increase hourly rates paid to childcare providers for the government's childcare entitlement offers and reflects the costs of inflation and national living wage increases.

- £500 million over the next three years to transform 'Start for Life' and family help services in half of the council areas across England. This will fund a network of Family Hubs, Start for Life services, perinatal mental health support, breastfeeding services, and parenting programmes.

- Over £200 million a year for the continuation of the holiday activities and food programme, providing enriching activities and healthy meals for disadvantaged children during school holidays.

https://foundationyears.org.uk/2021/10/key-spending-review-announcements-and-the-early-years-recovery-programme/

ECSDN Response:

The Early Childhood Studies Degrees Network (ECSDN) is encouraged by this increase in funding and investment in early childhood and look forward to further detail regarding how this will be allocated.

We welcome further clarification on the following messages within the 'Early Years Recovery programme' outlined in the Foundation Years Factsheet (foundationyears.org, 2021):

> *Deliver a universal training offer, together with targeted support to leaders and practitioners, to create a more sustainable, self-supporting system;*

> *Strengthen specialist expertise and leadership in the sector by boosting skills to develop children's early language and maths, as well as their personal and social development;*

> *Improve the capacity of the early years workforce to support children with special educational needs;*

> *Train practitioners to support parents with home learning, which is one of the biggest drivers of early outcomes and future attainment.*

The Early Childhood Studies Degrees Network (ECSDN) recognise that our graduates are extremely well placed to support this agenda due to the holistic nature of our degrees. We therefore look forward to seeing how the Early Years Recovery Programme will support the workforce in terms of pay and status.

Early Childhood Studies is an academic discipline with interdisciplinary and transdisciplinary working at its centre. Undergraduate, postgraduate students and alumni are equipped with outstanding knowledge and experience, and their expertise are essential in advocating for the health, well-being and education of all children and their families.

We believe that our work in producing Early Childhood Graduate Practitioner Competencies (ECSDN, 2018) which 'make a significant contribution to strengthening a graduate-led Early Childhood workforce that is responsive to workforce needs and improves outcomes for children' compliment the priorities outlined in the spending review. We therefore welcome further communication regarding our shared aims and commitment to a well-qualified and highly valued early childhood workforce.

Dr Helen Simmons (ECSDN Vice Chair Policy, Lobbying and Advocacy) and Philippa Thompson (ECSDN Co-Chair)

- How are parents supported through the spending review?
- How are practitioners supported through the spending review?
- Why is it important that the ECSDN responded to the spending review?

Political intervention: support or surveillance?

What the reports, initiatives and campaigns highlighted in the previous section and current political directives regarding early childhood have in common is a heavy focus on parenting. Parenting intervention strategies within national and international early childhood directives are described as 'wholly admirable' by Penn (2019, p. 3) in her consideration of the World Health Organisation (WHO) International Child Development Steering Group (ICDSG) – 'Advancing Early Childhood Development: from Science to Scale'. A commitment to reducing child suffering and improving child health is, of course, welcome and essential. But, as outlined by Penn (2019, p. 3), we do need to carefully consider any embedded messages within national and international intervention strategies:

> The assumption that someone from the outside has to intervene with a detailed, targeted, technocratic programme, and that the application of this programme will somehow change the balance between poor and rich countries, and enable poor countries to perform better in the long term, is an absurdity in the light of the economic figures.

When supporting parents, it is important that we do not facilitate messages encouraging the 'problematization' (Rose, 1999, p. xi) and 'professionalisation' (Furedi, 2008, p. 180) of modern parenting. Parenting is a unique experience with many complexities, and parenting agenda has been challenged by some from an ethical perspective, particularly in relation to the recognition of diversity in families and their circumstances. Holloway and Pimlott-Wilson, for example, have raised concerns about parenting education that is 'based on the assumption that parenting is a context free skill' (2012, p. 96).

Concerns have also been raised regarding dominant narratives embedded into parenting education that may have 'been shaped by middle-class values, with working-class parents being encouraged to behave in middle-class ways' (Holloway & Pimlott-Wilson, 2012, p. 96) with Johnston and Swanson (2006, p. 22) agreeing that 'there are clearly racial and class biases in the social construction of good and bad mothers'. It is possible that, through the political representation of science and more specifically, neuroscience, we are losing sight of the individual at the heart of the support.

With progression in our understanding of how babies' brains develop and therefore advice for new parents regarding developing of attachments and early social interaction, we need to ensure that we recognise the many factors that can impact the lives of families – culture, context and environment should not be underestimated. When reflecting on global discourses of parenting intervention, Penn (2019, p. 12) considers the following areas as essential for investigation:

- *The understanding and nuances of child rights in different circumstances*

- *Cultural sensitivity, and the place for local knowledge and livelihoods (context and history)*

- *The nature and the role of the language(s), especially the language of instruction in any project of schooling*

- *The importance of the arts – which is almost entirely ignored in conventional programming*
- *Intergenerational interdependence (family circumstances and views)*
- *The importance of gender and gender-based roles and their relation to childcare*
- *The rules, structures, and processes of those who seek to intervene*
- *The wider political climate and its impact*
- *The nature of evaluation, who does it, what criteria are used and how it is used.*

Keller (2018, pp. 11414–11419) also raise the following important points, regarding parenting intervention strategies:

- *Many intervention programmes aimed at fostering good parenting and infant/ childcare are based on principles of attachment theory expressed as positive parenting practices.*
- *Scientifically, these programmes derive their applicability and effectiveness on data from a small and narrow sample of the world's population; assume the existence of fixed developmental pathways and pit scientific knowledge against indigenous knowledge.*
- *Parenting programmes in Western countries apply attachment-based principles of positive parenting to families no matter what their sociocultural background may be.*
- *To understand the quality of parenting strategies, the cultural beliefs and practices in which they are embedded, that is, the local context and the living conditions of the local people, need to be understood.*

As we continue to develop strategies to support parents, nationally and globally, we can use the above areas for investigation to ensure a reflective and ethical approach. It is all too easy to fall into a rigid, one-size-fits-all approach in supporting families, but we need to ask ourselves if this is helpful. Real support is not judgemental or full of narratives that bear no resemblance to the lives of the families we are aiming to help. By listening and considering context, environments and our own ethical practice, we can move forward with meaningful support for families. An example of this could be through considering, with a critical eye, the theory that is deeply embedded into our practice.

REFLECTION

Individually, or in small groups, consider the following questions in relation to planning support for parents:

(Continued)

(Continued)

Why is it important that 'local context' and living conditions should be understood when supporting parents?

What other factors should be considered when planning support for families?

What could be the implications when these factors are not considered?

Valuing family and community history

As reflective **practitioners**, a key part of supporting parents is to ensure their inclusion in the planning and facilitation of provision. This needs to be more than a tokenistic gesture and instead ensure that culture, context and beliefs are truly embedded into the fabric of practice. This inclusion must also go deeper than the immediate families and consider the importance of generational learning as a key to unlocking the rich and diverse histories that help to form local communities.

With current initiatives, including, as highlighted earlier in this chapter, The Best Start for Life (DHSC, 2021) advocating for Family Hubs that support children and families, there is a real opportunity to learn from global approaches that have placed local narratives at the centre of the development of provision. Kjørholt, Matafwali and Mofu (in Kjørholt & Penn, 2019, p. 167), for example, used grandparents' memories of childhood in rural Zambia as 'a point of departure to create dialogue and implement a local-orientated approach to the development of Early Childhood Development (ECD) centers'. In their approach, Kjørholt, Matafwali and Mofu recognised the importance that history, oral traditions, songs and play has in forming local identities and values. The approach used the following four elements as a starting point when planning the provision:

1 Local Language

2 Locally Knowledge as expressed by play and oral traditions, such as stories, riddles, songs.

3 A child-to-child approach: older children participating as teachers

4 A generational approach to education and parenting – grandparents as staff in ECDs.

Kjørholt, Matafwali and Mofu (in Kjørholt &Penn, 2019, p. 169)

Learning from the past will inform the future, and providing a space for children and families to be supported within an environment that recognises the impact of local culture is an essential part of this. This generational-led approach may also help policy writers to recognise the importance of including the local community and families in the planning of provision. It is all too easy to take a top-down approach in initiatives and planning, but we must continue to ask who the real experts are.

As stated by Kjørholt, Matafwali and Mofu (in Kjørholt & Penn, 2019, p. 169):

> For policies and practices related to early childhood, this (approach) implies respect and humility related to the value of often 'hidden' languages, history and local epistemologies of knowledge embedded in everyday life, to a great extent often overlooked in global investment thinking.

Critically reflective practice and engagement with respectful approaches such as this will help us to facilitate a provision which is meaningful and appropriate to the environment that it forms part of and the people that are at the heart of it.

CASE STUDY: FOCUS ON RESEARCH

Simmons (2020), 'Surveillance of Modern Motherhood: Experiences of universal Parenting Courses', explored the experiences of mothers of children aged 0–3 years who attended universal parenting courses in the United Kingdom.

The key findings from the research as follows:

1 Parenting courses can provide opportunities for new mothers to build daily structures and social networks and reduce feelings of isolation.

2 Some negative experiences of parenting courses occur when practitioners are considered 'pushy' or 'non-neutral', particularly regarding sensitive areas such as breastfeeding or the reaching of developmental milestones. It is important that professionals delivering universal parenting courses are well-qualified, critically reflective practitioners who understand the needs of new mothers and young children and can deliver appropriately individualised support.

3 Participants recognise a place within society for parenting courses when they are practical, supportive, individualised and neutral rather than formulaic, homogenous or grounded in psychoanalytical or neurodevelopmental underpinnings, which can promote feelings of judgement or added pressure.

4 Findings link to the wider 'parenting culture' with societal pressures, motherhood ideologies, support or comparisons between mothers and other aspects of interpersonal surveillance, for example, social media and celebrity culture, adding to the challenge of finding confidence and agency within the role.

5 Self-surveillance is identified as the most powerful aspect of modern motherhood. Challenges include a reluctance to discuss 'taboo' aspects of motherhood

(Continued)

(Continued)

such as challenges with instant attachment following birth and the internalisation of social and cultural pressures.

6 It is important to note that, although there are clear levels of surveillance that are embedded into society, there is also evidence of agency and autonomy in the responses to these levels which were developed through strong social networks, support systems and the retaining of identity.

- Using the research outlined here, along with the 'Valuing family and community history' section above, how could parenting courses be planned to use a local-orientated approach?

- Why is it important that the practitioners who deliver parenting courses are critically reflective?

- What may be examples of 'parenting culture' and how are they potentially impacting on the experiences of new mothers?

Social networking and maternal identity

Along with valuing family and community history, localised support opportunities provide an important opportunity for parents to meet other parents. The importance of adult interaction cannot be underestimated, particularly for new mothers who may not otherwise have a chance to see another adult during the day. Recent research (Simmons, 2020) identified the following reasons why new mothers attended a Universal Parenting Course:

- Adult interaction
- The importance of having structure to a day
- Feeling isolated
- Social interaction for child
- A place to breastfeed
- Specific need to developmental reason
- Need to practical advice

Simmons (2020, p. 74)

Out of the above reasons, the need for adult interaction was, by far, the main factor identified for seeking additional support from a parenting course. Interestingly, this support was not sought out of a desire to learn more about baby brain development or to learn about the theory behind developmental milestones, but to seek out a support network at a potentially isolating time. The need for 'camaraderie' (participant response, Simmons, 2020, p. 76) played an important role in the early days of motherhood.

The opportunity to share stories and practical tips and find honesty and humour in the experiences during the transition to a new chapter of their lives is of great importance. This is something that was not possible during the global pandemic, and the impact of this on the mental health of parents is something that we are yet to see the full extent of. With the restriction of not only social networking opportunities but also support from health care and early childhood professionals, the planning for initiatives that address the impact of this on maternal identity and mental health needs to consider the aspects of support that mothers themselves feel is the most important.

Douglas and Michaels (2005, p. 250) describe motherhood as something that is its most enjoyable as a 'collective experience' with Davis (2012, p. 212) agreeing that opportunities for social interaction and support that is led by parents will ensure 'mutual pleasure in the delight that motherhood can bring, but also with the aim of alleviating some of the difficulties and inequities that they face'.

REFLECTION

In May 2022, Professor Jacqueline Dunkley-Bent, Chief Midwifery Officer in England, wrote a blog titled 'Bringing awareness to maternal mental health'. In the piece, she highlighted that one in four new and expectant mothers can be impacted by a wide range of perinatal mental health problems. Dunkley-Bent reflected on the theme of 2022s Maternal Mental Health Week as 'The Power of Connection' and how this is particularly important, post pandemic:

> The COVID-19 pandemic demonstrated the importance of the connections we develop with our communities. This is especially true for new and expectant mothers.

To read the full blog:

https://www.england.nhs.uk/blog/bringing-awareness-to-maternal-mental-health/

- If you were involved in the Mental Health Awareness Week, what strategies might you consider for promoting the 'power of connection'?

- Why is it so important that these strategies encourage connections within a community?

- Along with health professionals and early childhood practitioner-led activities and support, how can some of your strategies from the first question promote motherhood as a potentially 'collective experience' (Douglas & Michaels, 2005, p. 250)?

The role of the practitioner

As critically reflective practitioners, it is essential that the current political attention on parenting is considered with a critical eye. Support for parents is welcome and necessary but a top-down, one-size-fits-all approach and any notion of 'expert' is something that needs to be reflected upon carefully.

'Cultural sensitivity, and the place for local knowledge and livelihoods (context and history)' (Penn, 2019, p. 12) along with parental autonomy, family context and childhood uniqueness all need to be considered when planning and implementing support for parents.

Through policy and practice that is dominated by strong positivistic, scientific narrative, practitioners may find themselves working with children and families in a way that does not always sit comfortably with them, and they may not always recognise why this is. Through reflective practice and reflexivity, practitioners can engage with a range of theoretical lenses and ensure that the support that is offered reflects the needs of the people they are working with. On a practical level, this will include opportunities to meet families and engage in activities such as the local-oriented approach highlighted in the earlier section.

As early childhood practitioners, it is important that we are not 'blinded by the science' (Wastell & White, 2017) that is embedded into the policy world with 'fundamental assumptions and myths' (p. ix). Parents need support from empathetic, proactive practitioners who are encouraged to see through the constructions and misrepresentations of science and support families on an individualised basis.

According to Faircloth (2021, p. 39), it is under this 'developmental, psychological rationale, that parenting is understood as the source of, and the solution to, a whole range of problems, at both individual and societal levels'. With a focus on political intervention with all aspects of parenting, particularly new parenting, the role of autonomous and confident practitioners is more important than ever. This is not an easy ask, at a time where early childhood practitioners continue to be dominated by the same regulatory political discourse, finding agency and flexibility is a huge challenge and requires support through strong leadership and professional development opportunities.

For practitioners, this confidence can also develop through engagement with policy and workforce debate at a critical level. As explored by Moss (2017, p. 19), this will form part of the 'resistance movement', whereby practitioners can engage with theory and policy whilst using their experiences and knowledge to recognise that there are 'different ways of speaking the truth' (Moss, 2017, p. 19). This requires, as stated by Whalley (2007, in Fitzgerald & Maconochie, 2019, p. 412), a degree of 'constructive discontent' to support children and families in a way that is appropriate to their specific context. Whalley's concept 'urges early childhood professionals to critically question and even challenge policy in order to maintain the focus on the highest quality provision and practice'.

REFLECTION

With a commitment to supporting early childhood practitioners to develop a strong sense of professional identity, autonomy and confidence, in 2018, the ECSDN developed the 'Early Childhood Graduate Practitioner Competencies'.

With recognition of the importance of a graduate-led workforce for children and families, the nine competencies are assessed through placement tasks, observations of practice and academic assignments. Early childhood graduate practitioners are leaders in practice and agents of change for children and families. Through successful completion of their degree and competencies, the early childhood graduate practitioner will:

> *Critically apply high-level academic knowledge of pedagogy and research evidence, to the holistic development of infants and young children (0–8), in a practice context that is respectful of the child, their family and community.*

> *ECSDN (2018, p. 13)*

- How may the Early Childhood Graduate Practitioner Competencies support the professional identity of early childhood practitioners?

- Why is it important for early childhood practitioner to critically apply a high level of academic knowledge and research evidence, to the holistic development of infants and young children?

- How may this support a practice context that is respectful of the child, their family and community?

Conclusion

This chapter has considered the rise in political attention on parenting, including new directives which centre on localised support for parents. Throughout this chapter, this support has been reflected upon in a way that could promote the active inclusion of parents in future initiatives. This includes ensuring that parents' voices are heard, and that political attention recognises that these voices are diverse and rich in experiences, context and culture. Messages embedded into parenting intervention must ensure true inclusion that facilitates generational input along with family and community history within local support strategies.

Community support for new parents, particularly new mothers, has an essential role in reducing isolation and promoting adult interaction, all of which play an important part in navigating the early days of motherhood. Opportunities to form trusting relationships with health professionals and early childhood practitioners are crucial but, the research and experiences of new mothers show that, this support needs to be led by parents rather than anything too formulaic or homogeneous. Additionally, opportunities to develop honest and open relationships with other parents can make a real difference in the lives of new parents; finding humour, sharing experiences and forming friendships can reduce feelings of isolation and increase connectedness during this period in a new parent's life.

This chapter has also explored the importance of the role of the early childhood practitioner in supporting parents. Practitioners who are critically reflective, engaged in policy and qualified as leaders and agents of change will support parents with a confidence that means they are able to see beyond the textbook or rigid political directives and provide meaningful and individualised support for the children, families and communities they work with.

Further reading

Keller, H. (2018). Universality claim of attachment theory: Children's socioemotional development across cultures. *Proceedings of the National Academy of Sciences, 115*(45), 11414–11419.

Kjørholt, A. T., & Penn, H. (2019). *Early childhood and development work: Theories, policies and practices.* Cham: Palgrave Macmillan.

Vandenbroek, M., De Vos, J., Fias, W., Mariett Olsson, L., Penn, H., Wastell, D., & White, S. (2017). *Constructions of neuroscience in early childhood education.* London: Routledge.

Useful websites

Early Childhood Studies Degrees Network (ECSDN). (2022). *About us.* Retrieved from: https://www.ecsdn.org/

The National Centre for Family Hubs. (2022). *The best start for life.* London: Anna Freud National Centre for Children and Families.

References

Allen, G. (2011). *Early intervention: The next steps, an independent report to her Majesty's government by Graham Allen MP.* London: The Stationary Office.

All Party Parliamentary Group (APPG). (2015). *Conception to age 2: First 1001 days. Perinatal inquiry – Evidence sessions on first 1001 days.*

Burman, E. (2008). *Deconstructing developmental psychology* (2nd ed.). London: Routledge.

Clarke, B., Younas, F., & Project Team and Family Kids and Youth. (2017). *Helping parents to parent.* London: Social Mobility Commission.

Davis, A. (2012). *Modern motherhood: Women, family and England 1945–2000.* Manchester: Manchester University Press.

Department for Health and Social Care (DHSC). (2021). *The best start for life, a vision for the first 1001 critical days: The early years healthy development review report.* Retrieved from: https://assets.publishing.

service.gov.uk/government/uploads/system/uploads/attachment_data/file/973112/The_best_start_for_life_a_vision_for_the_1_001_critical_days.pdf (Accessed 8th April 2022).

Douglas, S. J., & Michaels, M. M. (2005). *The mommy myth: The idealization of motherhood and how it has undermined all women.* New York, NY: Free Press.

Dunkley-Bent, J. (2022). *Bringing awareness to maternal mental health.* Retrieved from: https://www.england.nhs.uk/blog/bringing-awareness-to-maternal-mental-health/ (Accessed 8th July 2022).

Early Childhood Studies Degrees Network. (2018). *Early childhood graduate practitioner competencies.* ECSDN.

Faircloth, C. (2021). *Couples transitions to parenthood: Gender, intimacy and equality.* London: Palgrave MacMillan.

Furedi, F. (2008). *Paranoid parenting: Why ignoring the experts may be best for your child.* Wiltshire: Continuum.

Fitzgerald, D., & Maconochie, H. (2019). *Early childhood studies: A students guide.* London: SAGE.

Gerhadt, S. (2004). *Why love matters.* London: Routledge.

Holloway, S., & Pimlott-Wilson, H. (2012). 'Any advice is welcome isn't it?' Neoliberal parenting education, local mothering cultures, and social class. *Environment and Planning, 46,* 94–111.

Johnston, D. D., & Swanson, D. H. (2006). Constructing the 'good mother': The experience of mothering ideologies by work status. *Sex Roles, 54,* 509–519.

Keller, H. (2018). Universality claim of attachment theory: Children's socioemotional development across cultures. *Proceedings of the National Academy of Sciences, 115*(45), 11414–11419.

Kjørholt, A. T., Matafwali, B., & Mofu, M. (2019). The knowledge is in your ears, in the stories you hear from the grandparents': Creating intercultural dialogue through memories of childhood. In **A. T. Kjørholt & H. Penn** (Eds.), *Early childhood and development work: Theories, policies and practices.* Cham: Palgrave Macmillan.

Moss, P. (2017). Power and resistance in early childhood education: From dominant discourses to democratic experimentation. *De Gruyter Open, 8*(1), 11–32.

Penn, H. (2019). Patronage, welfare, tenders, private consultancies and expert measurement: What is happening in early childhood education and care. In **A. T. Kjørholt & H. Penn** (Eds.), *Early childhood and development work: Theories, policies and practices.* Cham: Palgrave Macmillan.

Rose, N. (1999). *Governing the soul: The shaping of the private self* (2nd edn). London: Free Association Books.

Simmons, H. (2020). *Surveillance of modern motherhood: Experiences of universal parenting courses.* Cham: Palgrave Macmillan.

Simmons, H., & Thompson, P. (2021). *ECSDN spending review response: Early years funding: Autumn spending review 2021.* ECSDN. Retrieved from: https://www.ecsdn.org/category/ecsdn-response/ (Accessed 8th July 2022).

Wastell, D., & White, S. (2017). *Blinded by science, the social implications of epigenetics and neuroscience.* Bristol: Policy Press.

2 THE POTENTIAL OF CO-PRODUCTION

KATARZYNA FLEMING AND PENNY BORKETT

CHAPTER OBJECTIVES

By the end of this chapter, you will be able to:

- Understand the principles of co-production and how they are related to partnerships with parents/carers in the context of early childhood
- Identify practices that can enable effective and inclusive partnerships with parents in early childhood
- Consider your own positionality as a practitioner and reflect on your assumptions/attitudes to develop your practice in relation to partnerships with parents in early childhood

KEY DEFINITIONS

Co-production

Co-production is a model of partnership working where public services are planned, designed, commissioned and delivered in an equal and reciprocal relationship between practitioners, people using services and their close communities.

Inclusive partnerships

A partnership where all professionals work together in a reciprocal relationship to support a child or family.

Parents

Any person who has parental responsibility or has care of a young child during early childhood (from conception to eight years of age).

Practitioner

A person who is qualified to work with children (from conception to 8 years old) across health, education and social care.

Special educational needs and disability (SEND)

A child or young person has Special Educational Needs and Disabilities if they have a learning difficulty and/or a disability that means they need special health and education support, we shorten this to SEND.

Homogenised

When you assume that all children in a group/who have a similar SEND will all behave in the same way.

Lived experience

Knowledge about the world which has been ascertained through direct firsthand experiences.

Introduction

This chapter explores the potential of **co-production** in enabling **inclusive partnerships** with **parents** of children categorised as having **Special Educational Needs and Disability (SEND)** within the context of early childhood and beyond. While the focus here is predominantly on the **lived experience**s of families with children with SEND, we argue that the discussed potential of co-productive partnerships can also aid relationships with families in all settings from conception through to the age of 25.

Firstly, we present an overview of partnerships working within the field of early childhood and relevant policies; we then introduce and discuss co-production, a concept focused mainly within health and care services, and how it can change the relationship between all agencies and the families concerned.

Models of parent–practitioner partnerships in early childhood

One of the central principles of the Early Years Foundation Stage (EYFS) Statutory Framework (DfE, 2021) is the importance of building strong relationships with parents, and it is vital that this is in place early on in a child's life as they may be leaving parents for the first time. This is particularly essential if a child has or is considered to have a SEND.

Importantly, quite often relationships between parents and **practitioners** have very different perceived outcomes regarding development and it is vital that there is agreement about levels of support for children and their parents. Awareness of these differences can prevent unnecessary tensions; therefore, it is helpful to establish those outcomes at the onset of the relationships with a clear acknowledgement of the value of parental input in decision-making processes. It is also important that practitioners understand and give due regard and support to the role of parents of children with SEND and view them as an integral part of the relationship as well as acknowledge a recognition that parents may have many different roles and these different parental identities can have the potential to alter the relationship (Wolfendale, 1993).

Bronfenbrenner's (1979) ecological systems acknowledges that child development does not happen in a vacuum but is linked and embedded within every aspect of a family's life. He views development as circles within each other, which all interact as the child goes through life, similar to the ripples made when a stone is thrown into water. A short synopsis below supports understanding in relation to parents of children with SEND but is recommended to consider Bronfenbrenner's theory more closely:

- First ripple: Microsystem – relates to the child and their family

- Second ripple: Mesosystem – relates to all practitioners who work with the family across health, education and social care

- Third ripple: Ecosystem – relates to policies which have an impact on the child and family, for example, EYFS and the SEND Code of Practice which have more of an indirect impact on the child and family

- Final ripple: Macrosystem – relates to the political, societal and local priorities endemic in the country and may have an impact on the way that a family lives.

REFLECTION

The world has recently been living through the COVID-19 pandemic (2019–2022). The impact on children and families, particularly those with SEND, has been raised in both political and educational arenas.

Using the four 'ripples', can you use Bronfenbrenner's theory to consider how this impacted children and their families across a setting known to you and, in a broader sense, their place in society?

Liz Brooker (2010), within the context of early childhood, introduced practitioners to the Triangle of Care (Brooker, 2010), suggesting this model to support non-hierarchical relationships between the child, parent and practitioners in the setting. The Triangle of Care takes the view that the child, practitioner and parents have an equal voice and accentuates the importance of consistent communication between all parties. However, the original triangle drew no regard for other agencies working with the child. In 2021, Borkett advocated the triangle of extended care which adds to the original triangle the roles of family support, therapists and education professionals whose work is also integral to the family. As with the original, it is non-hierarchical and ensures that each party has equal status. For some parents and practitioners, the notion of a non-hierarchical relationships may be difficult initially. However, when this approach is adopted, it makes for a far more inclusive relationship between all parties.

Hickey, Richards, and Sheehy (2018) advocate that the main principles of co-production are power sharing, and the ability for all involved to have a say in decisions that affect them, as well as respect and the valuing of every person involved in the partnership, and reciprocity whereby each person participates and is listened to and their views are heard and acknowledged. Within the context of early childhood, this change can be achieved by implementing the principles of the Extended Triangle of Care (Borkett, 2021), which can help to foster non-hierarchical relationships between the child, parent and practitioners in the setting. The Extended Triangle of Care accentuates the important role of multi-agency working as a good early childhood practice. Despite an array of often differing priorities and agendas of multi-agencies, Walker (2018) argues that effective communication is imperative to multi-agency working for the best outcomes for children. One way to achieve more effective communication in partnerships could be to apply the four pillars of co-production as a value-based approach to all partnerships (Fleming, 2021).

What is co-production?

Co-production was first defined by Eleanor Ostrom in 1970s (Ostrom, 1996, p. 1), and although a well-established concept internationally, in the United Kingdom, co-production has been adopted more in health and social care than within education (Voorberg, Bekkers, & Tummers, 2015). Namely, within the social care services, co-production has been defined in the Care Act 2014 as operating

> *when an individual influences the support and services received, or when groups of people get together to influence the way that services are designed, commissioned and delivered.*

> *(DoH, 2014, p. 17)*

Likewise, within health services,

> *Co-production means delivering public services in an equal and reciprocal relationship between professionals, people using services, their families and their neighbours. Where activities are co-produced in this way, both services and neighbourhoods become far more effective agents of change.*

> *(Boyle & Harris, 2009, p. 11)*

Although varied in wording, all definitions advocate for service users to be active partners in designing, planning and/or delivering services. To enable equality of the relationships, and for citizens to become active agents in how these services are produced (Needham, 2008), the contributions of all parties need to be given an equivalent value (Cahn, 2004).

Cahn (2004, p. 24) asserts that through the **four main pillars of co-production**, inclusive partnerships can be achieved. These include the following:

1 People as assets who are recognised as bringing something valuable to contribute to the collective 'good' in society.

2 Redefining cultures and structures in operation to ensure social justice for marginalised groups and sustainability of democratic ethos.

3 Reciprocity where two-way exchanges prevail (i.e. 'you need me' is turned into 'we need each other').

4 Social capital of the collective.

These core values could be transferred into partnership working where parental expertise is acknowledged through reciprocal practice and where a culture of collaboration enriches the lives of children with SEND. This requires a shift in power from practitioners in early childhood to parents to be enacted in practice (Realpe & Wallace, 2010), which can be problematic as it would rely upon practitioners parting with some of their inherited power. Despite the Special Educational Needs and/or Disability Code of Practice's (CoP) (DfE & DoH, 2015) guidance on the inclusion of parental contributions in decision-making processes, ways of communicating between families and services require transformation (Needham, 2008). When applied effectively, co-production can serve as a 'therapeutic tool' (Needham, 2008, p. 223) where all members of the partnership, through a facilitated sharing of perspective and experience, come to new understandings of what the partnership means to others and how it impacts upon them. Therefore, the partnerships will not only involve consulting recipients of services on their views but would enable the services to be shaped and designed as a result of these views (Fairlie, 2015). The ownership of that involvement would, in return, increase citizens' trust in services that they have jointly designed, planned or delivered (Needham, 2008).

Early intervention

Early intervention is a key policy element promoted for young children in a range of ways around the United Kingdom. This may be offered through home visits, the receiving of early years education and childcare at a younger age or through other agencies such as speech and language, physiotherapy and occupational therapy working alongside parents. The common aspect is the recognition that money spent in early childhood can see significant benefits as children move into adulthood. One important aspect of early intervention is multi-agency working, which recognises that if children are given support early on in their lives, this has an impact into adulthood.

Over the years, how early intervention is offered to families has changed as governmental priorities have altered and local authority budgets have been tightened. It is reported that parents like to be involved with early intervention programmes as they support families at a time in their lives when maybe they may have received news of their child's diagnosis and need a knowledgeable adult to support them. They continue to state that the ongoing support through home visits and visits to other professionals gives tremendous support to parents when they may be feeling very vulnerable and alone. However, there is some criticism of these home-based programmes. Rix, Paige-Smith and Jones (2008, p.70) suggest that at times there may be a 'tension between play and therapy' whereby some parents can feel that they are, at times, more of a therapist than a parent. Bridle and Mann (2000), both parents of children with SEND and receiving a home-based programme, felt that, at times, the activities that would support their children took over, which resulted in parents feeling guilty for not engaging in everyday activities. Whilst Rix, Paige-Smith and Jones praise early intervention for the fact that the family is central to the programmes, they also suggest that sometimes these should take more account of siblings and the extended family. They stress the need for parents:

> to have a sense of control over their family life and to recognise that effective intervention strategies result from their own actions, strengths and capabilities (2008, p. 66).

Clearly, there is still more to do to enhance relationships between parents, families and the plethora of practitioners who might be involved in early intervention. The concept of co-production is potentially a way to view these relationships more democratically and that encourages all to listen and share sensitively important information relating to the child at the centre.

REFLECTION

Use a mind-mapping activity to explore the many roles that all parents but especially those of children with SEND have to play, particularly in relation to health, education and social care providers.

Consider how these may change the role of the parent to be experts in a range of fields, for example, teacher, physiotherapist and speech therapist.

- How do you think parents may respond both positively and negatively to navigating these differing roles?

- How could early childhood practitioners support parents with this?

Co-production and educational policy in the United Kingdom

While parental engagement is at the forefront of our discussion, the remit of part-nerships must include children's voices and contributions as guided by the policy (e.g. the SEND CoP (2015) or Birth to 5 Matters (2021)). Boddison and Soan (2022) argue that co-productive working is 'an illusion' as the current SEND system prevents the settings from implementing the values of co-production from the outset of relationships with families before any targets or agendas are firmly set in place.

Within the SEND CoP (2015), co-production is mentioned only once under the work between local authorities and families in the construction of the local offer (DfE & DoH, 2015). This opportunity to design the local offer in partnership with parents and agencies has achieved varied outcomes due to inadequate training for prac-titioners (Palikara, Castro, Gaona, & Eirinaki, 2019). The need for a significant developmental change in practice, if the code is to ever achieve its goals (APPG for SEND, 2021), is reflected in the myriad of proposed changes in the recent SEND Green Paper (HM Government, 2022) that aim for co-productive partnerships on the local governmental, institutional and individual levels. Therefore, we propose to explore the relevance of co-production within the context of early childhood through Cahn's (2004) four pillars of co-production later on in the chapter.

Co-productive partnerships draw on the value-based approaches where all con-tributors of the partnerships are considered valuable and are treated as an asset to the community of practice, where reciprocity is at the core of all interactions and where the goal of those interactions is to create a positive change for all involved (Fleming, 2021). This forms the bedrock of high-quality practice in early childhood as advocated for in a wide range of early childhood literature (Fitzgerald, 2004; MacNaughton & Hughes, 2011a; Ward & Perry, 2020).

Although it is essential to recognise the individual context of settings and families and their impact on partnerships, Fleming (2021) argues that fostering the same values in the formation of mentioned partnerships can result in more equitable and inclusive partnerships where all contributors are recognised for their input into the development of a just community of practice.

REFLECTION

Assess your own assumptions and attitudes towards working in partnership with parents. Consider:

- How do I address parents when I discuss their child? – am I often using 'mum'/'dad' instead of their actual names?

- Do I make assumptions about the families, rather than always listening to their stories/circumstances?

- Do I ensure I always perceive each family as unique despite their resemblance to other families I have met/worked with?

- Do I always ensure I learn something unique about each family and build on the positive connections to enable their sense of belonging to our learning community?

Barriers to co-production

Since the growing interest in co-production and its relevance to improving public services (Alford, 2014; Boyle & Harris, 2009; Cahn, 2004; Fairlie, 2015; Pestoff & Brandsen, 2010; Realpe & Wallance, 2010), its practical limitations have not been examined empirically at length (Fenwick, 2012). This leaves the ideal of co-production within the sphere of rhetoric and a prescriptive framework, rather than a well-established practical model. Beside the premise that both sides of the partnership must share enabling and participatory values, perceptions and attitudes (Williams, Seong-Cheol Kang, & Johnson, 2016), the issue of responsibility and accountability for delivery of services where outcomes of this delivery might be unexpected or undesirable continues to be an obstacle to the reciprocity and the ideal of equal partnerships underpinning co-production (Bell & Pahl, 2018; Fairlie, 2015; Fenwick, 2012; Needham, 2008). How equal and reciprocal this functioning might be is also continually determined by the dilemma professionals face between the demands to care and demands to contain, control and manage scarce resources (Fenwick, 2012; Needham, 2008). Therefore, it is imperative that practitioners engage in a deep reflection on how those barriers are considered when co-productive practice is initiated to establish what values drive the partnership working and to identify the changes required for reciprocal, equitable and therefore inclusive partnerships. This reflection can lead to a realisation that practitioners' resistance to work co-productively is evident in the setting; this resistance might occur as a result of practitioners potentially perceiving their expertise and experience as being undermined by having to share the domain of provision design and delivery with unqualified parents (Seligman & Darling, 2007). This threat could be translated to practitioners supporting children with SEND, as they may feel that their professional qualifications and their experience of a range of children with SEND are superior to parental knowledge and expertise of their children. The uncertainties of the roles in this scenario can result in practitioners' reluctance to adopt approaches that they may feel would distort their professional status. It is also unclear whether the families always wish to be actively involved in co-producing services (Fairlie, 2015), and it is reported that some citizens might wish to undertake tasks that require or develop their self-efficacy, whereas others might refuse it (Bovaird, Flemig, Loeffler, & Osborne, 2019). Therefore, it is even more crucial to build relationships with families where open and honest communication can take place to establish parental wishes about the extent of their contributions, at the same time fostering an ethos of openness and invitation to valued participation in all decision-making processes.

The role of the practitioner

Central to Bronfenbrenner (1979), the EYFS (DfE, 2021) and the Triangle of Care (Brooker, 2010) are the child and their family in receiving support that is appropriate to them and their needs and the recognition that this might change over time. However, Gibbs (2005) suggests that at times, practitioners can make parents feel vulnerable and anxious as they are expected to speak and share information about their child. They may feel that they do not have enough specialised knowledge about their child and their needs or indeed that they are being listened to. The need for practitioners to view families as individuals who require different areas of support at different times in a child's life is vital, but these kinds of relationships may take time to develop particularly if a child does not receive a diagnosis of SEND until later on in life.

Whenever support is needed, it is vital that parents' voices are heard in the services that they are offered. Parents need to feel confident that no question is too small and, as the EYFS (DfE, 2021) recognises, that practitioners recognise that they know their child and are aware of their specialist needs (Kagan, Lewis, Heaton, & Cranshaw, 1999).

MacNaughton & Hughes (2011b, p. 6) suggest that at times, practitioners can be guilty of 'homogenizing children' or not taking notice of their 'lived experience' due to the structural barriers of an undervalued workforce or maybe they do not recognise the importance of inclusive practice or may not have received any training around working alongside families.

Examples of this could be when practitioners think that all children on the autistic spectrum learn and behave in the same way or assume that the support given to parents of children with SEND should be exactly the same rather than acknowledging differing needs. MacNaughton and Hughes (2011b, p. 6) also discuss the idea of 'silencing', which suggests that professionals can make parents feel that they are being excluded and not listened to. Maconochie and Branch recognise that when agencies work together to support children with SEND, the health needs of the child improves. However, they also acknowledge some of the challenges of working together such as breakdowns in communication, the clarification of roles and responsibilities and the need to gain the families' 'trust and mutual respect' (2018, p. 270).

The following suggests using the co-productive four pillars (Cahn, 2004) as a way to develop early childhood practice across social care, health and education:

Everyone is an asset

All mission statements and policies that refer to partnerships with parents explicitly acknowledge parental contributions to all aspects of the provision. Parents should be actively encouraged (verbally, in a written form or through the ethos of the setting) to share their knowledge of their children, to contribute to the development and review of policies and practices in the setting and to express their views openly and honestly and those contributions are celebrated and welcome.

Redefining culture and structures for social justice

Practitioners are required to engage in a deep reflection on the culture in their setting and to evaluate the existing power dynamics between the service and families. Settings need to engage in reflective activities as part of staff training where they explore conversations about their own positionality, attitudes and deep-seated beliefs about the partnerships. Practitioners should also consider the impact of political directives that add to the barriers that practitioners face in being autonomous and critically reflective. From there, parents could be invited to engage in similar reflection, before the joint reflections take place.

Reciprocity where two-way exchanges prevail

The change from 'you need us' to 'we need each other' has to permeate through all aspects of the provision and be visible across the setting. This transformation requires time, consistency of messages and approaches to partnerships from all involved (Realpe & Wallace, 2010). Assuming that parents and children know they are valued participants in the setting can result in ambiguities and messages of inclusive partnerships may be lost. Therefore, as a setting, consider whether the reciprocity is explicit in your policy, mission statements, communication through newsletters or home-setting diaries (Mann et al., 2020). It is crucial to not assume that every parent will be expecting to be equally involved in the reciprocal exchanges – the individual and unique circumstances of families need to be recognised here, but not assumed (Seligman & Darling, 2007).

Social capital is where the collective knowledge, strengths and expertise of citizens are utilised to support the development of safe, thriving and supportive communities.

It is essential that the learning community develops a culture of learning with and from parents, where no one has to 'know it all' all the time – instead, we can rely on each other to contribute to the 'knowing' in the best way that supports our learning community (Mann et al., 2020).

As mentioned above, all agencies are required to be involved in effective communication. If parental expertise is utilised for training purposes, consider how this input can be recognised as professional knowledge and therefore remunerated accordingly.

CASE STUDY

A new family has joined your setting. They are from an ethnic minority background and have a good level of spoken English language. Their 3-year-old son has three more older siblings attending local primary school. Following close observations for 6 weeks, you are concerned that the boy displays some signs of withdrawal from group activities and a lack of willingness to participate in songs and nursery

(Continued)

(Continued)

rhymes. You have also noticed he often repeats the same phrases, sometimes in what appears to be an odd context.

A. Considering the four pillars of co-production outlined above, reflect on how you can support the child and his family through a potential referral process for additional support.

B. Consider how this scenario will relate to the triangle of extended care explored in this chapter.

Conclusion

This chapter has focused on the crucial relationships needed when parents and practitioners work together, to support children in early childhood, especially if they have or are thought to have SEND. It has introduced the Extended Triangle of Care (Borkett, 2021) and discussed how these can be used to ensure parties work democratically for the good of the child at the centre of all relationships remembering that they have a voice in decisions that affect them. It has introduced and encouraged an understanding of the principles of co-production and how these can shape relationships between parents and practitioners. Practitioners have been challenged to question their own positionality and stereotypes about parents and to recognise and celebrate the differences in all.

As students or practitioners within early childhood education, health and care services, it is necessary to engage in partnerships with parents. The final part of this chapter suggests how the pillars of co-production can support those developing partnerships. As discussed, it is essential that practitioners engage in a deep reflection where they evaluate and challenge their assumptions and how these impact on their ways of working in partnerships. Importantly, co-productive partnerships aim at equal value of contributions and therefore indicate the value of both sides of the relationship – the knowledge, expertise and experience of practitioners are as valuable and essential as those of parental lived experiences. Historically, parental input has been marginalised as lacking professional value with practitioners dominating the decision-making processes (Seligman & Darling, 2007). While we recognise that co-productive partnerships require a shift in power dynamics and traditional ways of working together, we encourage practitioners to be open to question and adapt the cultures and to foster an ethos of reciprocity in all aspects of partnerships. Despite some limitations in research and practice, the chapter demonstrates that co-productive partnerships can serve as vehicle to

- enable inclusive culture where the partnership is recognised as one whole, rather than both sides, in a reciprocal approach,

- ensure that all involved feel they belong to the collective learning community and

- ensure that decision-making processes are democratic and reflect the voices of all participants, and as a result, the services enrich and respond effectively to the needs of diverse communities of our society.

Finally, this case study should enable further reflection on the place of co-productive partnerships in an early childhood setting.

Further reading

Borkett, P. (2021). *Special educational needs in the early years – A guide to inclusive practice.* London: SAGE.

Brandsen, T., Steen, T., & Verschuere, B. (2018). *Co-production and co-creation: Engaging citizens in public services.* London: Taylor & Francis.

MacNaughton, G., & Hughes, P. (2011). *Parents and professionals in early childhood settings.* Berks: McGraw Hill.

Useful websites

The Early Years Coalition. (2021). Birth to 5 matters – Non-statutory guidance for the EYFS. Retrieved from: https://birthto5matters.org.uk/

https://councilfordisabledchildren.org.uk/

https://www.specialneedsjungle.com/

The National Network of Parent Carer Forums. Retrieved from: https://nnpcf.org.uk/

Centre for Studies on Inclusive Education. Retrieved from: http://www.csie.org.uk/

References

Alford, J. (2014). The multiple facets of co-production: Building on the work of Elinor Ostrom. *Public Management Review, 16*(3), 299–316.

All-Party Parliamentary Group for SEND. (2021). Forgotten. Left behind. Overlooked. The experiences of young people with SEND and their educational transitions during the Covid-19 pandemic in 2020. Report Spring 2021.

Bell, D. M., & Pahl, K. (2018). Co-production: Towards a utopian approach. *International Journal of Social Research Methodology, 21*(1), 105–117.

Boddison, A., & Soan, S. (2022). The coproduction illusion: Considering the relative success rates and efficiency rates of securing an education, health and care plan when requested by families or education professionals. *Journal of Research in Special Educational Needs, 22*(2), 91–104.

Borkett, P. A. (2021). *Special educational needs in the early years – a guide in inclusive practice.* London: SAGE.

Bovaird, T., Flemig, S., Loeffler, E., & Osborne, S. P. (2019). How far have we come with co-production—and what's next? *Public Money & Management, 39*(4), 229–232.

Boyle, D., & Harris, M. (2009). *The challenge of co-production.* London: New Economics Foundation.

Bridle, L., & Mann, G. (2000). Mixed feelings: A parental perspective on early intervention. *Article presented at the national conference of early childhood intervention Australia.* Brisbane 2000.

Bronfenbrenner, U. (1979). *The ecology of human development. Experiments by nature and design.* Cambridge, MA: Harvard University Press.

Brooker, L. (2010). Constructing the triangle of care: Power and professionalism in practitioner/parent relationships. *British Journal of Educational Studies, 58*(2), 181–196.

Cahn, E. S. (2004). *No more throw-away people: The co-production imperative.* Washington, DC: Essential Books.

Department for Education. (2021). *Statutory framework for the early years foundation stage setting the standards for learning, development and care for children from birth to five.* Retrieved from: https://assets. publishing.service.gov.uk/government/uploads/system/uploads/attachment_data/file/974907/EYFS_framework_-_March_2021.pdf

Department of Health (DoH). (2014). *Care and support statutory guidance. Issued under the care act 2014.* Retrieved from: https://assets.publishing.service.gov.uk/government/uploads/system/uploads/attachment_data/file/315993/Care-Act-Guidance.pdf

DfE (Department for Education) & DoH (Department of Health). (2015). *Special educational needs and disability code of practice: 0 to 25 years.* Retrieved from: https://www.gov.uk/government/uploads/system/uploads/attachment_data/file/398815/SEND_Code_of_Practice_January_2015.pdf

Fairlie, S. (2015). 'Co-production: A personal journey'. *Mental Health Review Journal, 20*(4), 267–278.

Fenwick, T. (2012). Co-production in professional practice: A sociomaterial analysis. *Professions and Professionalism, 2*(2), 1–16.

Fitzgerald, D. (2004). *Parent partnerships in the early years.* London: A&C Black.

Fleming, K. (2021). *Exploring inclusive partnerships: Parents, co-production, and the SEND code of practice (2015).* PhD thesis. Sheffield Hallam University.

Gibbs, N. (2005). Parents behaving badly. *Time, 165*(8), 40–49.

Hickey, G., Richards, T., & Sheehy, J. (2018). *Co-production from proposal to paper.* Retrieved from: https://media.nature.com/original/magazine-assets/d41586-018-06861-9/d41586-018-06861-9.pdf

HM Government. (2022). *SEND review: Right support, right place, right time.* London: HM Government.

Kagan, C., Lewis, S., Heaton, P., & Cranshaw, M. (1999). Enabled or disabled? Working parents of disabled children and the provision of child-care. *Journal of Community & Applied Social Psychology, 9,* 369–381.

MacNaughton, G., & Hughes, P. (2011a). *Parents and professionals in early childhood settings.* Berks: McGraw Hill.

MacNaughton, G., & Hughes, P. (2011b). *Parents and professionals in early childhood settings.* Berks: Open University Press.

Mann, G., Hodge, N., Runswick-Cole, K., Gilmore, S., Mavropoulou, S., & Fleming, K. (2020). Inclusive education in the 21st century: Developing productive partnerships with parents and carers (336–357). In L. Graham (Ed.), *Inclusive education for the 21st century: Theory, policy and practice.* Sydney: Allen & Unwin.

Needham, C. (2008). Realising the potential of co-production: Negotiating improvements in public services. *Social Policy and Society, 7*(2), 221–231.

Ostrom, E. (1996). Crossing the great divide: Co-production, synergy, and development. *World Development, 24*(6), 1073–1087.

Palikara, O., Castro, S., Gaona, C., & Eirinaki, V. (2019). Professionals' views on the new policy for special educational needs in England: Ideology versus implementation. *European Journal of Special Needs Education, 34*(1), 83–97.

Pestoff, V., & Brandsen, T. (2010). Public governance and the third sector: Opportunities for co-production and innovation?. In *The new public governance?* (pp. 239–252). London: Routledge.

Realpe, A., & Wallace, L. M. (2010). *What is co-production.* London: The Health Foundation.

Rix, J., Paige-Smith, A., & Jones, H. (2008). 'Until the cows came home': Issues for early intervention activities? Parental perspectives on the early years learning of their children with down syndrome. *Contemporary Issues in Early Childhood, 9*(1), 66–77.

Seligman, M., & Darling, R. B. (2007). *Ordinary families, special children: A systems approach to childhood disability.* London: Guilford Publications.

Voorberg, W. H., Bekkers, V. J., & Tummers, L. G. (2015). A systematic review of co-creation and co-production: Embarking on the social innovation journey. *Public Management Review, 17*(9), 1333–1357.

Walker, G. (2018). *Working together for children: A critical introduction to multi-agency working.* Great Britain: Bloomsbury Publishing.

Ward, U., & Perry, B. (Eds.). (2020). *Working with parents and families in early childhood education.* London: Routledge.

Williams, B. N., Kang, S.-C., & Johnson, J. (2016). (Co) Contamination as the dark side of co-production: Public value failures in co-production processes. *Public Management Review, 18*(5), 692–717.

Wolfendale, S. (1993). *Assessing special educational needs.* London: Bloomsbury.

3 UNDERSTANDING FOOD ALLERGIES AND ANAPHYLAXIS

PHILIPPA THOMPSON

CHAPTER OBJECTIVES

By the end of this chapter, you will be able to:

- Critically reflect on your own practice when working with children and families identified with food allergies and anaphylaxis in relation to SEND.
- Demonstrate an understanding of the ways that anaphylaxis and food allergies have an impact on children and parents in early childhood.
- Consider the role of the early childhood practitioner when working together with parents of children with food allergies and anaphylaxis.

KEY DEFINITIONS

Anaphylaxis

The most severe form of allergic reaction which can be life threatening.

Autoethnography

A research method based on qualitative analysis of personal experience for reflection and understanding of wider global societal, political and cultural issues.

ECEC

Early Childhood Education and Care.

Food allergy (FA)

This is 'caused by your immune system handling harmless proteins in certain foods as a threat. It releases a number of chemicals, which trigger an allergic reaction'. https://www.nhs.uk/conditions/food-allergy/causes/

Parent

Any person who has parental responsibility or has care of a young child during early childhood (from conception to eight years of age).

Peanuts

Peanuts are classed as a legume and belong to the same family as lentils, beans and peas.

Practitioner

Adult who is qualified to work with children (from conception to eight years of age) across health, education and social care.

Protectionist response

The response to young children and families with medical needs. The central focus is on safety rather than autonomy and shared control.

Psychosocial

This approach in research considers a person's or group of people's social environment impact alongside their psychological influences.

Tree nuts

Nuts that grow on trees as opposed to ground nuts (peanuts) include almonds, Brazil nuts, cashews, hazelnuts, pecans, pistachios and walnuts.

Introduction

This chapter is written from two perspectives. The first is **autoethnographic**, as a parent of a son diagnosed as **anaphylactic**, with a severe food allergy (FA) to **tree nuts** and **peanuts**. The second as having worked in the discipline of early childhood for over 30 years as a researcher, lecturer and practitioner. Benford and Tait (2017) state that the relationship between **practitioner** and **parent** is key to the well-being of the child in early childhood, and this philosophy has never felt more meaningful when understanding how to support those parenting a child with **food allergies** and **anaphylaxis**.

The chapter is written from the clear position that parents of children with anaphylaxis are marginalised. Hamilton (2021, p. 1) states that 'Marginalisation can be understood as both a process, and a condition, that prevents individuals or groups from full participation in social, economic and political life'. Children and families living with FAs and anaphylaxis would not instinctively be seen as being in a marginalised group, and this chapter seeks to challenge current thinking. The following seeks to move current understanding away from a **protectionist response** to these families (Greene, Prior, & Frier, 2001) and enable an understanding of the lived experiences of these parents and their children. The following themes aim to support readers to look through a different lens. It is always difficult to understand the lives of others when it is not a lived experience, but critical reflection and empathy are valuable tools to begin to further inclusivity of children and families with FAs and anaphylaxis.

The chapter will consider the key themes that are prevalent both in the literature and pertinent to the daily experiences of both children and parents living with anaphylaxis. Firstly, it is important to consider the context of anaphylaxis and FAs with early childhood. The initial theme considers the statistics available globally and how this is underpinned by research. Secondly, the impact on parents is reviewed from a research position. Understanding the significant impact this has at home is a way for early childhood practitioners to reflect on their own practice and potential unconscious bias. The following theme suggests how the positioning of both parents and practitioners in policy and practice has a significant impact on the well-being of all involved. The positioning of parents as 'either deficient or as active agents' (Sims-Schouten, 2016, p. 1393) when engaging with early childhood settings is problematic and can lead to a misunderstanding of relationships that are multi-dimensional. Finally, policy and practice in early childhood and the role of the practitioner are the themes that aim to support and develop practice in early childhood by supporting both practitioners and students to reflect on how they work together with parents to ensure a positive experience and a high level of well-being for the child.

Context of anaphylaxis and food allergies

According to Anaphylaxis UK,

> *Anaphylaxis is a severe and often sudden allergic reaction. It can occur when someone with allergies is exposed to something they are allergic to (known as an allergen). Reactions usually begin within minutes and rapidly progress but can occur up to 2–3 hours later.*

> *Anaphylaxis.org (2022)*

Anaphylaxis is the most severe form of food allergic reaction and can be unpredictable and fatal (Chooniedass, Temple, Martin, & Becker, 2018; Vale, Smith, Said, Mullins, & Loh, 2015). However, many children learn how to manage this and to minimise the risk with the support of adults enabling them to make independent decisions.

For families living with anaphylaxis and FAs, this is a frightening condition where action needs to be taken quickly and with a knowledge of symptoms and response. For those parenting a child between the ages of 0 and 8 years, this is at a time when children may be just beginning to learn to recognise the symptoms themselves and more crucially their own individual symptoms. However, in early childhood, children may not be able to articulate clearly or find themselves potentially in a situation where they do not feel comfortable stating out loud that they can feel an oncoming reaction, for example, where they have been asked to sit quietly and listen in the classroom.

FAs affect around 2 million people in the United Kingdom and 5%–8% of children (Muraro et al., 2014). FAs affect between 6% and 8 % of children under 3 years in Europe and North America (Walsh, 2017a; National Institute for Health and Care Excellence (NICE), Quality standard [QS118], 2016). FAs are now understood globally to present an increasing health issue (Sanagavarapu, 2018; Vale et al., 2015), and research over the last decade in medical journals has increased significantly.

Legislation dates back to the mandatory provision of food allergen information, first introduced in 1996 by the Food Standards Agency. The latest Special Educational Needs and Disabilities (SEND) Code of Practice (Department for Education (DfE) and DoHSC, 2015) recognises that children with anaphylaxis need definitive support in all education and care settings (maintained schools; private day care; childminders; children's centres; maintained nursery schools; academies; free schools and voluntary providers). However, much of this legislation continues to refer strongly to schools rather than the wider variety of settings belonging to early childhood. It is also concerning that the latest SEND Green Paper (2022) makes no specific mention of children with FAs and anaphylaxis.

Whilst a requirement for legislation with regards to FAs and anaphylaxis has been necessary, it is important to understand that there is still work to be developed around the reasons behind the introduction of this legislation. It would appear that it has been driven by two key foci:

- Statistics arising of fatalities from FAs and anaphylaxis.

- Incidences causing anaphylaxis and FA reactions.

This reflects a protectionist response where legislation considers how to keep children safe from harm but does not consider the social and emotional impact of living with anaphylaxis and an FA (Greene, Prior, & Frier, 2001) and how it may impact upon relationships between parents and practitioners.

REFLECTION

- Have you learnt anything that has provoked your thoughts from reading the introduction and the first theme?

- Have your previous responses to parents/children/friends with anaphylaxis been influenced by a protectionist perspective?

- Create a list of honest emotions that you have felt when you are with a friend or responsible for a child who has FAs and anaphylaxis. Consider how this may have influenced your relationship.

Parenting a child with anaphylaxis: The impact

As a practitioner, it may be difficult to understand a home situation where FAs dominate life and experiences for all family members. This may also make it difficult to focus on the needs of the parent whilst their child is under their care. However, all successful parent partnerships work when all partners try to understand the differing perspectives and role requirements. The additional dilemma for parents when making choices around who will be responsible for their child is the plausible fear of their child having a serious allergic reaction when they are not there to support their child and, in some circumstances, apply lifesaving medication.

It is also important to consider the social and emotional impact of parenting a child between the ages of 0 and 8 (and beyond) and how this can affect parental relationships with the setting. Research on the **psychosocial** impacts of parenting a child with FAs and anaphylaxis has been documented from a clinical medical perspective over the past 10 years. This has also been linked with research on the health-related quality of life (HRQL) for both parents and children. Very little research has focussed on early childhood, and yet it is reported that the most reactions occur in children of this age (Akeson, Worth, & Sheikh, 2007; Cummings et al., 2010).

In recent years, there has been an acknowledgement, in health research, that parenting a child with FAs can impact on the family's quality of life (QoL). This has resulted in several HRQL studies including the influential EuroPrevall project (Fernandez-Rivas et al., 2015) developed by the Community Research and Development Information Service (CORDIS) funded by the European Union. Prior to this, Cohen, Noone, Muñoz-Furlong, and Sicherer (2004) identified four key factors that were significant for those parenting a child with FAs and anaphylaxis:

- parental emotions
- parents' experiences of family, social events and school
- time-consuming roles and responsibilities
- parental health and nutrition concerns

The initial shock of your child being diagnosed and experiencing any allergic reaction that is food related can take some time to come to terms with. After this, parents often begin to change and manage what happens in their own home environment and that of close family. However, when parents think about returning to work and their child starts transitioning to early childhood environments, the fear returns and the organisational burden becomes heavier (Gillespie, Woodgate, Chalmers, & Watson, 2007). In this context, early childhood practitioners could play a significant role in improving the trusting relationships required between the key person and the parent (Elfer, 2013).

The impact of parenting a child with anaphylaxis and FAs can be illustrated by a few examples, but it must be remembered that for each family, the experience will be different. The following examples serve to help towards understanding, but regular conversations and noticing when parents seem to be struggling are the suggested route.

For many, the idea of family celebrations and wider celebratory events are exciting and times to look forward to. For those dealing with FAs and anaphylaxis, celebrations that involve food cause emotions such as fear, loss and anxiety. Accepting the invitation inevitably means checking what food will be available, what extra food may need to be brought and raising awareness of FAs and often several conversations with whoever is making the food. At children's parties, parents can often find themselves in the kitchen of a soft play provider checking labels with concerned caterers rather than mixing with other parents. Added to this could be a lack of understanding and support from wider family members, which can again add to the anxiety at a usually celebratory time. One Australian study (Sanagavarapu, 2017) highlights the support needs of mothers when their children are starting school, linking the implications of anxiety of family and social events to early childhood practice. Often when children begin to mix more socially from a young age, then a plethora of birthday and other 'playdate' invitations are extended, adding an extension of social anxiety for parents. Children with FAs and anaphylaxis can also be excluded from these invitations through the fear of other parents, and this can create anxiety around isolation (Cohen et al., 2004; Singley & Hynes, 2005; Valentine & Knibb, 2011).

Global and UK policies in early childhood all highlight the need for an Anaphylaxis Management Plan or a Personalised Care Project provided by health practitioners with a depth of knowledge. However, it is often reported that it is parents who are left to explain complex medical information to early childhood practitioners once the care plan has been sent out (Moneret-Vautrin et al., 2001; Nurmatov, Worth, & Sheikh, 2008). As each individual case may produce differing reactions, and with each child the reactions could differ as they get older, policy needs to be sensitive to the needs of the unique child (DfE, 2021). Good practice would suggest talking to parents before their child starts in the setting to talk through the care plan and how their child currently manages their medication, how they feel about food and how parents would like to work with the setting to support practitioners, themselves and their child.

Anaphylaxis a hidden disability?

Parents of young children with anaphylaxis in England struggle to gain recognition for their child as having SEND despite the medical need being recognised on the current SEND Code of Practice (DfE & DoH, 2015). Often there is no obvious outward impact on the child and the disability can be hidden from others. Parents, however, live with their child on a daily basis and know the impact the FA has and is having on their child and it is important to listen without prejudice. Parents have possibly already had to deal with being framed as a 'fussy parent' or been exposed to media/social media false suggestions that the anaphylaxis is not real (despite medical evidence to the contrary). This can provide an immediate barrier to relationships with family members, friends and practitioners. Additionally, the difficulty of practitioners recognising when an immediate medical response is required, but not the social and emotional impact, can also cause problematic partnerships.

Parental positioning in early childhood: Politics and practice

To understand the difficulties a minority group may face, it is important to understand how they are positioned within early childhood, particularly in education settings where they may experience the most difficulty. Health settings such as the local medical centre and hospital can often provide a supportive place for parents as they are enabled to understand their child's allergy and receive advice on the use of medication. However, it can sometimes still be a battle for some parents to gain a diagnosis for their child.

Cottle and Alexander (2014) report that in early childhood, parents can be positioned by practitioners in a simplified way as either inactive or active in terms of their engagement with early childhood settings. There is a danger in this over-simplification as these relationships are extremely complex for many, not only involving culture and class but also having a child with medical needs can add further complications. This has the potential to lead to social isolation for parents and children (Cottle & Alexander, 2014; Osgood, Albon, Allen, & Hollingworth, 2013; Sims-Schouten, 2016).

Partnerships with parents may also be problematic due to the complex positioning of parents in a wide range of roles by society. It is difficult for parents to understand where they are positioned and how their partnership works when they are considered as responsible for supporting their children to achieve academically to generate early childhood setting improvement (Nakagawa, 2000). In the meantime, parents are also positioned by government as essential elements of the workforce (Grover, 2005), with a pressure to return to work on those who have completed maternity/paternity/adoption leave. Finally, Wright (2012), Barnes and Power (2012), and Cain (2016) all discuss the positioning of parents as achievers of social and economic success, again providing a pressure to raise children in particular ways including attendance at work. Taking time out to attend medical appointments for your child, supporting the setting with advice on FAs and anaphylaxis and being on call for any allergic reaction can make a parental role problematic. Gupta et al. (2013) report how parents have turned down job opportunities that involve travelling any distance or accept part-time work instead due to having to be present at school/setting events for safety purposes and taking on the role of 'expert' on their child's condition. These pressures on time and the anxiety faced leaving a child with other carers can have a significant impact on QoL and potentially on their relationship with practitioners.

It is also important to note that in English Early Childhood Education and Care (**ECEC**) settings, there is an expectation from the Office for Standards in Education, Children's Services and Skills (Ofsted) that all settings have policies that support children with SEND or those with medical conditions. There is however no requirement for a specific allergy policy. An amendment of The Human Medicines

Regulations (2012) stated that all schools could have spare adrenaline on site, providing reassurance to parents of the children affected. Noticeably, settings outside the maintained sector were not included in this legislation and are therefore still reliant on parents and children to bring adrenaline auto-injectors (AAIs) every day. This confusion creates an uncertain environment for a parent to bring a child with FAs and anaphylaxis.

The final position that is familiar in early childhood is that the parent is considered as their child's first and most enduring educator. There is a pressure on parents, particularly once their child starts at school, that they should be focussing on their child's learning. For many parents their focus is different and on their child's happiness and well-being. For the parents of a child with anaphylaxis, there is a strong tendency to focus on the danger aspects. These could be snack time, school dinners, packed lunches and food treats that may be provided for birthdays and other celebrations. This sounds strange to some, but perhaps imagine coming into a significant life-threatening situation at least twice a day and reflect on how this may feel and the long-term effect it could have. Would the focus be on learning or survival in this instance?

This complex positioning suggests that the parental role is already being defined by early childhood practitioners and settings before children and parents begin their partnership journey with them. Research evidence demonstrates that there is a strong focus on a parent's ability to support their children's learning and that 'parent participation has moved from the psychological to the political arena' (Sims-Schouten, 2016, p. 1392). Parenting a child with FAs and anaphylaxis moves immediately into this political game which is difficult for both practitioners and parents.

The confusion of policy and practice

The reactive, protectionist response to fatalities and medical research has potentially resulted in a confusing categorisation for both parents and early childhood settings of FAs and anaphylaxis into two differing areas:

1 As a purely medical condition

2 As a disability

The most recent SEND review (2022, p. 21) reports on how 'children and young people felt they had not received enough understanding or tailored support for their needs. When children and young people did not get the support they wanted, they often felt excluded, unable to form relationships with children their own age, and in some cases bullied'. The report continues to discuss the idea of co-production (see Chapter 3) continuing on from the 2015 SEND report that parents and children should be 'engaged in the decision-making process around the support that they receive and the progress they are making' (2022, p. 29). However, disappointingly, there is no mention of children with medical conditions such as anaphylaxis, so the confusion for practitioners and parents continues.

REFLECTION

There is evidently confusion about best practice for children and parents in early childhood practice. Some well-meaning settings have attempted to support children and reassure parents by introducing systems at mealtimes to keep children safe. This may include different coloured plates such as red plates for those with allergy and green plates for those who do not. Reflecting on this approach, consider the following questions:

- Is this practice inclusive or designed more for adult control (protectionism) rather than the children and parents?

- Would you use this colour-coded system for any other disability, for example, a red cushion on the carpet for a child with autism? It is likely that you would say no to this so why do you think it is considered acceptable for children with allergies?

- Have you considered your unconscious bias about parents who have a child with allergies? How have you heard them spoken about by other practitioners? Why do you think this is?

Can you think of more inclusive ways for children and parents to feel less isolated?

The role of the practitioner

The role of the practitioner in early childhood as both carer and educator and how this is defined in legislation and research is a complex one. Early childhood settings across health, education and care have a wide range of differing expectations and methods when engaging with parents. The early childhood practitioner as carer of a child with FAs and anaphylaxis incurs high responsibility, which can lead to adding stress to relationships with parents. Supporting a child with anaphylaxis in a setting can be a complicated and stressful role for practitioners who may also not have the required medical training.

Policy in early childhood comes with the expectation of outcomes and performance, and when children with medical needs may have persistent absences due to medical appointments and having had minor or significant reactions, it is understandable that resentment can be part of the parent/practitioner relationship. Parents of children with FAs need to develop strong, trusting relationships with practitioners for them to feel that their child will be safe in a space outside their own home (Cummings et al., 2010).

It should be stated that there has been a development of global practitioner understanding of FAs and anaphylaxis in recent years (Chooniedass, Temple, Martin, & Becker, 2018). Training for staff to use AAIs, although costly to providers, is available to many. Parents have the right to be informed about staff training and provision, and it is important that this is communicated. Some settings ask parents to train them, but this can put parents in a difficult position. They have been taught themselves by health professionals and are not necessarily confident enough to train others. One of the key roles for the practitioner is to return to what many are already aware of, and as stated in many curriculum frameworks, that each child is unique. As each individual case may produce differing reactions, and with each child the reactions could differ as they get older, policy and practice need to be sensitive to this.

CASE STUDY

Yang was diagnosed with a severe nut allergy and anaphylaxis aged four years old following a reaction whilst at home. His parents administered liquid medication at home as they had some awareness of allergies but knew that it was important for adrenaline to be administered in hospital as soon as possible. That night the weather was reported as severe ice and ambulances were struggling to get to emergencies, so the family drove themselves to the local children's hospital. Dad drove whilst mum sat in the back of the car with Yang and talking on the phone to emergency services watching carefully for further signs of throat swelling and trying to remain calm. On arrival at the hospital, the correct medication was administered and Yang was observed overnight. Following this, he was diagnosed with anaphylaxis and has had regular 6-monthly visits for tests and updates ever since.

For parents, this was a huge change to their lifestyle. Going out to eat became too frightening as at the time there were no allergens listed on menus. Travelling abroad by plane was too risky. Most of all, leaving Yang in the care of others where food was available became a huge exercise in trust. The parents began to live with the fact that their child could have an allergic reaction at any time that could be fatal and they may not be with them. Yang had just started school and also went to a childminder for two days a week after school. The childminder spent her own time reading up on everything, sent a letter to all parents about nut products in any food sent and kept a spare EpiPen in the house. She went on EpiPen training immediately and spoke to the parents whenever she was unsure. They felt as if they were learning together.

However, the school experience was very different. The school would not recognise Yang as having any special needs and in fact raised an issue with his attendance as he had to miss school after the reaction and with regular appointments afterwards. Yang became withdrawn after being a very sociable, talkative child and when asked by his parents stated that he could not stop thinking about his EpiPen as it was locked in the school office. At four, he understood that his medication was too far away in an emergency and this left him unable to focus on friendships and learning. The emotional impact of the allergy was far more wide reaching than just the reaction.

(Continued)

(Continued)

Questions

- How much did you know about FAs before you read this chapter? Have you begun to reflect on your personal perceptions and in what way?

- If you were working with children and parents dealing with anaphylaxis, how do you think you would approach this?

- How else do you think anaphylaxis might impact on family life in early childhood?

Conclusion

This chapter aims to support students and practitioners to develop a deeper understanding of the needs of this group of parents and children often overlooked in policy and practice. Whilst early childhood practitioners are encouraged to engage more effectively with families, government policy with an emphasis on improving developmental outcomes for children has the potential to encourage further marginalisation of parents of children with FAs and anaphylaxis.

Policy is extremely complex in early childhood as governance is spread across a range of government departments, including education, health, work and pensions. Current research literature suggests that these complexities in governance and policy writing can impact upon family experiences and QoL from conception to the age of eight years (Cohen et al., 2004). There is evidence that there is still a lack of public policy that supports the safety of those with FAs and anaphylaxis, although recent publicity has influenced restaurants and airline practice to try and provide further safety. For parents, this lack of decision-making and policy introduction can be the cause of anxiety, and for many, a supportive and caring early childhood practitioner can have a significant impact on many areas of their QoL. The role of the early childhood practitioner is highly skilled and the significance of a quality, caring relationship cannot be underestimated.

Further reading

Ford, L. S., Turner, P. J., & Campbell, D. E. (2014). Recommendations for the management of food allergies in a preschool/childcare setting and prevention of anaphylaxis. *Expert review of Clinical Immunology, 10*(7), 867–874.

Polloni, L., Baldi, I., Amadi, M., Tonazzo, V., Bonaguro, R., Lazzarotto, F., Toniolo, A., Gregori, D., & Muraro, A. (2022). Management of children with food-induced anaphylaxis: A cross-sectional survey of parental knowledge, attitude, and practices. *Frontiers in Pediatrics, 10*, 886551.

https://www.gov.uk/government/publications/supporting-pupils-at-school-with-medical-conditions–3

Useful websites

https://www.allergyuk.org/

https://www.anaphylaxis.org.uk/

https://www.nhs.uk/conditions/baby/weaning-and-feeding/food-allergies-in-babies-and-young-children/

References

Akeson, N., Worth, A., & Sheikh, A. (2007). The psychosocial impact of anaphylaxis on young people and their parents. *Clinical & Experimental Allergy*, *37*(8), 1213–1220.

Anaphylaxis. (2022). *About anaphylaxis*. Retrieved from: https://www.anaphylaxis.org.uk/ (Accessed 9th August 2022).

Barnes, C., & Power, M. (2012). Internalising discourses of parenting blame: Voices from the field. *Studies in the Maternal*, *4*(2), 1–21.

Benford, J., & Tait, C. (2017). Working in groups with parents of young children; growing together at the Pen Green Centre. In **M. Whalley** (Ed.), *Involving parents in their children's learning: A knowledge-sharing approach*. London: SAGE.

Cain, R. (2016). Responsibilising recovery: Lone and low-paid parents, universal credit and the gendered contradictions of UK welfare reform. *British Politics*, *11*(4), 488–507.

Chooniedass, R., Temple, B., Martin, D., & Becker, A. (2018). A qualitative study exploring parents' experiences with epinephrine use for their child's anaphylactic reaction. *Clinical and Translational Allergy*, *8*(1), 43.

Cohen, B. L., Noone, S., Muñoz-Furlong, A., & Sicherer, S. H. (2004). Development of a questionnaire to measure quality of life in families with a child with food allergy. *Journal of Allergy and Clinical Immunology*, *114*(5), 1159–1163.

Cottle, M., & Alexander, E. (2014). Parent partnership and 'quality' early years services: Practitioners' perspectives. *European Early Childhood Education Research Journal*, *22*(5), 637–659.

Cummings, A. J., Knibb, R. C., Erlewyn-Lajeunesse, M., King, R. M., Roberts, G., & Lucas, J. S. (2010). Management of nut allergy influences quality of life and anxiety in children and their mothers. *Paediatric Allergy and Immunology*, *21*(41), 586–594.

Department for Education. (2021). *Statutory framework for the early years foundation stage*. Retrieved from: https://www.gov.uk/government/publications/early-years-foundation-stage-framework--2

DfE (Department for Education) & DoH (Department of Health). (2015). *Special educational needs and disability code of practice: 0 to 25 years*. Retrieved from: https://www.gov.uk/government/uploads/system/uploads/attachment_data/file/398815/SEND_Code_of_Practice_January_2015.pdf

Elfer, P. (2013). *Key persons in the nursery: Building relationships for quality provision*. London: David Fulton Publishers.

Fernández-Rivas, M., Barreales, L., Mackie, A. R., Fritsche, P., Vázquez-Cortés, S., Jedrzejczak-Czechowicz, M., . . . Kompoti, E. (2015). The EuroPrevall outpatient clinic study on food allergy: Background and methodology. *Allergy*, *70*(5), 576–584.

Gillespie, C. A., Woodgate, R. L., Chalmers, K. I., & Watson, W. T. (2007). 'Living with risk': Mothering a child with food-induced anaphylaxis. *Journal of Paediatric Nursing*, *22*(1), 30–42.

Greene, H. L., Prior, T., & Frier, H. I. (2001). Foods, health claims, and the law: Comparisons of the United States and Europe. *Obesity Research, 9*(S11), 276S–283S.

Grover, C. (2005). The National Childcare Strategy: The social regulation of lone mothers as a gendered reserve army of labour. *Capital & Class, 29*(1), 63–90.

Gupta, R., Holdford, D., Bilaver, L., Dyer, A., Holl, J. L., & Meltzer, D. (2013). The economic impact of childhood food allergy in the United States. *JAMA Pediatrics, 167*(11), 1026–1031.

Hamilton, P. (2021). *Diversity and marginalisation in childhood: A guide for inclusive thinking 0-11.* London: SAGE.

HM Government. (2022). *SEND review: Right support, right place, right time.* London: HM Government.

Moneret-Vautrin, D. A., Kanny, G., Morisset, M., Flabbee, J., Guenard, L., Beaudouin, E., & Parisot, L. (2001). Food anaphylaxis in schools: Evaluation of the management plan and the efficiency of the emergency kit. *Allergy, 56*(11), 1071–1076.

Muraro, A., Hoffmann-Sommergruber, K., Holzhauser, T., Poulsen, L. K., Gowland, M. H., Akdis, C. A., ..., van Ree, R. (2014). EAACI food allergy and anaphylaxis guidelines. Protecting consumers with food allergies: Understanding food consumption, meeting regulations and identifying unmet needs. *Allergy, 69*(11), 1464–1472.

Nakagawa, K. (2000). Unthreading the ties that bind: Questioning the discourse of parent involvement. *Educational Policy, 14*(4), 443–472.

National Institute for Health and Care Excellence (NICE), Quality standard [QS 118]. (2016). Retrieved from: https://www.nice.org.uk/guidance/qs118

Nurmatov, U., Worth, A., & Sheikh, A. (2008). Anaphylaxis management plans for the acute and long-term management of anaphylaxis: A systematic review. *Journal of Allergy and Clinical Immunology, 122*(2), 353–361.

Osgood, J., Albon, D., Allen, K., & Hollingworth, S. (2013). 'Hard to reach' or nomadic resistance? Families 'choosing' not to participate in early childhood services. *Global Studies of Childhood, 3*(3), 208–220.

Sanagavarapu, P. (2017). Young children's knowledge of food allergy and transition to school. *Cogent Education, 4*(1), 1304617.

Sanagavarapu, P. (2018). Experiences and support needs of mothers of children with food allergy during the transition to school. *Early Childhood Education Journal, 46*(5), 523–534.

Sims-Schouten, W. (2016). Positioning in relationships between parents and early years practitioners. *Early Child Development and Care, 186*(9), 1392–1405.

Singley, S. G., & Hynes, K. (2005). Transitions to parenthood: Work-family policies, gender, and the couple context. *Gender & Society, 19*(3), 376–397.

The Human Medicines Regulations. (2012). Retrieved from: http://www.legislation.gov.uk/uksi/2012/1916/contents/made

Valentine, A. Z., & Knibb, R. C. (2011). Exploring quality of life in families of children living with and without a severe food allergy. *Appetite, 57*(2), 467–474.

Vale, S., Smith, J., Said, M., Mullins, R. J., & Loh, R. (2015). ASCIA guidelines for prevention of anaphylaxis in schools, pre-schools and childcare: 2015 update. *Journal of Paediatrics and Child Health, 51*(10), 949–954.

Walsh, J. (2017a). *National Institute for Health and Care Excellence (NICE), quality standard [QS118], 2016.*

Wright, A. (2012). Fantasies of empowerment: Mapping neoliberal discourse in the coalition government's school's policy. *Journal of Education Policy, 27*(3), 279–294.

4 RACE AND INEQUALITY IN EARLY CHILDHOOD HEALTH

VALERIE DANIEL

CHAPTER OBJECTIVES

By the end of this chapter, you will be able to:

- Understand the impact of race and inequality on early childhood health.
- Understand the root causes of health inequities in early childhood.
- Understand the barriers to addressing race and inequality in early childhood health.

Consider some strategies for addressing race and inequality in early childhood health.

KEY DEFINITIONS

BAME

Black, Asian and minority ethnic (BAME). The collective term widely used for the 'non-White' population by government departments, public bodies, the media and others.

Bias

Bias is a natural inclination for or prejudice against an individual or group of people. Bias is often learned and is often preconceived and unreasoned. Bias can be conscious or unconscious, but it involves either consciously or unconsciously stereotyping groups of people based on false beliefs or assumptions.

Ethnicity

Ethnicity focuses on the culture of people from specific geographic regions, including their language, heritage, religion and customs.

Parents

Any person who has parental responsibility or has care of a young child during early childhood (from conception to eight years of age).

Practitioner

A person who is qualified to work with children (from conception to 8 years old) across health, education and social care.

Race

Race is the concept of categorising people into groups based on physical characteristics, especially skin colour, as well as ascribing social meaning to these groups.

Racial disproportionality

Describes when certain racial groups are over- or under-represented 'at levels that are disproportionate to their numbers in the overall child and family population' (Courtney & Skyles, 2003, p. 2).

Racial disparity

Describes unequal treatment of certain groups due to their race, which potentially increases disproportionality. Unequal treatment refers to differential resource allocation, access and services between racial groups (Putnam-Hornstein, Needell, King, & Johnson-Motoyama, 2013).

Introduction

This chapter will consider child health equity and what it would mean for every child in the United Kingdom to have what they need to be as healthy as possible. It would seem entirely feasible that all children in the United Kingdom should have access to basic health determinants like clean water, sanitation and adequate nutrition, so why would there be irrefutable evidence (BMA 2021; Marmot, Allen, Boyce, Goldblatt, & Morrison, 2020; Opondo, Jayaweera, & Hollowell, 2019; Perry et al., 2021) of vast health inequities in early childhood? The simple answer to this question is that social and economic factors also play a major role in shaping children's health outcomes. Early childhood development is a critical element in health equity: the earliest years of a child's life can determine lifelong vulnerability or create opportunities for children to thrive and grow. Childhood development is influenced by a range of socioeconomic factors which include family income, breastfeeding and nutrition, parenting skills and styles, parental stress and adverse childhood experiences, early childhood care and education, parents' education and more. The topic of discussion for this chapter is that race is an undeniable influence in the socioeconomic factors that affect early childhood health. We do not need any more research studies to prove that healthcare inequalities exist between ethnic groups in the United Kingdom, and it is time for full recognition that childhood mortality, morbidity as well as differentials in health care are undeniably correlated to race and ethnicity. As a result, a child's right to protection, nurture and care and to be as healthy as possible is determined by *ad hoc*, individual healthcare providers, rather than a healthcare system that works to eradicate race and ethnicity as a key factor in the likelihood of suffering from childhood disease, having ongoing health vulnerabilities *and/or* dying before adulthood. We can agree that racism is a public health crisis, therefore conceptualising racism in health is of utmost importance for reducing early childhood health inequalities.

Principles and values

Working in health care comes with the underpinning principles of research ethics, public health ethics, organisational ethics, personal ethics and also professional values which include the following:

- Doing good and avoiding harm
- Expertise and competence
- Fairness and equity
- Honesty and integrity
- Entitlements and rights
- Responsibility and reliability
- Professional compassion and respect

As the United Kingdom aims for all citizens to spend more time in 'good' or 'very good' health, the key purpose of health care is to help the public to maintain and maximise good health. As early childhood practitioners, we know that good health is crucial to quality of life for children and essential for healthy growth and development. The National Occupational Standards in Children's Care, Learning and Development (2015) were designed to provide a set of principles and values for working with young children across a range of settings and services.

The standards are outlined below:

Principles

- The welfare of the child is paramount.
- Practitioners contribute to children's care, learning and development, and this is reflected in every aspect of practice and service provision.

- Practitioners work with parents and families who are partners in the care, learning and development of their children and are the child's first and most enduring educators.

Values

- The needs, rights and views of the child are at the centre of all practice and provision.

- Individuality, difference and diversity are valued and celebrated.

- Equality of opportunity and anti-discriminatory practice are actively promoted.

- Children's health and well-being are actively promoted.

- Children's personal and physical safety is safeguarded, whilst allowing for risk and challenge as appropriate to the capabilities of the child.

- Self-esteem, resilience and a positive self-image are recognised as essential to every child's development.

- Confidentiality and agreements about confidential information are respected as appropriate unless a child's protection and well-being are at stake.

- Professional knowledge, skills and values are shared appropriately in order to enrich the experience of children more widely.

- Best practice requires reflection and a continuous search for improvement.

National Occupational Standards (2015) [Online] Retrieved from: http://www.ukstandards.org.uk.

These policy frameworks promote principles and values that should drive the actions of all practitioners involved in early childhood health. So why is inequality still such a strong feature in early childhood health? Essentially, policy frameworks and practice need to hold hands and harmoniously walk together, if there is to be any hope of reducing early childhood health inequalities.

REFLECTION

- Discuss the importance of ethics in healthcare practice.

- Evaluate tensions, conflicts and possible complicity within and between your personal and professional value system as related to healthcare practice.

The dynamics of race

By 1964, there were approximately one million people from Commonwealth countries living in the United Kingdom. Most of them were responding to the

British Government's call for workers after Britain was devastated by war and needed workers to help restore the post-war economy. However, racially charged public statements made about West Indian immigrants being 'undesirable and burdensome' during this time contributed to serious damage in Britain coming to terms with having a multi-racial dynamic. It could be suggested that this was nearly 55 years ago, so why is this still a topic of discussion? The answer to that is, the legacy of suspicion and mistrust has persisted to present times. Prejudice does not go away just because time has passed, or because a policy framework and legislation say it should not exist. Let us not forget that people put policy into practice, people who have their own sets of beliefs, values and motivations which are constantly nurtured by coded racism and the promotion of racial stereotypes. Without thinking, the attributes of White equals good and Black equals bad are reinforced in a society where blackness is already seen as inferior and threatening. Tatum (1997) argues that this message is so prevalent in our society, that it is like 'smog in the air. Sometimes it is so thick it is visible, other times it is less apparent, but always, day in and day out, we are breathing it in' (p. 6). Samuel Johnson, a British author, born in 1709, famously said 'prejudice, not being founded on reason, cannot be removed by argument' and I will add neither can it be removed by laws. Johnson also said 'the chains of habit are too weak to be felt until they are too strong to be broken'. This aptly describes coded racism: subtle, socially constructed and habitual. Subliminal messages form a part of our everyday understanding of the world and helps our unconscious minds to make snap judgements from even well-meaning people and more complexly, from some Black and ethnic minority people.

Distortions of race

The vast majority of Black and ethnic minority adults who are born in the United Kingdom start out in a system that is unfairly stacked against them because of the engrained ideology of biological superiority between ethnic groups, which is the basis of structural racism. Structural racism creates a chasm between communities of people who have deeply opposing views and who simply do not trust each other's motives. So sadly, trust is a casualty of structural racism; the loss of trust in people and public systems that are meant to support **all** citizens. These distortions about race filter into early childhood health. Obviously, without trust, it will be difficult to reduce poor early childhood health outcomes.

Cerdeña, Plaisime, and Tsai (2020) reaffirm research that tells us that 'race is a poor proxy for human variation'. They also explain that ;genetic research shows that humans cannot be divided into biologically distinct subcategories' (p. 1125). However, the persistence of race-based health care which characterises race as an essential biological variable translates into inequitable care for ethnic minority adults and children alike. Cerdeña et al. (2020) propose an approach of 'race-conscious' health care, which would be defined as healthcare 'practice and pedagogy that accounts for how structural racism determines illness and health' (p. 1127) (Figure 4.1).

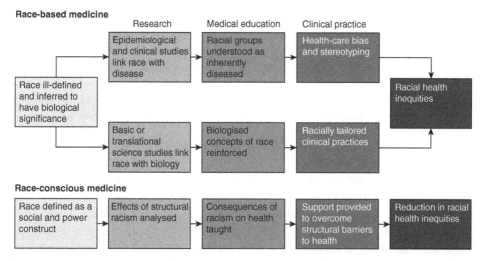

Figure 4.1 Race-based health care vs race-conscious health care (Cerdeña et al., 2020)

Source: Reproduced by kind permission of Elsevier Inc.

REFLECTION

Race-based services rely on information that promotes Black and Brown people as genetically different from White people. This perception has its legacy in European colonialisation, when the concept of 'race' was developed as a tool to divide, control and assert the idea of biological inferiority of people with melanated skin tones.

- Discuss why and how the socially constructed concept of race, originally designed as a dividing tool, can impact on early childhood health outcomes?

- How might coded racism affect practitioners in their assessments and practice?

- How might unintentional racial bias impact on early childhood health outcomes?

Think critically and discuss how race-conscious health care could transform early childhood health outcomes.

Structural and societal patterns of racism in early childhood health

We know that biological and environmental factors play a key role in childhood health risks and outcomes, but we have to ask if these are enough to explain the significant disparities in health outcomes between racial groups. If there is to be sustainable change in childhood health outcomes, we have to consider whether everyone has access to and receives the same quality of healthcare intervention. Do we live in a society where there is inconsistency in addressing healthcare needs? Does a lack of accessibility to services and a lack of trust in the healthcare system impact negatively on some community groups and how they deal with their own personal health needs? These are questions that need to be thoroughly explored to implement the right kind of actions to reduce early childhood health inequalities.

Structural inequality is such a fundamental feature of UK society, that it has almost ceased to be perceptible in everyday life by those who benefit from it, and when it is blatantly exposed by events like the global pandemic, it is outrightly denied or there is a failure to recognise it in its truest form. A classic example of this is the highly contested report of the Commission on Race and Ethnic Disparities (2021) (CRED). CRED was established in 2020 and tasked to look at race and ethnic disparities in education, employment, crime and policing and health in the United Kingdom in the wake of Black Lives Matter protests following the murder of George Floyd. The report confirmed that the United Kingdom does not yet enjoy racial equality but fell short of acknowledging structural racism as a key element of inequality. So as we do not as yet have racial equality in the United Kingdom, there are some questions that need to be asked to explore the disparities in early childhood health outcomes in the United Kingdom.

REFLECTION

- What evidence is there that indicates that the current inequality in the United Kingdom does impact on the early childhood healthcare system?

- How can we detangle racial discrimination from other social factors that affect early childhood health outcomes in the United Kingdom?

- How might the healthcare provider/receiver relationship contribute to communication disparities and population-level early childhood health disparities?

- Discuss whether unconscious bias of healthcare providers could potentially be a part of the solution to early childhood health disparities?

Racial disproportionality in healthcare outcomes is routinely documented in the United Kingdom and this includes early childhood health; however, the relentless denial of institutionalised racism means that race-based disparities are poorly defined. This creates an unstable basis for when race is relevant and when it is not, in healthcare practice. Jones (2000) notes that this 'impedes the advance of scientific knowledge, limits efforts at primary prevention, and perpetuates ideas of biologically determined differences between the races' (p. 1212). We know that racial disproportionality and racial disparities in early childhood health outcomes are avoidable, so the question to ask is whether **all** children matter in the United

Kingdom. The gut response from anyone reading this would automatically be 'Yes! of course **all** children matter!' but sadly the disparities in early childhood health outcomes in the United Kingdom tells us differently. What does research tell us about the links between structural racism and early childhood health disparities? Jones (2000) provides a theoretical framework for us to explore this question (Figure 4.2).

Jones further highlights institutionalised racism as structural because it is pervasively codified into institutions of custom, practice and law, which also serves to complicate the identification of race-associated discrimination and often displays as inherited disadvantage with Black and ethnic minority communities. She specifies that the link between socioeconomic status and race stems from the historical legacy of racism 'but persists because of contemporary structural factors that perpetuate those historical injustices' (p. 1212). Jones (2000) advises us that institutional racism manifests as:

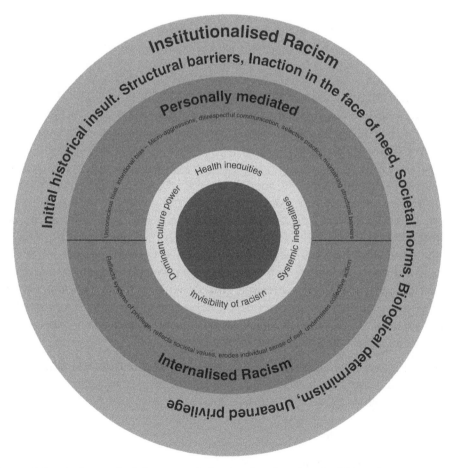

Figure 4.2   A theoretical framework for levels of racism in UK society

Source: Adapted from Jones (2000). Three levels of racism; institutionalised, personally mediated and internalised.

- 'Inaction in the face of need'.

- Lack of 'access to power' including 'differential access to information (including one's own history), resources (including wealth and organizational infrastructure), and voice (including voting rights, representation in government, and control of the media)'.

- 'Differential access to quality education, sound housing, gainful employment, appropriate medical facilities, and a clean environment' (p. 1212).

Jones (2000) also presents us with an allegory of a gardener with two plant boxes, which appeals to me because of the powerful message regarding institutionalised/ structural racism without triggering an emotive response. Read 'A Gardener's Tale' below:

CASE STUDY: A GARDENER'S TALE

Let us imagine a gardener who has two flower boxes, one that she knows to be filled with rich, fertile soil and another that she knows to be filled with poor, rocky soil. This gardener has two packets of seeds for the same type of flower. However, the plants grown from one packet of seeds will bear pink blossoms, while the plants grown from the other packet of seeds will bear red blossoms. The gardener prefers red over pink, so she plants the red seed in the rich, fertile soil and the pink seed in the poor, rocky soil. And sure enough, what I witnessed in my own garden comes to pass in this garden too. All of the red flowers grow up and flourish, with the fittest growing tall and strong and even the weakest making it to a middling height. But in the box with the poor, rocky soil, things look different. The weak among the pink seeds do not even make it, and the strongest among them grow only to a middling height. In time, the flowers in these two boxes go to seed, dropping their progeny into the same soil in which they were growing. The next year the same thing happens, with the red flowers in the rich soil growing full and vigorous and strong, while the pink flowers in the poor soil struggle to survive. And these flowers go to seed. Year after year, the same thing happens. Ten years later, the gardener comes to survey her garden. Gazing at the two boxes, she says, 'I was right to prefer red over pink! Look how vibrant and beautiful the red flowers look and see how pitiful and scrawny the pink ones are'.

Using the Jones (2000) allegory of 'A Gardener's Tale' alongside the Jones (2000) theoretical framework for levels of racism in UK society, identify the elements that represent the following:

- Institutionalised racism

- Personally mediated racism

- Internalised racism

Discuss the relevance of 'A Gardener's Tale' to early childhood health outcomes in the United Kingdom.

Who is the gardener? Discuss where the dangers lie and what powers the gardener has to make change.

The wider issues

Research tells us that intergenerational social disadvantage that often results in early childhood health disparities is perpetuated by structural racism; however, causal explanations for racial disparities are rarely examined. This can result in disparate early childhood health outcomes often being discussed or documented without being contextualised within the different social environments that require intervention in tandem, to positively impact on childhood health outcomes. Some of these are:

- The **physical environment**, for example, housing and pollution in densely populated ethnic minority areas.

- The **economic environment**, for example, lack of employment, low-income employment and family income.

- The **social environment**, for example, culture, social status, race, gender and immigration status.

- The **service environment**, for example, education, health care, social services, over-policing of ethnic minority communities and under-policing of ethnic minority areas.

Environmental health research is used to inform human health and well-being, but it has to be noted that structural racism affects the translation of health policies and the various environmental protections for communities who are disproportionately affected. Recent public health disasters like the Grenfell Tower fire in 2017 demonstrate the far-reaching impact of inaction on physical, social, economic and service environments that largely affect poorer and ethnic minority communities. At last count, 75 people died in the Grenfell fire, 57 of them were from Black and ethnic minority communities and 18 of them were young children. 'Redressing structural racism in environmental epidemiology will require implementation of systemic remedies at all levels of education and research' (Perry et al., 2021, p. 6). Their recommendations are as follows:

- Acknowledge racism in public health research

- Include affected communities in decision-making

- Develop requirements and standards for discussing 'race' in research

- Embrace a more holistic approach to analysis
- Partner with community members to conduct research

REFLECTION

- How can we as practitioners identify racism that impacts on the health outcomes and well-being of young children?

- Discuss whether 'race' is an independent risk factor for early childhood health outcomes and how misinformed racially tailored health care might drive poor early childhood health outcomes and increase health inequities.

Research recommendations

This section will explore some of the consequences of ignoring race as a determinant of early childhood health inequalities and will highlight some recommendations that have evolved out of research. Racial health inequalities can begin from conception and continue throughout childhood and into adulthood. We know that many of these inequalities are driven by socioeconomic factors, and trying to address social issues as separate from racial issues as suggested by CRED (2021) leaves a massive gap in capacity to make real change in health outcomes for all children. Social and racial issues for ethnic minority communities are not mutually exclusive. We need to accept that ignoring race in early childhood health inequalities is hugely significant and socially consequential. 'It should be taught that racial health disparities are a consequence of structural racism' (Cerdeña et al., 2020, p. 1127).

The British Medical Association (BMA, 2021) did an analysis of the CRED Race Report and the findings highlighted issues like ethnic minority disparities in the healthcare workforce. While the Race Report celebrates the contributions of ethnic minority healthcare workers in post-war Britain, it does not in any way address the racial disproportionality of ethnic minority healthcare workers who continue to be over-represented in lower pay grade roles and grossly under-represented in higher pay grade roles. Under-representation at leadership levels in public systems helps to quieten a significant number of the voices that are needed to make a difference to race-based early childhood health outcomes.

The role of the practitioner

The BMA (2021) advocates for 'cultural transformation' across all aspects of health care 'including selection, attainment, progression, assessments, individual experiences, staff diversity and staff training'. This 'cultural transformation' should also include parent partnership. As practitioners, we know the importance of recognising parents as an invaluable source of information on their children and a rich source of information on their individual culture. Without a deep and respectful value for parent partnerships, early childhood health care will prolong negative and preventable risks to childhood health outcomes. BMA (2021) also informs that race is a significant factor in proper ethnic minority representation across the teaching faculty and also in career progression into more senior roles.

Lack of ethnic minority representation in healthcare education and senior medical roles serves to stem the experience and knowledge of ethnic minority healthcare professionals from having an impact and can reinforce racial inequality and worsen early childhood health outcomes.

- Sachs and Rigby (2021, p. 3) reporting on asthma care recommend these actions among others:

- *'Anti-prejudice training for healthcare staff as the general prejudice that some groups face impacts their asthma care.*

- *Myth busting in communities to help support the sharing of accurate information and avoid delayed diagnosis'.*

As practitioners we cannot ignore health care that is based on racial stereotyping (e.g. Black people have longer nerve endings and thicker skin than White people so they feel less pain). When extrapolated, this essentially says that Black children feel pain to a far lesser degree than White children! Think about this and the impact it might have on pain management in some early childhood diseases. Without cultural transformation, these false theories will continue to be used to justify cuts to resources for those who need them the most. Cerdeña et al. (2020, p. 1126) recommends that 'race should not be used to make inferences about physiological function' in healthcare practice but that race should be used 'to assess for experiences of discrimination and refer to affinity-based support services'. Marmot (2010, p. 14) makes six recommendations which cover stages of life, healthy standard of living, communities and places and ill health prevention; their highest priority recommendation was: 'Give every child the best start in life', an important aspect for practitioners to reflect upon.

Acknowledging racial bias in healthcare systems is of the utmost importance for practice. However, race-neutral interventions and colour-blind healthcare practice as a means of mitigating bias and racial discrimination are a misguided concept that stems from the belief that treating everyone as equally as possible without regard to race, culture or ethnicity is the best way to end discrimination. As well-meaning as this intention may be, this perspective does more harm than good. Being 'blind' to race and ethnicity is essentially being blind to racism in health care which 'corrupts knowledge production and limits access to equal treatment' (Yearby, 2021, p. 24). Being specific about racial disadvantages in social policies is important in respect to the role this could play in reducing racially discriminatory early childhood health outcomes.

REFLECTION

Consider the early childhood healthcare settings you are familiar with and reflect on the following:

- How have you observed 'cultural transformation' taking place?

- How do you think health care could acknowledge racial bias?

- Have you considered how you refer to collective parents and families, for example, White or BAME, and what implications this has?

Conclusion

Racial disproportionality and disparities in early childhood health are both complex and multi-factorial, for example:

- The risk of neonatal and infant mortality is twice as high in Black African and Pakistani babies as White British babies (Opondo et al., 2019, p. 8).

- In 5131 paediatric heart operations, Asian infants were 52% more likely to die than White infants (Sinha, Khan, Messahel, & Kar, 2021, BMJ blog).

- In children with renal failure, national registry data demonstrate that South Asian and Black children were less likely to receive a pre-emptive renal transplant than White children (Sinha et al., 2021, BMJ blog).

Sinha et al. (2021) emphasise that the health disparities in these examples cannot be solely attributed to socioeconomic factors, and with regards to adverse birth outcomes, socioeconomic factors can only account for a quarter of the disparities in outcomes across infants from different ethnic groups. They recommend deleting the collective concept of 'BAME' as patterns of ethnic variation in health are extremely diverse. 'BAME' data as a collective reduce children to being 'White or non-White', which impairs the development of the best health care based on particular needs.

White normativity is so pervasively engrained in public health research that 'White' is automatically selected as the referent group in statistical analysis without any consideration of the purpose of doing so or the effect of choosing to do so. On top of White normativity, a systematic review on the impact of healthcare algorithms on racial and ethnic disparities in health and health care has found that race and ethnicity are used in the algorithms that influence clinical decision-making and patient outcomes, however, they conclude that 'because race and ethnicity are socially constructed, their inclusion as variables within healthcare algorithms may lead to unknown or unwanted effects, including the potential for exacerbation and/or perpetuation of health and healthcare disparities' (Department of Health and Human Services, 2022, p. 1). This is of concern for us in the United Kingdom because technology is perceived as fundamental to the ongoing transformation of the health and care sector and is 'central to the delivery of health and care for both adults and children' (NHS, 2016).

We should note that health inequities are avoidable and can be reduced, but this is subject to political will, a children's rights perspective and passionate advocates for quality health care for all children despite their social circumstances. It bears repeating that understanding how to make changes to childhood health inequalities requires time and deep thought to the function of race and how it continually reproduces and normalises the idea of a natural social hierarchy within society. Race is an agenda that also persistently nurtures the idea of inherent racial differences based on biological factors or genetic coding that denotes human attributes like intelligence, character, physical abilities and personality traits. We know that research has debunked these myths, so as early childhood practitioners, there is a duty on us to persist in doing what is right, even on those occasions when it is easier, quicker and far more convenient to do what everyone else is doing. As practitioners, we need to make the right choices for the right reasons, and there is no better reason than doing right by a child no matter the social circumstances they were born into, live in or the colour of their skin.

Further reading

Alegria, M., Vallas, M., & Pumariega, A. J. (2010). Racial and ethnic disparities in paediatric mental health. *Child and Adolescent Psychiatric Clinics of North America, 19*(4), 759–774.

Ayodeji, E., Dubicka, B., Abuah, O., Odebiyi, B., Sultana, R., & Ani, C. (2021). Editorial perspective: Mental health needs of children and young people of Black ethnicity.[1] Is it time to reconceptualise racism as a traumatic experience? *Child and Adolescent Mental Health, 26*(3), 265–266.

British Medical Association (BMA). (2022). *Race inequalities and ethnic disparities in healthcare.* Retrieved from: https://www.bma.org.uk/advice-and-support/equality-and-diversity-guidance/race-equality-in-medicine/race-inequalities-and-ethnic-disparities-in-healthcare (Accessed 8th August 2022).

Useful websites

https://www.gov.uk/government/publications/inequalities-in-child-development

https://stateofchildhealth.rcpch.ac.uk/key-priorities/reduce-health-inequalities/

https://adc.bmj.com/content/104/10/998

https://www.instituteofhealthequity.org/resources-reports/give-every-child-the-best-start-in-life

References

British Medical Association (BMA). (2021). *A missed opportunity: BMA response to the race report.* Retrieved from: https://www.bma.org.uk/media/4276/bma-analysis-of-the-race-report-from-the-commission-on-race-and-ethnic-disparities-june-2021.pdf (Accessed 11th August 2022).

Cerdeña, J. P., Plaisime, M. V., & Tsai, J. (2020). From race-based to race-conscious medicine: How anti-racist uprisings call us to act. *Lancet, 396*, 1125–1128.

Commission on Race and Ethnic Disparities (CRED). (2021). *Commission on race and ethnic disparities: The report.* Cabinet Office, Government UK.

Courtney, M., & Skyles, A. (2003). Racial disproportionality in the child welfare system. *Children and Youth Services Review, 25*(5–6), 355–358.

Department of Health and Human Services. (2022, December 05). Impact of Healthcare Algorithms on Racial and Ethnic Disparities in Health and Healthcare. Retrieved from: https://effectivehealthcare.ahrq.gov/products/racial-disparities-health-healthcare/protocol

Jones, C. P. J. (2000). Levels of racism: A theoretic framework and a Gardener's Tale. *American Journal of Public Health, 2000*(90), 1212–1215.

Marmot, M. (2010). *Fair society, healthy lives: The Marmot review: Executive summary, review of health inequalities in England post-2010.* London: The Institute of Health Equity.

Marmot, M., Allen, J., Boyce, T., Goldblatt, P., & Morrison, J. (2020). *Health equity in England: The Marmot review 10 years on.* London: The Institute of Health Equity.

National Health Service. (2016). *Digital health transformation programme.* Retrieved from: www.england.nhs.uk/digitaltechnology/child-health (Accessed 8th August 2022).

National Occupational Standards. (2015). *Repository for all approved national occupational standards.* Retrieved from: http://www.ukstandards.org.uk (Accessed 8th August 2022).

Opondo, C., Jayaweera, H., & Hollowell, J. (2019). Variations in neonatal mortality, infant mortality, preterm birth and birth weight in England and Wales according to ethnicity and maternal country or region of birth: An analysis of linked national data from 2006 to 2012. *Journal of Epidemiology and Community Health, 74*(4), 336–345.

Perry, M. J., Arrington, S., Freisthler, M. S., Ibe, I. N., McCray, N. L., Neumann, L. M., . . . Trejo Rosas, B. M. (2021). Pervasive structural racism in environmental epidemiology. *Environmental Health, 20*, 119.

Putnam-Hornstein, E., Needell, B., King, B., & Johnson-Motoyama, M. (2013). Racial and ethnic disparities: A population-based examination of risk factors for involvement with child protective services. *National Library of Medicine, 37*(1), 33–46.

Sachs, J., & Rigby, E. (2021). *Children, young people and families' experiences of chronic asthma management and care.* Young People's Health Partnership. Retrieved from: https://ayph.org.uk/lets-hear-from-young-people-and-their-families-about-their-experiences-of-managing-asthma/ (Accessed 8th August 2022).

Sinha, I., Khan, H., Messahel, S., & Kar, P. (2021). Ignoring systemic racism hinders efforts to eliminate health inequalities in childhood. *BMJ Blogs.* Retrieved from: https://blogs.bmj.com/bmj/2021/04/27/ignoring-systemic-racism-hinders-efforts-to-eliminate-racial-health-inequalities-in-childhoo/

Tatum, B. D. (1997). *'Why are all the Black kids sitting together in the cafeteria?' and other conversations about race.* New York, NY: Basic Books.

Yearby, R. (2021). Race based medicine, colorblind disease: How racism in medicine harms us all. *American Journal Bioethics, 21*(2), 9–27.

5 UNDERSTANDING AND SUPPORTING ADOPTIVE FAMILIES

JENNY BOLDRIN

CHAPTER OBJECTIVES

By the end of this chapter, you will be able to:

- Demonstrate an understanding of the potential needs of adopted children, including consideration of the lasting impact of early and sustained trauma.
- Explore adoption through multiple ecological lenses, including children, parents and siblings.
- Explore the role of life story work in supporting the identity, well-being and belonging of adopted children.
- Critically reflect on the varied and complex reasons behind adoption disruption.

KEY DEFINITIONS

Parents

Any person who has parental responsibility or has care of a young child during early childhood (from conception to eight years of age).

Practitioner

A person who is qualified to work with children (from conception to 8 years old) across health, education and social care.

Looked-after child

A child who is the legal responsibility of the local authority due to relinquishment by birth parents or removal by the local authority to protect the safety and welfare of the child.

(Continued)

(Continued)

Adoption

The process by which a looked-after child's permanency plan results in them transitioning to an adoptive placement where adoptive parents assume all legal parental rights. Also includes transnational adoptions whereby children are adopted internationally, although this is less common in the United Kingdom.

Permanence

The process of finding a looked-after child a permanent, stable and loving home to offer consistency of care.

Introduction

This chapter will introduce the unique and often complex reality of adoptive families. By exploring some of the dominant discourses surrounding the ecology of adoption, early childhood **practitioners** are challenged to critically reflect on what adoption means for children and families at the centre of the process.

At the heart of this chapter are relationships, particularly the complex relationships and narratives at play within adoptive family dynamics. Relationships are rarely straightforward and those shaped through adoption are no exception. It is important to consider how an understanding of the relationships lost and formed through adoption can support professional practice.

Adopted children and families are one of the most vulnerable and marginalised groups in society (Gore-Langton & Boy, 2017), often subject to a lack of professional understanding of their complex and unique needs. Children entering adoptive families are often characterised as the lucky ones (Syne, Green, & Dyer, 2012), making a fresh start and living out the fantasy of a forever family, leaving little room to acknowledge the lasting and long-term impact of trauma and loss upon their lives. This chapter will provide opportunities to reflect on how, through sensitive and respectful partnership working, professionals can work to become attuned to the needs of adoptive families and ensure they are represented and empowered through early childhood practice.

Relational and developmental trauma

Government statistics suggest that over two thirds of the children in local authority care in England are there because of abuse or neglect, with 'family disfunction', 'family in acute stress' and 'absent parenting' also highlighted as significant contributors to the statistics (Department for Education, 2021).

The role of trauma within the early life of looked-after and adopted children is often described as *relational trauma* (Chiu, Lam Ho, Tollenaar, Elzinga, & Zhang, 2019) as the abuse being inflicted is often done so by trusted caregivers or those who the child relies upon for survival. Trauma perpetuated within a caregiver relationship is considered especially problematic for development as these relationships exist for children to establish the fundamental psychological principles of trust, emotional regulation, social interaction and self-image. Such processes are integral to the formation of attachments within early childhood, and the damage done by their absence has the potential to be lifelong and profound (John et al., 2019; Ryan, Lane, & Powers, 2017). According to Howe (2005), the feeling of safety and security brought about by the responses and reliability of a caregiver allows exploration of the world and subsequent connections in development. Where security and safety are removed, cognitive, emotional and social development is threatened with physiological efforts predominantly being concentrated on survival and safety.

For children moving into adoptive placements, early life experiences will be a determining factor in their ability to navigate their transition, form new relationships and feel a sense of psychological well-being. Golding (2020, p. 371) reminds us that:

> *Abuse, neglect, exposure to frightened and frightening parents, separation and loss all erode sense of safety, destroy trust in others and lead to defensive adaptations which whilst aiding survival reduces resilience.*

According to Fresno et al. (2018), children living in states of persistent and complex trauma will often develop assessment strategies to cope with their situations, creating conditioned reactions to perceived threats within their environment. Such reactions are not easily undone and may require consistent therapeutic interventions from parents and professionals. Fagan (2011) warns that even children who are seemingly responding to new relationships and environments within adoptive placements can easily experience behavioural relapses in the face of seemingly minor stressors, as their psychological conditioning instinctively takes over. John et al. (2019, p. 121) agrees, claiming that children exposed to complex trauma through early childhood will often experience post-traumatic stress responses through later life, including:

- *Re-experiencing – distress at trauma reminders such as nightmares*
- *Avoidance – avoiding the thoughts and feelings associated with the trauma*
- *Negative alterations in cognition and mood – 'persistent negative emotional states'*
- *Alterations in reactivity – emotional outbursts, anger and trouble concentrating.*

Chiu et al. (2019) assert that one of the most influential and long-lasting consequences of early childhood trauma is the child's internalised self-image, or *self-schema*. Shaped by our interactions with those around us, our self-schema is formed through our mental constructions of experiences. Those who have experienced persistently negative early interactions surrounding love, attachment and self-worth are at risk of creating a dysfunctional self-schema, the effects of which could last into adulthood.

As we begin to see, understanding childhood trauma and its impact is not a straightforward task for practitioners. Golding (2020) warns that abuse and neglect can lead to a range of difficulties which are complex, confusing to understand and often misdiagnosed. Not considering the role of early trauma in a child's needs may lead to inappropriate labelling and grouping under the umbrella of Special Educational Needs (Gore-Langton & Boy, 2017), whereas applying a generic label of *trauma* is also unhelpful and assumes that all children experience and respond to trauma in the same way. Instead, practitioners must be prepared to treat each child individually and use comprehensive assessment and specialist support to create appropriate interventions.

The UK Trauma Council (2022) describes the link between early childhood trauma and mental health as 'latent vulnerability' as the effects can be initially hidden and only emerge in the face of potential triggers in later life.

Consider the following:

1 What can early childhood settings put in place to ensure practitioners have a thorough understanding of the potential impact of trauma on children's later well-being, behaviour and outcomes?
2 How could this knowledge and understanding impact your own perceptions of behaviour management practices?
3 How can practitioners work with parents to gain a better understanding of the potential needs of children?

Adoptive parents: Why their story matters

Adoption represents a journey for all those involved, one which is not solely focused on the adoption itself, but rather constitutes a tapestry of experiences leading up to and following the period of placement. Understanding the often complex narratives of adoptive parents prior to their decision to adopt can be transformative in understanding the support they may require.

Research suggests that most couples who choose to adopt do so because of infertility (Long, Jones, Jomeen, & Martin, 2022), indicating the potential for trauma and grief to be present within their pre-adoption narrative. Cudmore (2005) suggests that infertility can lead to damaged self-esteem and feelings of shame, which could potentially be compounded by the notion of not being able to fulfil societal, cultural and familial expectations (Jakhara, 2018). According to

Tasker and Wood (2016), practitioners should therefore give consideration to the relational challenges potentially faced by those embarking on the adoption journey. Challenges may be characterised by:

- Relationship strain as a result of long-term infertility.
- The stress of pre-adoption assessment and matching processes.
- The loss of internal biological representations of family.

Becoming a parent via adoption is uniquely positioned from more traditional biological routes, and acknowledging not only the physical but also psychological and emotional journeys of adoptive parents is fundamental in understanding the level of support they need. Long et al. (2022) warn that a lack of understanding of contextual differences can result in adoptive and biological transitions being grouped, leading to the more specific needs of adoptive parents being overlooked.

Weistra and Luke (2017, p. 229) explore the impact of social support and stigma on the experiences of parents navigating the journey through adoption. Their findings suggest that stigma could be associated with two aspects of the experience:

1 *Perceived attitudes* towards adoption from society

2 *Self-image* that results from perceived attitudes

Specific findings point to a perception that becoming a parent via adoption is somehow *second best* to biological routes, and that parents may experience feelings of failure for their deviation from the norm. Weistra and Luke (2017) go on to suggest that the pressure felt by adoptive parents to be perfect may often result in an unwillingness to ask for support. Cudmore (2005) agrees, asserting that this may begin pre-placement as adopters feel unable to talk openly about prior infertility grief due to concerns about how their capacity to parent will be viewed by social workers.

Cudmore (2005) suggests the fantasy of parenthood and vision of the perfect family can lead to unrealistic expectations and perceptions of the reality to follow, an issue felt more strongly by adopters of children with Special Educational Needs (Moyer & Goldberg, 2015). The overwhelming desire to be parents can lead to adopters positioning themselves unrealistically as being equipped to parent children with more complex needs than they are able to. Moyer and Goldberg (2015) found that this can often be felt more significantly by same-sex adopters who report feeling at risk of discrimination and pressured to accept harder to place children for fear of waiting longer to be matched. They therefore advocate that support for parents throughout adoption should, in part, focus on cognitive flexibility to ensure parents have the capacity to adapt their expectations to the frequent changes they may encounter.

For those working with adoptive families, a recognition of the needs of the parents will play a crucial role in supporting the well-being and outcomes of their children (Hamilton & Forgacs-Pritchard, 2021). The needs of parents are often masked by the more immediate and obvious needs of children; however, understanding that adoptive parents will be on a complex and challenging journey themselves is central to providing targeted support. Kohn-Willbridge, Pike, and O de Visser's (2021) findings indicate parents often struggle with feelings of powerlessness, uncertainty, isolation and physical and emotional fatigue through their day-to-day reality. Through a culture of respect and active listening, professionals should work to position themselves within the support network for the whole family, stay alert to the challenges parents may be facing and be sensitive to parents who may not feel able to ask for support.

REFLECTION

Weistra and Luke (2017) report that 93% of adoptive parents feel a lack of under-standing of adoption within society. They suggest that more needs to be done to bridge the gap between our understanding of biological and adoptive parenting. They critique the misleading portrayal of adoption through the media and suggest further public education is required to bridge the gap in society's understanding.

Based on this view, reflect on the following questions:

1 How can early childhood settings represent adoption as a celebrated and respected family model?

2 Do current models of partnership working with parents that you have experi-enced allow for respectful and active listening when working with parents who may find asking for support challenging?

3 So far through this chapter, how has your own understanding of adoption been influenced?

Siblings in adoption

Hamilton and Forgacs-Pritchard (2021, p. 559) refer to *all* the relationships sur-rounding the adoptive family as a 'complex tapestry'. Taking time to consider the nature of sibling relationships is therefore essential to truly view adoption through an ecological and holistic lens.

Sibling relationships within an adoptive family may be characterised by one or more of the following:

- Birth siblings adopted together into one family unit at simultaneous or different times.

- Birth siblings separated within the care system but with contact arrangements which must be facilitated by adoptive parents. They may be in separate adoptive placements or a mixture of adoptive and foster settings.

- Birth siblings who no longer have contact with one another.

- A child joining a family through adoption where there is already one or more birth children.

- Multiple children joining a family through separate adoption orders from different families.

Sibling relationships are amongst the most influential an individual can experience in their lifetime (Meakings, Coffey, & Shelton, 2017) and are often characterised by fluctuations of intense emotion. Rivalry, jealousy, conflict, love, protection and joy are regularly intertwined throughout normative sibling dynamics, aiding in children's emotional development and providing space to negotiate social terrains through childhood and into adolescence (Selwyn, 2019). Sibling relationships within the adoption arena are rarely straightforward and are often associated with the coexistence of losses and gains, therefore carrying the potential for heightened intensity within normative emotional experiences. Bowen's family systems theory (1978) suggests that each family is a complex interdependent unit and family members are affected by the emotional well-being and needs of others within the unit. When traumatised children enter an adoptive family, their trauma and related behaviours do not disappear and may instead be further compounded by the adoption process itself (Hunsley, Ekas, & Crawley, 2021). Bowen's theory suggests that the subsequent emotional behaviours and needs of the adopted child will be felt by all members of the family unit, including siblings.

The decision to place birth siblings together or apart has been subject to frequent debate. The Children and Families Act (2014) advocates for siblings to be placed together where it is in the children's best interest. However, according to Selwyn (2019), our understanding of the dynamics of sibling relationships through adoption is limited and therefore decisions regarding placement should be made individually through rigorous assessment. Hegar (2005) has suggested that the presence of siblings may aid children in being able to cope within their environment and adapt to stressful situations. However, as Sharpe (2014) and Selwyn (2019) remind us, not all sibling relationships are positive and may instead serve to perpetuate the trauma and abuse which has been the dominant characteristic of their early life experience together.

Research exploring the decision to adopt a sibling group has demonstrated that parents may attribute their decision to several motivating factors (Frost & Goldberg, 2020; Selwyn, Saunders, & Farmer, 2010):

- Adopters feeling that a 'family' constitutes more than one child, therefore being motivated to create their ideal family model.

- A long-term desire to have multiple children and a dislike of the process, therefore not wanting to repeat it.

- A view that placing siblings together is better for children and an unwillingness to be responsible for causing separations.

- Wanting to support social care systems based on the knowledge that sibling groups are harder to place.

- A perception that the waiting process would be shorter if willing to adopt a sibling group.

Wherever the motivation lies, Hamilton and Forgacs-Pritchard (2021) assert that adoptive parents often experience a steep learning curve in their parenting skills due to the varied and frequent challenges they face when supporting multiple children with different needs. As a result, they argue that practitioners must recognise that adoptive parents of sibling groups will require specialised and individualised support which acknowledges the complexity of their reality.

Life story work: Identity and intrapersonal relationships

Having a secure sense of identity is a fundamental factor in an individual's feeling of well-being and belonging. Our relationships with ourselves, those around us, our context and our history are crucial aspects of our emotional security (Rose & Philpot, 2005). The ability to reminisce about our past relationships, family ties and contexts allows us to trace back along, what Hooley, Stokes, and Combes (2016, p. 220) describe as an 'autobiographical' journey, forming the foundations of our response to the question 'who am I?' Children who have travelled through the care system are likely to find this process more challenging, if not impossible. The pain of recalling trauma, frequent transitions and gaps in the store of memories can all be factors which create a disconnect between an adopted child's history and their sense of self. The simple feeling of what it is like to have a mother and father and to live alongside them can be a confusing concept which requires careful exploration in a way which acknowledges the uniqueness of each child's lived reality (Rose & Philpot, 2005).

Life story work (LSW) has grown from an understanding that disconnecting children from their past, and not allowing them the age-appropriate methods of exploring their narrative of self, can be catastrophic to children's overall development (Booth, 2022; Davies & Hodges, 2017). According to Rose and Philpot (2005), an adopted child requires time to understand and make sense of what has happened to them, ultimately working towards an acceptance of the past to move towards the future. According to Gore-Langton and Boy (2017) and Watson, Latter, and Bellew (2015a, 2015b), practitioners have an important role to play in supporting LSW through enabling children to discuss their history in a safe and secure environment and are well placed to create inclusive spaces which allow children to express their uniqueness and celebrate adoption as a valid form of family emergence.

REFLECTION

Ecomapping is a strategy used by professionals within social care to support children to explore the relationships in their life, including past and present connections. A relationship key is used to communicate the nature of the relationship as a means of opening dialogue surrounding the child's identity and self-image.

Take time to explore the map in Figure 5.1, which demonstrates a basic ecomap for Jake, an adopted child. Reflect on how Jake's adoptive parents can strengthen their relationship with Jake based on your understanding of LSW. How do you feel professionals could work to enable that process? What are the implications for Jake in having such varied and complex relationships in his life?

You may wish to create your own ecomap as a way of exploring the process.

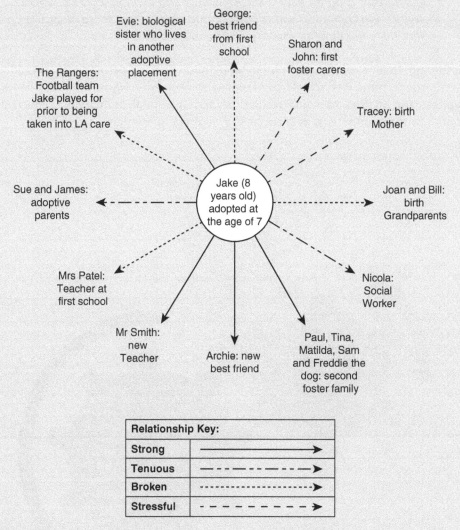

Figure 5.1   Ecomap

The role of the practitioner

Early childhood practitioners can support adoptive families by ensuring they remain open and accepting of the need for personalised provision, being mindful not to group adopted children or families based on any presumption of need. Working with adoptive families requires practitioners to be reflective, reflexive and responsive in their practice, ensuring families feel represented, heard and valued.

Practitioners have an important role to play in supporting the needs of adoptive families and therefore promoting permanence for the child (Goodwin, Madden, Singletary, & Laine Scales, 2020). Department for Education (2021, pp. 19–20) guidance states that the objective of permanence is:

> *to ensure that children have a secure, stable and loving family to support them through childhood and beyond and to give them a sense of security, continuity, commitment, identity and belonging.*

According to Brodzinsky and Livingstone-Smith (2019), permanence should be seen through three distinct, yet overlapping components. Figure 5.2 identifies and explores the themes of legal, residential and relational permanence which are central to the foundations of a successful adoptive placement.

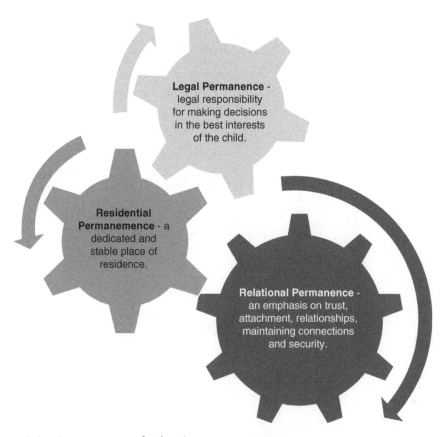

Figure 5.2   Components of adoption permanence

Brodzinsky and Livingstone-Smith (2019) are clear that the need to nurture relational permanence is key in supporting the family in an ongoing and holistic way. Rolock et al. (2021) agree and argue that, whilst legal and residential permanence is largely one sided, relational permanence is bidirectional and requires both the child and adoptive parents' influence to sustain the relationship. A child grieving the loss of prior relationships and attachments will need time, flexibility and understanding to be ready to accept and reciprocate relational permanence (Brodzinsky & Livingstone-Smith, 2019).

Goodwin et al. (2020, p. 119) assert that there is a need to normalize the adjustment process beyond what they describe as the *honeymoon period* and allow space to explore the tensions which may arise over time, emphasising that no two families will experience adjustment in the same way. Rolock et al. (2021) agree, asserting that post-permanency discontinuity should be identified as early as possibly to provide appropriate support from evidence-based services.

The support required to promote permanence will change over time and so professionals must be prepared to stay alert to the potential challenges families may be facing. According to Gore-Langton and Boy (2017), support should represent several overlapping pedagogical themes:

1 Identification of the child's needs – knowing the child

2 Prioritising relationships – acknowledging relational trauma and supporting reciprocal partnerships

3 Rethinking behaviour management – responding empathetically

4 Sensitive information sharing – having clear arrangements for communication sharing in place

5 Protection of families – being alert to bullying and discrimination

6 Support for staff – training and an acknowledgment of secondary trauma

UK legislative change has signalled a growing awareness of the need to support the unique needs of adopted children within educational provision. Most recently, the Children and Social Work Act (2017) placed an expectation on schools to appoint a designated person to be responsible for the progress of adopted children. However, Gore-Langton and Boy (2017, pp. 29–30) report that though there have been positive steps taken, support is still patchy and more needs to be done to truly *understand* families' needs, reminding us that *'when we tune in to children, we allow them to tune in to learning'*.

CASE STUDY

The following extracts are taken from Selwyn, Wijedasa, and Meakings (2014, pp. 193–194), *Beyond the Adoption Order Challenges, Interventions and Adoption Disruptions: Research Report.*

(Continued)

(Continued)

The GP's response has been brilliant. It felt like she had quite a holistic picture, because she spoke with Mike, she really listened to what he was saying, but at the same time when he left, she said and 'How's it for you because I can see that must be really challenging to manage'? Someone who just kind of acknowledges, whereas I felt that the adoption social 193 worker had no idea really, what it was that we were dealing with. And in fact, the adoption social worker didn't even meet Mike.

I always felt judged; always felt that we were failing. They never worked in partnership with us, it was always them versus us, and that was the worst time of all ... I think I'm traumatised by that. I think even now when I'm talking about it, I could cry because I was so hurt by their lack of sensitivity, their lack of recognition that she was our daughter and that we were fighting to hold on to her ... This little girl who is behaving barbarically we're not blaming her, but we can't do it in this way anymore. And that was a terrible time ... it was as if I had become the abusive mother.

Consider the following:

1 In the parents' descriptions, what is significant about the way they felt they were viewed?

2 What does it tell you about the responsibility of *all* professionals that parents have contact with?

3 In what ways might this influence your own professional practice?

Conclusion

This chapter has introduced some of the reasons why adoptive families require practitioners to take an individualised and personalised approach through their partnerships. To understand the distinct needs of each family, practitioners must work to consider the enduring legacy of past experiences and relationships. By exploring discourses surrounding trauma, identity, transition and permanence, it becomes clear that it is insufficient to view adoptive families through a static ecological lens. A true holistic understanding of need comes from the realisation that adoptive parents, adopted children and siblings will have experienced multiple ecologies and lived realities distinct from one another, all of which carry the potential to create a long-lasting impact on the adoptive family dynamic.

Adoptive families will benefit from practitioners who are skilled at active listening and base their pedagogy on a culture of partnerships and trust. Through sensitive and reciprocal relationships, practitioners can work to create inclusive and non-judgmental attitudes where children and families feel they belong.

Further reading

Gore-Langton, E., & Boy, K. (2017). *Becoming and adoption friendly school: A whole-school resource for supporting children who have experienced trauma or loss.* London: Jessica Kingsley Publishers.

Kohn-Willbridge, C., Pike, A., & O de Visser, R. (2021). 'Look after me too': A qualitative exploration of the transition into adoptive motherhood. *Adoption and Fostering, 45*(3), 300–315.

Selwyn, J., Wijedasa, D. N., & Meakings, S. J. (2014). Beyond the adoption order: Challenges, interventions and disruptions. Retrieved from: https://assets.publishing.service.gov.uk/government/uploads/system/uploads/attachment_data/file/301889/Final_Report_-_3rd_April_2014v2.pdf

Useful websites

Adoption UK – https://www.adoptionuk.org/

Anna Freud – National Centre for Children and Families – https://www.annafreud.org/

PAC UK – https://www.pac-uk.org/

References

Booth, R. (2022). Helping us heal; how creative life story work supports individuals and organisations to recover from trauma. *Journal of Social Work Practice, 36*(1), 119–127. doi: 10.1080/02650533.2021.2025349

Brodzinsky, D., & Livingstone-Smith, S. (2019). Commentary: Understanding research, policy, and practice issues in adoption instability. *Research on Social Work Practice, 29*(2), 185–194.

Children and Families Act. (2014). Retrieved from: https://www.legislation.gov.uk/ukpga/2014/6/contents/enacted

Children and Social Work Act. (2017). Retrieved from: https://www.legislation.gov.uk/ukpga/2017/16/contents/enacted

Chiu, C., Lam Ho, H., Tollenaar, S., Elzinga, B. M., & Zhang, T. (2019). Early relational trauma and self representations: Misattributing externally derived representations as internally generated. *Psychological Trauma: Theory, Research, Practice, and Policy, 11*(1), 64–72. doi: 10.1037/tra0000369

Cudmore, L. (2005). Becoming parents in the context of loss. *Sexual and Relationship Therapy, 20*(3), 299–308. doi: 10.1080/14681990500141204

Davies, M., & Hodges, J. (2017). Relationship renaissance: The use of attachment-based narrative and metaphor in life story work. *Adoption & Fostering, 41*(2), 131–141. doi: 10.1177/0308575917702831

Department for Education. (2021). *The children act 1989 guidance and regulations volume 2: Care planning, placement and case review.* Retrieved from: https://assets.publishing.service.gov.uk/government/uploads/system/uploads/attachment_data/file/1000549/The_Children_Act_1989_guidance_and_regulations_Volume_2_care_planning__placement_and_case_review.pdf

Fagan, M. (2011). Relational trauma and its impact on late-adopted children. *Journal of Child Psychotherapy, 37*(2), 129–146. doi: 10.1080/0075417X.2011.581467

Frost, R., & Goldberg, A. (2020). 'People said we were nuts . . . I understand what they were saying now': An exploration of the transition to parenthood in sibling group adoption. *Children and Youth Services Review, 116*, 1–11. doi: 10.1016/j.childyouth.2020.105209

71

Golding, K. (2020). Understanding and helping children who have experienced maltreatment. *Paediatrics and Child Health, 30*(11), 371–377.

Goodwin, B., Madden, E., Singletary, J., & Laine Scales, T. (2020). Adoption workers' perspectives on adoption adjustment and the honeymoon period. *Child and Youth Services Review, 119*, 1–9.

Gore-Langton, E., & Boy, K. (2017). *Becoming and adoption friendly school: A whole-school resource for supporting children who have experienced trauma or loss.* London: Jessica Kingsley Publishers.

Hamilton, P., & Forgacs-Pritchard, K. (2021). The complex tapestry of relationships which surround adoptive families: A case study. *Education, 3–13, 49*(5), 558–571. doi: 10.1080/03004279.2020.1742186

Hegar, R. L. (2005). Sibling placement in foster care and adoption: An overview of international research. *Children and Youth Service Review, 27*, 717–739.

Hooley, K., Stokes, L., & Combes, H. (2016). Life story work with looked after and adopted children: How professional training and experience determine perceptions of its value. *Adoption & Fostering, 40*(3), 219–233. doi: 10.1177/0308575916661129

Howe, D. (2005). *Child abuse and neglect: Attachment, development, and intervention.* Basingstoke: Palgrave MacMillan.

Hunsley, J., Ekas, N., & Crawley, R. (2021). An exploratory study of the impact of adoption on adoptive siblings. *Journal of Child and Family Studies, 30*, 311–324.

Jakhara, M. (2018). *The journey to adopt a child – A mixed methods study comparing aspiring parents' perceptions of the adoption process with those of social workers and social work managers.* (Doctoral dissertation) Retrieved from: https://www-proquest-com.ezproxy.derby.ac.uk/docview/ 2516280856

John, S., Brandt, T., Secrist, M., Mesman, G., Sigel, B., & Kramer, T. (2019). Empirically-guided assessment of complex trauma for children in foster care: A focus on appropriate diagnosis of attachment concerns. *Psychological Services: Trauma Informed Care for Children and Families, 16*(1), 120–133.

Kohn-Willbridge, C., Pike, A., & O de Visser, R. (2021). 'Look after me too': A qualitative exploration of the transition into adoptive motherhood. *Adoption and Fostering, 45*(3), 300–315.

Long, T., Jones, C., Jomeen, J., & Martin, C. R. (2022). Transition to adoptive parenthood: A concept analysis. *Community Practitioner*, (Jan/Feb).

Meakings, S., Coffey, A., & Shelton, K. (2017). The influence of adoption on sibling relationships: Experiences and support needs of newly formed adoptive families. *British Journal of Social Work, 47*, 1781–1799.

Moyer, A. M., & Goldberg, A. E. (2015). 'We were not planning on this, but . . .': Adoptive parents' reactions and adaptations to unmet expectations. *Child & Family Social Work, 22*, 12–21. doi: 10.1111/cfs. 12219

Rolock, N., Ocasio, K., White, K., Cho, Y., Fong, R., Marra, L., & Faulkner, M. (2021). Identifying families who may be struggling after adoption or guardianship. *Journal of Public Child Welfare, 15*(1), 78–104. doi: 10.1080/15548732.2020.1831679

Rose, R., & Philpot, T. (2005). *The child's own story.* London: Jessica Kingsley Publishers.

Ryan, K., Lane, S., & Powers, D. (2017). A multidisciplinary model for treating complex trauma in early childhood. *International Journal of Play Therapy, 26*(2), 111–123.

Selwyn, J. (2019). Sibling relationships in adoptive families that disrupted or were in crisis. *Research on Social Work Practice, 29*(2), 165–175. doi: 10.1177/1049731518783859

Selwyn, J., Wijedasa, D. N., & Meakings, S. J. (2014). *Beyond the adoption order: Challenges, interventions and disruptions.* Retrieved from: https://assets.publishing.service.gov.uk/government/uploads/system/uploads/attachment_data/file/301889/Final_Report_-_3rd_April_2014v2.pdf

Selwyn, J., Saunders, H., & Farmer, E. (2010). The views of children and young people on being cared for by an independent foster-care provider. *British Journal of Social Work, 40*(3), 696–713.

Sharpe, R. (2014). *Together or apart? An analysis of social workers' decision making when considering the placement of siblings for adoption or foster care* (Doctoral dissertation). Retrieved from British Library: EThOS e-theses online service (uk.bl.ethos.633368).

Syne, J., Green, R., & Dyer, J. (2012). Adoption: The lucky ones or the Cinderellas of children in care? *Educational and Child Psychology, 29*(3), 93–106.

Tasker, F., & Wood, S. (2016). The transition into adoptive parenthood: Adoption as a process of continued unsafe uncertainty when family scripts collide. *Clinical Child Psychology and Psychiatry, 21*(4), 520–535.

UK Trauma Council. (2022). *How latent vulnerability plays out over a child's life.* Retrieved from: https://uktraumacouncil.org/resource/how-latent-vulnerability-plays-out-over-a-childs-life

Watson, D., Latter, S., & Bellew, R. (2015a). Adopted children and young people's views on their life storybooks: The role of narrative in the formation of identities. *Children and Youth Services Review, 58,* 90–98.

Watson, D., Latter, S., & Bellew, R. (2015b). Adopters' views on their children's life story books. *Adoption and Fostering, 39*(2), 119–134.

Weistra, S., & Luke, N. (2017). Adoptive parents' experiences of social support and attitudes towards adoption. *Adoption and Fostering, 41*(3), 228–241.

6 WORKING WITH LGBT+ PARENT-LED FAMILIES

AARON BRADBURY

CHAPTER OBJECTIVES

By the end of this chapter, you will be able to:

- Recognise the importance of creating a partnership with parents and carers who identify as LGBT+.
- Explore nurturing outcomes for the child, and professional bias when working with LGBT+ families.
- Consider parenting and positionality by exploring key concepts of professionalism within the early childhood sector.
- Reflect on anti-discriminatory practices to enable positive outcomes for the child and family.

KEY DEFINITIONS

Parents

Any person who has parental responsibility or has care of a young child during early childhood (from conception to eight years of age).

Practitioner

A person who is qualified to work with children (from conception to 8 years old) across health, education and social care.

LGBT+

The LGBT+ community is a loosely defined grouping of lesbian, gay, bisexual and transgender people.

Unconscious bias

Unconscious bias is a term that describes the associations we hold, outside our conscious awareness and control. Unconscious bias affects everyone.

Nurturing

Nurture is defined as the many environmental variables that affect a person, including their experiences in early childhood, family and social relationships, culture and community.

Gender stereotypes

A gender stereotype is a generalised view or preconception about attributes or characteristics that are ought to be possessed by people or the roles that are or should be performed by men and women.

Anti-oppressive practice

Anti-oppressive practice means that we take account of the impact of power, inequality and oppression on people and actively combat these.

Representative approach/representation

Representation in early childhood. The ability to symbolise is predicated upon the capacity for representation, which is, in turn, fostered by the infant's primary object relationships.

Introduction

This chapter looks at many aspects of working with parents and carers who identify as lesbian, gay, bisexual and transgender (LGBT+) within the early childhood sector. It explores aspects of working with parents who are under-represented in society, thinking about ways in which children and parents can be supported and practice can be enhanced.

Families come in all shapes and sizes, and it is a common misconception that they should all be treated the same. It is of course a myth that **LGBT+** families do in fact need to be treated differently. Being treated differently is not the answer, but treating them so that they are represented is. This chapter considers the many aspects of the role of an early childhood practitioner and what is needed to ensure that **LGBT+** parent-led families are given the space to be represented.

Initially, the chapter considers current practice and UK legislation in early childhood followed by an overview of the meaning and impact of **gender stereotypes** including a synopsis of the history of legislation surrounding this. Moving on the role of the parent in contemporary times is considered alongside how children's gender identity develops and how they may understand gender alongside parents and practitioners. The final part of the chapter supports practitioner understanding as to how they can understand **unconscious bias** and work towards positive relationships for the benefit of child, parent and themselves.

Current practice and legislation

As early childhood practitioners, we can always present a welcoming and collaborative approach with parents for the best outcomes for children. There are many benefits of working more closely with under-represented groups within early childhood. This has become more aligned to working in partnership with parents for maintaining a child-centred approach. Every child could be a part of a family which is **LGBT+**. **Early childhood practitioners** have an opportunity to prevent prejudices from occurring within everyday practice by ensuring that these children and their families feel valued and welcome. Ensuring that we actively celebrate and support all parents and children by applying a representative approach to advocate for all children and their families can improve practice. Every child should feel valued and have a sense of belonging within our early childhood settings and practices. However, recent and long-awaited societal changes in the United Kingdom have focussed legislative changes for LGBT+ parents. This highlights the continual work that is needed around inclusion for this group of families.

The law in the United Kingdom has gone through a dramatic change. Parents of the same sex can now be married, adopt and foster, which is very much more aligned to the nuclear families we have come to understand as the norm within our society. Changing the law does not lead to overnight changes within our practice. There is still a long way to go for us as a society including the use of gender-neutral language and changing prejudice. Ensuring challenge is made of the assumptions by some that **LGBT+** is to be feared and is dangerous for children is essential. Moreover, it provides children with opportunities to learn about the world that they live in, to thrive and to grow up to be valuable and caring citizens of our future. The use of neutral words such as family suggests the need for practitioners to advocate, which includes using the term **LGBT+** (Church, Hedge, Averett, & Ballard, 2016). Neutral phrases such as family structure and family circumstances are used when discussing family diversity and inclusion within practice. However, we must make it clear which family we are speaking of; this allows an element of **representation** from early childhood professionals.

When working with **LGBT+**-parented families, it is important to foster an understanding of respectful attitudes towards individuality and diversity. As early childhood practitioners, it is important to build an element of reflective thinking within the earliest years of early childhood. This supports young children and their families to build an inclusive society for the future where individual rights are respected. To achieve this, early childhood practitioners need to continually evaluate their attitudes and practices (Burt, Gelnaw, & Lesser, 2010) and to purposefully disrupt heteronormative thinking within the earliest of years and their learning environments (Taylor & Richardson, 2005).

Gunn (2009) defines heteronormativity as:

> *Heteronormativity is the concept that heterosexual sexuality is an institutionalised norm and a superior and privileged standard. It is perpetuated via discourses that position heterosexual sexuality as dominant and normative, and which construct heterosexual sexuality as the form of sexuality against which all others are compared.*

(p. 27)

LGBT+ parents in the 21st century

Children who are parented by LGBT+ parents were attending early childhood settings way before any success of changing of any law for equality with families and marriage. Looking at representation is nothing new, and it is a stark reality that we are still raising this in the 21st century. The Early Years Single Equality Strategy (EYSES) (2008), a document for early childhood educators, reminds us of the continual challenge and need to give our children an opportunity to learn about the world that they live in and to see the impact we can have on our children and families. It provided a comprehensive overview of working with children and families suggesting an Equality Named Co-ordinator (ENCO). This was someone who worked within the settings to make sure that children and parents were given **representation** and that these people had affective training to be able to do this.

Despite these enhancements, it is unclear how early childhood practitioners are in fact equipped to reflect the current narrative of inclusion, diversity and equality for **LGBT+** parents and their children. The EYSES (2008) is no longer a part of policy in English early childhood settings and does not currently appear to be high on the political agenda. Therefore, early childhood practitioners are left to make those judgement calls to support positive outcomes for all children, including using the Equality Act (2010) as a baseline to make sure that everyone is treated with equality within practice.

Breaking down gender stereotypes

Within early childhood, the question seems to be around how far **representation** for **LGBT+** awareness should become a priority for work with children and families. This is a controversial question that can raise strong responses when working with children in early childhood. From the 17th century, childhood has been presented as a period of innocence (Robinson, 2013), in which children should be protected from difficult and controversial adult concerns (Blaise, 2005; Renold, 2005). Any discussion around the representative nature of **LGBT+** education with young children, especially regarding discussions around gender, has become a turbulent landscape in current times, which can produce protest and clear resistance from professionals and certain parent groups (DePalma, 2016; Parveen, 2019).

While it is always important that any work with children is age appropriate, what is needed is a balanced, sensitive and sympathetic awareness from early childhood practitioners who can collaborate with other relevant professionals, working alongside parents and carers, who can support children and parents who identify as **LGBT+**.

Early childhood is a crucial stage of development for these discussions to start. **Early childhood practitioners** are in an ideal position to start to disrupt the landscape of gender normalising and the pedagogies and practices which are involved. The environment within the early childhood settings and practices from us can challenge **gender stereotypes**, whereby we can develop or create a **nurturing** and sympathetic environment for the development of gender variation and sexual orientation in later childhood and adulthood (Bradbury, 2022a; Luecke, 2011).

Knowing what LGBT+ means

For many, the acronyms can become quite confusing, and this is forever evolving. So, it is an important first step to understand what the term **LGBT+-parented family** means. An **LGBT+**-parented family includes at least one adult who identifies as an **LGBT+** parent and is raising at least one child. Children may also become part of these families in the context of same-sex relationships through many means including adoption, surrogacy or sperm donation. Children may be raised in different family structures where one parent identifies as **LGBT+** or both. There may be other significant family members such as birth parents, sperm donor and surrogate mother all sharing various arrangements for parenting (Surtees, 2017).

Families with transgender parents are an increasingly visible family structure, yet a significant moral panic has been created, suggesting that this is morally wrong or even detrimental for children. It is noticeable how detrimentally transgender parents, the **LGBT+** community, are discussed across media platforms and woven into discussions concerning feminism and safe spaces. The growing rhetoric from gender-critical and exclusionary radical feminists can demonstrate antipathy towards trans and non-gendered individuals. There also appears a misconception of what may be discussed in schools and settings with young children, which can cause panic and misinformation. Practitioners and curriculum focus on children as human beings first and foremost, by applying a non-judgemental, safe environment where children can be unique and themselves. It is important that an early childhood workforce considers any values or ideologies with balance and makes decisions on an individual basis. This provides an environment that works with care, compassion and nurture for the child rather than believing politicised views without knowing the facts in their widest context.

Parenting children of the 21st century who are LGBT+

There is now a generation of children and young people who can express themselves in a much more fluid way of interacting with others and within the wider society. A study by Bragg et al. (2018), in England, reports that there are many children in the 12–14 age range who now have an expansion of vocabulary of gender expression. These children also have voiced commitments to gender equality, diversity and the rights of gender and sexual minorities. Therefore, it is important that we do not lose sight of the changing nature and thoughts of our youngest in society. As practitioners, we must also move with the times, work alongside our young people and develop ways to understand them so that we can also support parents to understand too.

There are many ways that children are leading the way into the future with gender ideology and sexual orientation. It could be suggested that we can learn just as much from our children as we can in textbooks and research studies. Neary and Cross (2018) also deliver messages about how children are doing this and becoming activists of change. Change can upset the status quo, and it is this which many parents and early childhood practitioners feel threatened by. It is the not knowing and being done to rather than done with which causes many professional relationships to break down. Children can become advocates for fairness in society by enabling them to flourish and become their own unique person. Working with children in early childhood, it is important to value the importance of uniqueness and allow children to express freedom and joy.

Young children are developing an understanding of what it means to be unique, to be their individual selves and most importantly that they have a position within society to be themselves. This has become more apparent and discussed more openly within our practices. The unique qualities of a child are becoming much more explained and accessible to both parents and professionals in an equal measure. The Birth to 5 Matters: Non-statutory Guidance for the Early Years Foundation Stage (2021) puts the unique child at the centre of practice and states:

> Each child is unique, and while we are guided by an understanding of some general patterns of development from pre-birth into early childhood, progression is uneven and unfolds differently for each individual child. The complex differences for each child mean the pathways toward maturity should be seen more as a dancing around a ballroom than climbing a ladder.

(p. 18)

As adults, when parenting children, there is no infinite guide of how to respond and parent effectively. Children developing in the current context have a different experience to that of their parents and our own childhoods. Parents may approach us with questions or concerns that their child may be LGBT+. However, it is equally important that we do not make assumptions that children are **LGBT+** either. It is our role to support parents and the children to develop a keen sense of identity where they can flourish. However, at the same time, it could just be a child questioning their identity. It is a time when children are be able to find themselves, including who they are and which feelings they may have. Until a child states that they are, or might be, LGBT+ try not to make assumptions and let them disclose in their own time.

It is important to remember that children are finding their place within society as they grow and develop. Within early childhood, it is common for children to act out different scenarios in their play, in terms of their development during their social interactions. Being able to listen to children and taking time to fully understand what it is that they are saying, thinking and working alongside them to develop their full uniqueness within practice is an important way to really support children's uniqueness (Bradbury, 2022a).

CASE STUDY: FAMILY 1

When discussing the support they received from early childhood services, both parents united in speaking positively regarding this level of care, insisting that in terms of support, the system had not been prejudiced or negligent towards them as lesbian parents. In terms of how they were approached and treated by their son's early childhood workers, they also perceived this to have been equal to heterosexual families, and throughout their son's childhood, events such as Mother's and Father's Day had been dealt with tentatively and in a way which empowered all families. It was noted how most of their anxieties had been previously formulated from their schooling experiences and that their main worry had been regarding what mainstream schooling experience would have on their son, their hope that education would be more open and inclusive of the LGBT community. They described how significant they felt it was that the early childhood services and school where their son attended ensure their services and the school curriculum addresses big issues such as pride and LGBT families. They described how the school, placing such an emphasis on their curriculum sharing stories of diverse families and people, supported them and their son in feeling included and integrated into the school community.

A reflective exercise later in the chapter (after case study 2) will consider both case studies together.

Do young children understand and use gender?

Research is key to becoming informed and understanding where children are developmentally. Kohlberg's (1966) stages of gender development, whilst one perspective, suggest that a pre-school child is not yet at the gender permanence stage in relation to development, so it is important to recognise that children may be exploring their gender identity and do not necessarily know that they are a different gender. Early childhood practitioners have a part to play here perhaps with information sharing to support parents to know what the research is saying and how this links to child development.

When do children begin to recognise that men and women are different 'types' of people, and when do they link this information to other qualities to form basic stereotypes? Related to this is when do children recognise their own self.

Quinn et al. (2002) suggest that infants as young as three and four months of age distinguish between 'male' and 'female' faces, as demonstrated in habituation and preferential looking paradigms. However, for some children, the match between their assigned gender and gender identity is not so clear.

How does gender identity develop in children?

Through a developmental psychology lens, gender identity typically develops in stages which are aligned to age, but as always, this is also dependent on a wide range of social factors, so practitioners should consider this.

- At age two: Children become conscious of physical differences between boys and girls.

- At three: Most children can label themselves as a boy or a girl.

- By the age of four: Most children have a stable sense of their gender identity.

During this time, children learn gender role behaviours, what boys do and what girls do. The point here is that all children will tend to develop a clearer view of themselves and gender over a prolonged period. Research suggests (Fast & Olson, 2018) that children who assert gender diverse identity or development delay will know their gender as clearly and consistently as their developmentally matched peers and benefit from the same level of support, love and social acceptance.

REFLECTION

Taking on board your experiences of being an early childhood professional, how have you been able to support the discussion of supporting parents and carers when it comes to LGBT+?

Have you had any experiences of the following?

- Parents and carers who are questioning sexuality and gender with young children, either are against the discussion or for the discussion. How have you approached this and what points can you take forward to share with other professionals?

- Do children respond to an open and **nurturing** approach to **representation** around **LGBT+** discourses?

Nurturing the family structure for positive outcomes for the child

As an early childhood practitioner, **nurturing** needs to be at the heart of our practices. This critical link can be made by advocating for all children and families, so their voices are heard, celebrated and given every chance to feel valued.

Bradbury (2022b) explores the suggestion that **nurturing** an emotional relationship is the primary function needed for intellectual and social growth. This builds on the work of Bowlby (1988) and Ainsworth (1978), which uses science to help explore development of the human brain during its earliest years.

Focussing on **nurturing** through our practice allows us to see how systems and processes exclude children and their families just because they are different. When **LGBT+** parent-led families do not fit into what society see as the norm, then they can be excluded from day-to-day thinking and accessibility of services. This can have a long-term impact on both the child and their family (Katz-Wise et al., 2017). Children need to be given the chances to succeed through life by becoming resilient and confident human beings. It is a practitioner's role to reach out and give children the opportunities to encompass personal freedoms by exploring childhood to its fullest including opportunities.

Nurturing encompasses many things, but more importantly thinking about how programmes in early childhood support and connect with parents. It is important to enter this space and discuss with a focus of wanting to give children the best possible start in life. Learning is a process which needs to be fostered together. If parents are asking questions, this is a positive thing. It means that they are interested, no matter how this is presented. Early childhood practitioners can engage with this process and inform parents of their need to also nurture children with the benefits of child development.

Ways to incorporate a **nurturing** approach with practices:

- As experts in child development, it is important to take parents on the same journey. Explain aspects of child development, how it will help and inform their parenting. Enable parents to see the key benefits.

- Familiarise with contemporary concepts, such as keeping up to date with key aspects of working with parents and making your setting inclusive of **LGBT+** families and **LGBT+** parent-led families.

- Value practitioner expertise, but also value other perspectives. See the benefit of why **LGBT+ representation** and advocating for visual acknowledgement benefits all as a community.

- How do practitioners nurture parents so that the relationship between everyone is one which is in a partnership with no hierarchy?

- Think about how you are portraying **representation**, the language you are using, the engagement with all and most importantly the training you have received to engage with this. It is important to adapt, listen and work in partnership with parents.

The need for a comprehensive approach

Creating an inclusive environment in which families can state their **LGBT+** status would increase opportunities for early childhood practitioners to get to know them better, which consequently will reduce prejudices and stereotypes of **LGBT+**

parenting. Each family will come with its own individuality, home culture and ways of doing things. It is the practitioner's role to see this and value what it is that they bring and most importantly what they want for their child.

It is true that children become more accepting about **LGBT+** families once they discover the similarities between **LGBT+** families and their own. The notion of sameness which normalises the differences between those who are **LGBT+** parented and heterosexual families can result in hiding the stigma that **LGBT+**-parented families experience in society. Early childhood practitioners may become complicit in institutionalising stigma and further legitimising one dominant family paradigm over another (Cloughessy & Waniganayake, 2014). There should always be the commitment for valuing and respecting the diversity of individuals, families and the wider community. The community must sit at the heart of practice. The Birth to 5 Matters: Non-statutory Guidance for the Early Years Foundation Stage states (2021):

> *During the earliest years of a child's life certain attitudes and dispositions are being shaped. This is also clear that over time, parents, and carers views continually develop and shape over time. Children are influenced by their environments and the adults that are around them, in ways that often affect children's ideas about themselves. When it comes to gender and sexual orientation, early childhood professionals play a significant part in eradicating those stereotypical ideas about how they should be and who they should become. It is our role to not shy away from these conversations whether they are being led by parents or children, and instead challenge the effects of prejudice and discrimination.*

> *(p. 24)*

The role of the practitioner

Enabling a meaningful partnership with parents starts with our practitioner's own attitudes and practices that focus on the families' strengths and their individuality. It is important that all families are included and that **LGBT+** parent-led families are given a voice alongside others in the interests of equity. Like all parents, those who are **LGBT+** or have children who are **LGBT+** have their own goals, dreams and concerns about their child just like every other parent and family.

An essential element of practice is to explore why it is important to get to know parents. Recognition of their uniqueness is an essential element of practice. Asking the same questions to all families but thinking about continually asking the following may help us frame the need to get to know our families much more:

- 'What names does your child call you' (e.g. papa or mama)?
- 'How would you like us to refer to you when we speak to your child'?

- 'How would you like us to describe your family to others, children, etc.'?
- 'How would you like me to respond to questions about your family'?

CASE STUDY: LGBT+ PARENT-LED FAMILY – SEEING THE WORLD THROUGH THEIR EYES

Family 2

We knew that we would be treated differently. We have been married for 10 years. My husband is no longer my husband and is now my wife. It was a real personal and private experience which we managed to keep under the radar. Five years ago, my then husband asked if we should have children. We decided to try for a baby and Charlie was born. Charlie knows nothing different; his two mummies are exactly that. I do not use the word dad; we use the word mum. His mum is now going through a lengthy process of transitioning. It is this which brings me to my point. It is now that we come across questions from professionals. We have not faced any derogatory comments, but it is the assumptions that there is a father in the family home. We have had a professional say, do you still have connections with the father. To our child, he has two mummies. In fact, one is biologically a female born as a woman, and the other is transgender and is now a female, but we are aware that we will of course face some backlash at some point. The current way that transgender people are treated in society today makes me sad that Charlie will get some of this negativity. It keeps me up at night sometimes. If I am honest, I cry, so much for Charlie more than anything. He plays, he laughs and he will love with all his heart. It makes me heartbroken as it was not Charlie who chose his world, but we love him so much and give him so much. One day we will explain it to him but now we are on our journey together as a family and that is what matters.

REFLECTION

Case study 1 and 2 both reflect the current landscape for **LGBT+** families within the early childhood sector. What would you do to support parents and families to understand what has been discussed in both of the case studies?

How would you

- make your services more inclusive for all families?
- support children's understanding about **LGBT+** families?
- bring families together so that they can learn from one another?

Conclusion

This chapter is a snippet of how to support parents who identify as LGBT+. It comes from a place of inclusiveness for all children and their parents. It notes the importance of valuing the child primarily, but also valuing the expertise of our practices as early childhood practitioners. We must start somewhere, and that place must be us using our knowledge to change the script within early childhood. Parents need to be seen as key partners to supporting each other within a wider context of community. We all need to play our part for parents who identify as LGBT+ and for children who are questioning their position in society by creating a safe place where they can develop into their own unique selves. Of course, much of this work comes with caution. We should not be making bold statements of children, just like we would not with any other form of child development, but it is more about creating the environment where children can thrive and develop without any toxic stress. Times are changing, we must change with it. Otherwise, we need to question why we are in our roles in the first place. Nurture is key, and everyone deserves to be nurtured in early childhood practice. When this is done, it gives every child and parent the best possible opportunity to thrive.

Further reading

Grimmer, T. (2018). *Calling all superheroes: Supporting and developing superhero play in the early years.* London: Routledge.

Vollans, C. (2016). Fluid thinking. *Nursery World Magazine.* Mark Allen Group. Retrieved from: https://www.magonlinelibrary.com/doi/abs/10.12968/nuwa.2016.19.30

Warin, J. (2016). Pioneers, professionals, playmates, protectors, 'Poofs' and 'Paedos': Swedish male preschool teachers' construction of their identities. In S. Brownhill, J. Warin, & I. Wernersson (Eds.), *Men, masculinities and teaching in early childhood education; international perspectives* (pp. 95–106). Oxon: Routledge.

Useful websites

https://www.legislation.gov.uk/ukpga/2010/15/contents – The Equality Act (2010)

Mermaids: https://mermaidsuk.org.uk/ – A charity that supports transgender, non-binary and gender-diverse children and young people. mermaidsuk.org.uk

Stonewall: https://www.stonewall.org.uk/ – A large LGBT organisation working towards a world where all children and young people have access to an LGBT-inclusive education by providing resources, support, training and research.

References

Ainsworth, M. D. S. (1978). The Bowlby- Ainsworth attachment theory. *Behavioural and Brain Sciences, 1*(3), 436–438.

Blaise, M. (2005). A feminist poststructuralist study of children 'doing' gender in an urban kindergarten classroom. *Early Childhood Research Quarterly, 20*(1), 85–108.

Bowlby, J. (1988). *A secure base: Clinical applications of attachment theory.* London: Taylor & Francis.

Bradbury, A. (2022a). Nurturing in the early years – what the science tells us? *Early Education Journal, 96,* 7–9.

Bradbury, A. (2022b). Stephen Bavolek. In **A. Bradbury & R. Swailes** (Eds.), *Early childhood theorists today* (pp. 4–17). London: Learning Matters.

Bragg, S., Renold, E., Ringrose, J., & Jackson, C. (2018). 'More than boy, girl, male, female': Exploring young people's views on gender diversity within and beyond school contexts. *Sex Education, 18*(4), 420–434.

Burt, T., Gelnaw, A., & Lesser, L. K. (2010). Creating welcoming and inclusive environments for lesbian, gay, bisexual, and transgender (LGBT) families in early childhood settings. *YC Young Children, 65*(1), 97.

Church, J., Hedge, A., Averett, P., & Ballard, S. (2016). Early childhood administrators' attitudes and experiences in working with gay- and lesbian-parented families. *Early Childhood Development and Care, 188*(3), 1–17.

Cloughessy, K., & Waniganayake, M. (2014). Early childhood educators working with children who have lesbian, gay, bisexual and transgender parents: What does the literature tell us? *Early Child Development and Care, 184*(8), 1287–1280.

DePalma, R. (2016). Gay penguins, sissy ducklings...and beyond? Exploring gender and sexuality diversity through children's literature. *Discourse: Studies in the Cultural Politics of Education, 37*(6), 828–845.

Fast, A. A., & Olson, K. R. (2018). Gender development in transgender preschool children. *Child Development, 89*(2), 620–637.

Gunn, A. C. (2009). 'But who are the parents?' Examining heteronormative discourse in New Zealand Government early childhood reports and policy. *Early Childhood Folio, 13,* 27–30. Wellington: New Zealand Council for Educational Research.

Katz-Wise, S. L., Budge, S. L., Fugate, E., Flanagan, K., Touloumtzis, C., Rood, B., Perez-Brumer, A., & Leibowitz, S. (2017). Transactional pathways of transgender identity development in transgender and gender-nonconforming youth and caregiver perspectives from the Trans Youth Family Study. *International Journal of Transgenderism, 18*(3), 243–263.

Kohlberg, L. (1966). A cognitive-developmental analysis of children's sex-role concepts and attitudes. In E. **Maccoby** (Ed.), *The development of sex differences* (pp. 82–173). Stanford, CA: Stanford University Press.

Luecke, J. (2011). Working with transgender children and their classmates in pre-adolescence: Just be supportive. *Journal of LGBT Youth, 8*(2), 116–156.

Meleady, C. (2008). *Early years single equality strategy (EYSES): Essential advice and guidance.* Early Years Equality.

Neary, A., & Cross, C. (2018). *Exploring gender identity and gender norms in primary schools: The perspectives of educators and parents of transgender and gender variant 4 children.* Limerick: University of Limerick and the Transgender Equality Network of Ireland.

Parveen, N. (2019, March 4). Birmingham school stops LGBT lessons after parents protest. *The Guardian.* Retrieved from: https://www.theguardian.com/education/2019/mar/04/birmingham-school-stops-lgbt-lessons-after-parent-protests (Accessed on 1st August 2022).

Quinn, P. C., Yahr, J., Kuhn, A., Slater, A. M., & Pascalis, O. (2002). Representation of the gender of human faces by infants: A preference for female. *Perception, 31*(9), 1109–1121.

Renold, E. (2005). *Girls, boys and junior sexualities: Exploring children's gender and sexual relations in the primary school.* London: Routledge Falmer.

Robinson, K. (2013). Innocence, knowledge and the construction of childhood. *The contradictory nature of sexuality and censorship in children's contemporary lives.* New York, NY: Routledge.

Surtees, N. (2017). *Narrating connections and boundaries: Constructing relatedness in lesbian known donor familial configurations* (Doctoral thesis. University of Canterbury, Christchurch, New Zealand). Retrieved from: https://ir.canterbury.ac.nz/handle/10092/13321

Taylor, A., & Richardson, C. (2005). Queering home corner. *Contemporary Issues in Early Childhood, 6*(2), 163–173.

7 PERSPECTIVES ON MULTILINGUALISM

MARTIN NEEDHAM

CHAPTER OBJECTIVES

By the end of this chapter, you will be able to:

- Reflect on principles that can inform the development of strategies to support the languages children have access to at home.
- Help families to think about the benefits and challenges of supporting the languages spoken at home.
- Encourage children who only have access to English at home to take an interest in and develop a respect for other languages.

KEY DEFINITIONS

Bilingual learner

Someone who is learning in two languages.

English as an additional language (EAL)

Someone who is learning English in addition to, or alongside, a 'home' language.

Lingua Franca

A language that is adopted between speakers whose native languages are different.

Multilingual learner

Someone who is learning in more than two languages.

Parents

Any person who has parental responsibility or has care of a young child during early childhood (from conception to eight years of age).

Practitioner

A person who is qualified to work with children (from conception to 8 years old) across health, education and social care.

Teaching English to speakers of other languages (TESOL)

Usually a more systematic approach to teaching English language vocabulary and grammar.

Translanguaging

Combining different languages together.

Introduction

There is a great deal of literature exploring support strategies for children who have **English as an Additional Language (EAL)** and who are studying in contexts where English is the dominant language (Mistry & Sood, 2020; Murphy, 2011; Wang, 2014). Literature for early childhood **practitioners** and teachers often concentrates on strategies for supporting the acquisition of English language and literacy. This chapter will consider the importance, advantages and challenges of supporting the development of the home language(s) that children have access to, while seeking to identify some general principles for supporting this learning development. This chapter is prompted by concerns that English, as an increasingly dominant *lingua franca*, may displace or weaken fluency in children's home language(s). Families arriving into the United Kingdom with young children have been surprised at how quickly learning a home language can stall in the excitement of settling into a new home. This chapter considers some of the short- and long-term advantages of supporting multilingualism in early childhood. It explores some of the strategies that early childhood settings and families might adopt to help sustain home languages and thereby enhance children's thinking skills.

The chapter also reflects on educational attainment data (Commission on Race Equality, 2021; Mistry & Sood, 2020), implicating systemic bias and linguistic racism (Baker-Bell, 2020) towards certain groups as a significant problem undermining the benefits that multilingualism brings (Mistry & Sood, 2020). In England, those children and young people whose families responded to the calls to former colonies to migrate to England to reduce the labour shortages in 1960s and 1970s Britain often experienced racism and linguistic racism, resulting in some focussing on English rather than home languages. This is illustrated vividly through books that have been turned into the films such as *Blinded by the Light* (Manzoor, 2007) and *Brick Lane* (Ali, 2003). There continues to be a great deal of prejudice towards languages and accents of all sorts in the United Kingdom, and there is often pressure not just to speak English but also to 'fit in' with community and school dialects. Having worked as primary teacher in Hunza Valley in the mountainous Northern Areas of Pakistan in the 1990s, I speak a little Urdu, and Burushaski, which is a rare indigenous linguistic isolate specific to the area. Urdu has much in common with Hindi, providing a lingua franca across South Asia. My experiences in South Asia and of Urdu often lead to positive conversations about places and culture with children, **parents** and students who have South Asian connections. Some students from South Asian backgrounds who have grown up in the United Kingdom, by their early 20s, would like to be more fluent in the linguistic traditions of their families to access their family and cultural heritage more easily. Rare community languages, such as Burushaski, highlight what a precious thing languages are, since they provide deeper insights into a community's heritage, identity, knowledge and sense of self. The school children from the 1990s in the Hunza Valley are now parents themselves, switching comfortably and confidently between English, Urdu and Burushaski in their social media content. This chapter is dedicated to them, their children and their unique language; it is intended to encourage readers' confidence in supporting families seeking to sustain their linguistic heritages.

Bilingual learners: Magic and myths

Acquiring EAL, even where children are newly arrived into the United Kingdom, can appear to happen relatively straightforwardly (Mistry & Sood, 2020). When thrust into the daily routines of English-speaking educational settings, children acquire the language they are immersed in quickly. There is a seemingly magical relationship between the human language acquisition device (LAD) as identified by Chomsky (2006) and the language acquisition support system that is described by Bruner (1986). Young children acquire the fundamentals of their first language grammar and a vocabulary of around 6,000 words by the time they are six (Goswami, 2015). Chomsky (2006) suggests this occurs because brains and bodies are hard wired to pay attention to making meaning and anticipating what comes next from the visual, auditory and affective ques of the people around them. At the same time, Bruner (1986) posits that other humans recognise the need to make communication systems more accessible to young children and instinctively exaggerate and repeat elements of visual and communication in patterns that facilitate language acquisition. This learning occurs primarily, not through the formal teaching of grammar, but through children unconsciously picking up on patterns in speech as they are being inducted as apprentices into meaningful activities (Rogoff, 2003) such as daily classroom and playground routines by adults and peers.

Krashen's 1982 seminal work on second language development focusses on 'language acquisition' as compared to traditional second language teaching (Krashen, 1982). It encourages educators to create the types of immersive language learning contexts identified by Chomsky and Bruner. Krashen (1982) draws attention to the problems that arise when individuals monitor their own language production too closely, becoming overanxious and inhibited in the reception and production processes of communication (Dewaele & Li, 2020). Krashen's (1982) work also suggests that additional languages are acquired following similar sequences implying that key nouns and verbs might be a suitable initial focus with attention focussing on the grammatical details of prefixes and suffixes later. Krashen also advocates that language is acquired when the facilitator targets learning, which is just a little ahead of what the learner currently knows in fashion similar to Vygotsky's zone of proximal development (Vygotsky, 1987).

A **multilingual** education is seen as a strong benefit:

> *In an internationalised economy that is increasingly based on services, people need to be able to communicate with other people all around the world. International communication can be usually managed in English but knowing and being able to communicate in the first language of the interlocutor is often a great asset and calls for the mastering of several languages, besides English.*

> *(Hamby & Richards, 2012, p. 65)*

The ability to speak two languages is widely regarded as helping learners to understand how language structures work, making the learning of further languages easier. Diamond (2010) reports on research from Canada suggesting that a substantial sample of bilingual senior citizens were on average likely to develop Alzheimer's disease 5 years later than those who were monolingual. This is attributed to the enhanced cognitive function associated with a wider activation of neural pathways as a result of using two languages. Hamby and Richards (2012) discuss how a great many countries have adopted multilingual education policies, often because of increasing pressure to begin acquiring English at an early age, or where there are two strong national languages. Hamby and Richards (2012) show how Belgium and Canada have adopted immersive approaches to language learning, where a variety of subject lessons are taught largely in the target language. This has been shown to work more effectively in developing functional language competency as compared to traditional language teaching where learners may come to rely heavily on translation and may be anxious about word-for-word correspondence and correct grammar.

In England, concerns have often been expressed in the past, about children's ability to achieve as **bilingual** or EAL learners; however, the evidence over time is much more nuanced. The Effective Provision of Pre-School Education (EPPE) longitudinal study (Sammons et al., 2007) of more than 2,000 children progressing through pre-schools and schools around the turn of the century found that by Year 5 'Although children who needed EAL support were still showing slightly lower attainment in reading, the relative attainment "gap" compared with other children had decreased' (p. 4). Sammons et al. (2007) pointed out that attainment was much more closely associated with parental education, home background and income as compared to EAL. Mistry and Sood (2015) reviewed this and further evidence from the first decade of this century in England, suggesting that statistically there is relatively little difference in attainment between EAL children and others in KS1 and KS2 with increasing differences in attainment appearing in GCSE results. They suggested that expectations of achievement are more of an issue than English language proficiency, concluding that 'Learners with EAL are not a problem and settings need to challenge such a deficit model' (Mistry & Sood, 2015, p. 8). It is very important to note that EAL has been disassociated as label related to Special Educational Needs (Mistry & Sood, 2020).

In 2021, the Commission on Race Equality's independent report on Education and Training highlighted data, based upon public examination results from 2019, examining attainment differences between Asian, Black, Mixed and White groups (Commission on Race Equality, 2021). At this broad category level, Asian children achieve better results in GCSE and similar profiles at A Level to White young people, but they fared less well at University (Commission on Race Equality, 2021). However, the report foregrounds the problems of broad categorisations such as Black, Asian and minority ethnic (BAME) and draws attention to the statistically lower attainment of those from Bangladeshi, Pakistani and Black Caribbean backgrounds in GCSEs and A Levels. Once again, this latest data suggest that it is not the acquisition of English that underpins underachievement but a more complex mix of expectations around race, class, communities and classroom performances, which means that children from some backgrounds, although starting well in school, are falling behind as they progress through the education system.

The data sets discussed above do not comment on the retention of home languages. One aspect of this identified under-achievement may be the lack of recognition and respect being afforded to children's home languages (Baker-Bell, 2020; Cummins, 2001; Mistry & Sood, 2020). Baker-Bell (2020, p. 16) identifies *linguistic racism* and the pressures on Black students in the United States to use standard English in schools rather than Black language. Baker-Bell (2020) vividly portrays the sense of individuals and groups being devalued and othered, that is, engendered by such linguistic racism. If one or both parent's first and most fluent language is other than English, for children to lose the opportunity to exchange complex ideas in that language would mean missing out on opportunities throughout childhood and beyond to learn from parents' views and heritage. Messages of uncertainty or disinterest about languages from early childhood settings may accelerate powerful societal pressures to acquire English, arising from the domination of English in school communications and the media platforms that parents and children encounter. In the following theme, the importance of language to cultural recognition, identity and self-esteem is explored in more depth.

REFLECTION

Reflect on your own experiences and write three short examples of different children who are familiar to you identifying, how they share similar and different aspects of language development.

Multilingualism supporting identity and culture

At the level of individual family contexts that we are focussing on in this chapter, acquiring a 'home' language affords the immediate benefits of connecting with family heritage and family members. The failure of early childhood provision to support home languages may compromise family connections as well as under-mining self-confidence and identity. Anzaldua (2012) presents very persuasive examples of how Spanish speakers in the Southern United States have been oppressed by the suppression of Spanish in educational settings and the devaluing of Spanish and hybrid indigenous languages. She articulates the damage this cultural racism inflicts on individuals and how this undermines their identities.

> *So, if you really want to hurt me, talk badly about my language. Ethnic identity is twin skin to linguistic identity_ I am my language. Until I can take pride in my language, I cannot take pride in myself. Until I can accept as legitimate Chicano Texas Spanish, Tex-Mex and all the other languages I speak, I cannot accept the legitimacy of myself.*

(Anzaldua, 2012, p. 81)

Having staff that represent and use community languages is a huge asset, and where this is the case, setting aside chunks of time to talk to through topics in an immersive way with children in their home languages is helpful in supporting the legitimacy and status of languages as well as enhancing children's understanding. Many settings may have too few children speaking a particular language to have a member of staff champion them, but it is still possible to invite parents to

- spend time discussing topics in the classroom and or at home,
- help produce writing and displays in home languages,
- lend or recommend books, music, pictures, films and digital content in home languages and
- support visits to shops, business and religious or community centres where parents have connections.

These are all opportunities to recognise cultures and languages, to raise awareness and understanding among all children and staff.

Baker-Bell (2020) and Anzaldua (2012) both draw attention to languages that are created by people in a particular location and time, which are bound up in identity and include elements from different languages; these might be regarded as hybrid languages or acts of **translanguaging** (Creese & Blackledge, 2015). Each of these authors argues that pedagogy should allow space for and not suppress these language acts. In this chapter, the term **multilingualism** is used to convey the idea that many children are acquiring more than two languages as they learn to adapt their communications to the different audiences and contexts they encounter. Practitioners need to acknowledge children's identities and authentic voices as advocates for those with similar lived experiences and avoid correcting patterns of language which are not standard English. Practitioners should demonstrate an interest and ask about the languages children use at home and how they are used. Practitioners should try to learn some words and phrases from children and their families and seek out relevant texts in those languages.

Multilingualism supports learning and thinking

Examining topics first in one language and then again in a second language provides the opportunity to revise and check what has been comprehended from previous encounters with the topic, providing opportunities to recognise where one knows the vocabulary in one but not the second language. This is a good memory development exercise, and it supports the development of metacognitive (Bruner, 1986) awareness, that is, self-awareness of one's own thinking. It is clear from psychological studies of memory and patterns of revision (Smith, Cowie, & Blades, 2011) that such revision helps assimilate, accommodate and retain knowledge. Encouraging parents to review what their child has done in school can be helpful, and parents might welcome shared discussions with other parents about how to do this using two languages. Children might want to report on their day in English whilst walking home and then cover related topics later in a home language. For example, if children have covered farm animals during the day, this might be discussed on the way home and parents might share stories, songs or experiences about farming at bedtime.

Especially when working with young children, Krashen's second language learning principles (Krashen, 1982) suggest that separating language use into immersive blocks might be helpful rather than focussing on grammar and the direct translation of sentences; however, with older children, this can be helpful a shortcut to working out rules quickly and explicitly that is often neglected. Over time, children will start to notice how meanings are constructed differently using different structures and metaphors across different languages. This awareness will make for interesting reflections, encouraging children to ask more questions about why languages work in the way that they do, where words come from and how intonation, prefixes and suffixes change meanings. Native English speakers who are learning to teach English to speakers of other languages **(TESOL)** are often surprised at how much they have taken for granted and not noticed about how English is structured.

Having access to multiple languages encourages creativity by prompting thinking about the choice and order or words. Thinking flexibly about how to explain something when you are not fluent in a language can become an enjoyable and satisfying challenge. For those emersed in a language learning context, it is important to learn to relax, as trying to translate too closely from one language to another can be inhibiting. It is often better to find ways to use the words and phrases you do know, together with what you are hearing together to improvise communications; practice in performance is important to build up speed and confidence. Translanguaging can be helpful and often evolves quickly between speakers and in communities that are using two or more languages as they work out how best to share ideas. Thus, useful relevant words are pulled into a shared working vocabulary, and this playful use of languages creates interesting opportunities for creativity of expression and thought.

At home with multilingualism

Macrory (2006) presents a study of young children growing up in a bilingual home in the United Kingdom, showing how by 15 months children can recognise that they might need to use different words with different people. Macrory presents examples where parents focus on a different language each and try to keep their communications with their child to that language. Families who try this may find it is not always easy to maintain. The child may tend more toward using one language, especially where it is a dominant language with few additional immersive contexts in the other language beyond the home. There are many contexts where children acquire three languages because they experience them on a regular basis in meaningful social contexts with access to media resources in all three languages. The principle for learning would be that communication is usually conducted in one language in any situation with lots of contextual clues, and that translation is used only minimally. Translanguaging may occur, that is, one or more languages may get mixed together in conversations; this is probably best viewed as useful experimentation rather than something to be corrected or discouraged too directly. The point of communication is to be able to work out how best to convey ideas in particular situations with particular company and children will be judging the effectiveness of communications for themselves, because that is the way the LAD works.

Curdt-Christiansen (2009) discusses the challenges for a sample of Chinese families living in Canada in deciding language policies because of

> *Competing with mainstream ideologies, children's popular culture and peer influence on children's social values, resisting mainstream imposition, fighting for economic survival and struggling for legal status are the challenges that immigrant families face in combating language loss.*

> *(Curdt-Christiansen, 2009, p. 353)*

These challenges might lead to family language policies including how much time was spent on different languages, where they are spoken, who will use which languages and how much time might be allowed in different languages using different media. These are complex issues in practice with many variables including families' language proficiencies, children's dispositions and local environments. Families are likely to welcome opportunities to share their experiences of family language policies and practice with other families and practitioners.

95

CASE STUDY

Consider the following examples of parents discussing the approach to supporting their own children's language development.

Interview extracts from parents attending a parent and child group talking about their approaches to supporting their children's language. One parent focussed on supporting English as much as possible at home, the other seeking to focus on their mother tongue and heritage knowing. Both give good reasons for their choices.

Observation extract 1: Yasmeen (mother) and Ahmed (child aged 15 months)

Ahmed hears the sound of the push alongs moving in the outside yard, and he moves over to the nearby door and watches.

'Brrrm bruum ... ba', says Ahmed.

'Car janeo?' [Do you want to go in the car?] 'Car jaeo' [go to the car] 'chello' [let's go]

'Baba' [daddy], says Ahmed. Yasmeen comments that he is always saying daddy at home.

Mum helps Ahmed out of the apron and into his coat and outside he sits on a ride on quad bike waiting for it to move, pressing the handle and pushing a little with his feet but not very seriously. Mum explains that his father bought him a motorised quad bike and she thinks that he is waiting for it to move.

'Ahmed iska batieah' [sit in this one], mum holds open the door a larger car, which she says he liked last week when she pushes him along in it. He stays sting in the car only briefly before getting a skittle from the boot of the car; he climbs out of the car and picks out another skittle from the boot and he shows them to mum; and she smiles and he then walks in a circle around the yard tapping the skittle together. He moves back towards his 'bang', she says, and he offers them to her and she takes one and taps it gently against the other skittle that Ahmed is still holding. He continues tapping the skittles together talking to himself. Mum finishes talking and stands the skittle up that Ahmed offers, 'come on, ... kieya hay? [What is this] one two wee', as Ahmed knocks the skittles over. 'One two, one two skittles wee', mum stands them up again, 'niche karo! [Knock it down]'. Ahmed knocks it down and mum stands them up again. 'Wee niche karo', this is repeated several times, and Ahmed kneels and then crawls along with one skittle and gives it back to mum to stand up.

Interview extract 1: Yasmeen

Martin: *You use two languages quite a lot; how conscious are you of the use of language?*

Yasmeen: *I started doing it consciously at first because I want it to be important in his life. Communication skills are like vital specially being an Asian child and then he is trilingual as well, we've got like three languages at home and I like really wanted him to be able to distinguish between the different languages and everything so I started just really wanting to do that but once I started it all just came naturally for me I have always tried to put communication top of the list, I've noticed he can understand both languages at home and because I have seen the change in him like he can understand I try to emphasise it more and more. It started off consciously and once I know that he has grasped it. Now he knows what I am talking about then everything comes naturally. I want him to be a good communicator whatever he does it's like trying to find a balance you don't want to push him too much but then I do want to really really encourage him whatever he learns that is fine whatever he doesn't learn then that's just the way he has learned basically. I don't know many other people in a similar situation. I have a friend and she didn't speak any English to her daughter none whatsoever and sometimes I look at her daughter and she finds it really difficult to understand English she looks at you blankly if you say what is this. I don't want Ahmed to be like that and focus on just one language and because they are young, they are like sponges aren't they. They can absorb a lot of information I've taken like totally the opposite approach, and I've said I'm not going to do that with him.*

Observation extract 2: Shafiqa (mother) and Afzal (child, 30 months)

Afzal and Imtiaz stand next to each other by a washing-up bowl that has been placed outside on a table with plastic cups, plates, pans and jugs. They quietly take items and place them in the water looking around. Afzal tentatively picks up a blue metal-enamelled pan and puts it down again. Martin encourages them to put more items into the water by asking shall we wash this pan up as well? Martin puts the pan in the water and rinses it out showing Afzal how clean it is. Afzal and Imtiaz continue to play side by side dipping things in the water and pouring the water out. Mum, who has gradually withdrawn and gone to sign into the register, returns but maintains a little distance, commenting to her friend that Afzal is playing nicely and indicating that she would keep her distance for a while.

Interview extract 2: Shafiqa

Shafiqa: *The last few weeks he has been very clingy, his dad went to India, he was all quiet all of a sudden 'cause he misses his dad, and he was asking about his dad. And Imtiaz's mum said that she used to bring him here and he used to get upset and start to cry so what I thought was I'm going to bring him here because he is*

(Continued)

(Continued)

going to start nursery soon and to settle him, I think it's best to let him move off from me.

I'm quite old now in our generation. I don't think we got English like a first language 'cause my mum is like Punjabi, Punjabi speaking, so I remember when I was at nursery, you know when like you haven't got much English. So, I was like quiet. So, I want him to know the English I want him to know what is happening around him and what is not happening. That was like scary for me because I didn't get that for myself. So, I want him to get that language first.

A lot of the Asians do want to speak Punjabi first because that is our mother tongue language, but I speak English myself you see, because I want him to know all the basics in English first. I still speak Punjabi as well and I have started to speak Punjabi to him as well now. I think of Afzal, and I think if he goes to Nursery and if he hasn't got that language, he like isn't going to be with it. He is going to be like shy and quiet and I don't want him to have that.

Martin: *So, independence is something you're trying to promote?*

Shafiqa: *Yeah, that's it yeah. He's been doing that from a very young age, trying to do things for himself. But in a situation like this he just stands back and watches everything.*

REFLECTION

Reflecting on the content of this chapter, consider how you might respond in discussion with each of these parents.

What if any suggestions you would make in each case?

The role of the practitioner

Practitioners should be ready to explore with children's caregivers the language experiences children are exposed to in their home environments and families' approaches to supporting language and literacy learning (Wang, 2014). Early childhood practitioners can brief themselves on strategies for supporting both English and home language acquisition so they can share this knowledge with families.

Settings can show that they value children's home languages and cultures by asking about home languages; seeking resources to support home languages including books, signs and images and supporting discussions of topics at home by providing information about what is happening in the setting. Practitioners should consider learning some phrases in other languages from children and their families.

Settings can consider ways to engage with colleagues, partners or volunteers who are speakers of languages to support other languages. Education policy is often focussed helping children to succeed in English; practitioners should also think about helping families to keep in touch through cultural connections across generations, across continental divides and across time.

Practitioners can encourage children from monolingual home contexts to be interested in other languages; children should feel speaking more than one language is not unusual and is perceived as something that is achievable and valued. Activities that can be beneficial for everyone include learning simple phrases such as greetings, my name is, I am five years old, numbers and colours in the home languages of children. Learning nursery rhymes from different cultures and reviewing modern contemporary images of places, cultural objects and artworks can be important ways of starting to address societal cultural biases, if done well. Parents can be very helpful in supporting settings to do these things well.

REFLECTION

First, identify the ideas from this chapter that you will consider implementing in the future.

Second, add some bullet points against each identified idea, outlining actions that you might take to implement them.

Conclusion

This chapter has tried to identify a range of reasons why early childhood settings should be proactive in supporting families' language policies (Curdt-Christiansen, 2009). There are good ethical (Baker-Bell, 2020), pedagogic (Krashen, 1982) and pragmatic reasons (Mistry & Sood, 2020) for encouraging multilingualism. Some parents will be confident and eager to work with settings to support their children, while others will find this more challenging. Considerable negotiation may be needed to think things through, but this should not be a point for nervousness and inaction. Prejudice towards other languages is deeply embedded in English society, leading to racism which is harmful to all. Promoting multilingualism is essential to fulfilling children's right to have their cultural identities respected and for building self-esteem and a sense of belonging. Promoting multilingualism is something that could help all children to develop a healthy curiosity, interest and respect for languages and the way they work.

Further reading

Baker-Bell, A. (2020). *Linguistic justice Black language literacy identity and pedagogy*. New York, NY: Routledge.

Mistry, M., & Sood, K. (2020). *Meeting the needs of young children with English as an additional language*. Abingdon: Routledge.

Useful websites

National Literacy Trust: Bilingual quick tips

https://literacytrust.org.uk/early-years/bilingual-quick-tips

Teachers TV: The Multilingual Classroom – YouTube

https://www.youtube.com/watch?v=nzoKIHMRjRM

References

Ali, M. (2003). *Brick Lane*. London: Penguin Random House.

Anzaldua, G. (2012). *Borderlands La Frontera* (4th ed.). San Francisco, CA: Aunt Lute Books.

Baker-Bell, A. (2020). *Linguistic justice Black language literacy identity and pedagogy*. New York, NY: Routledge.

Bruner, J. (1986). *Actual minds, possible worlds*. Cambridge, MA: Harvard University Press.

Chomsky, N. (2006). *language in mind*. Cambridge, MA: Cambridge University Press.

Commission on Race Equality. (2021). *Independent report education and training updated 28 April 2021*. Retrieved from: https://www.gov.uk/government/publications/the-report-of-the-commission-on-race-and-ethnic-disparities/education-and-training (Accessed 4th August 2022).

Creese, A., & Blackledge, A. (2015). Translanguaging and identity in educational settings. *Annual Review of Applied Linguistics*, *35*, 20–35.

Cummins, J. (2001). Bilingual children's mother tongue: Why is it important for education? University of Toronto 2001, February. *Sprogforum*, *7*(19), 15–20. Retrieved from: https://inside.isb.ac.th/nativelanguage/files/2015/11/Bilingual-Childrens-Mother-Tongue.pdf (Accessed 11th August 2022).

Curdt-Christiansen, X. L. (2009). Invisible and visible language planning: Ideological factors in the family language policy of Chinese immigrant families in Quebec. *Language Policy*, *8*, 351–375.

Dewaele, J., & Li, C. (2020). Emotions in second language acquisition: A critical review and research agenda. *Foreign Language World*, *196*(1), 34–49.

Diamond, J. (15 October 2010). The benefits of multilingualism bilingual rearing of children, instead of confusing them, may bring lifelong advantages. *Science*, *330*(6002), 332–333.

Goswami, U. (2015). *Children's cognitive development and learning*. York: Cambridge Primary Review Trust.

Hamby, P., & Richards, M. (2012). The paradoxical visions of multilingualism in education: The ideological dimension of discourses on multilingualism in Belgium and Canada. *International Journal of Multilingualism*, *9*(2), 165–188.

Krashen, S. (1982). *Principles and practice in second language acquisition.* Oxford: Pergamon Press.

Macrory, G. (2006). Bilingual language development: What do early years practitioners need to know? *Early Years, 26*(2), 159–169.

Manzoor, S. (2007). *Greeting from Bury Park.* London: Bloomsbury.

Mistry, M., & Sood, K. (2020). *Meeting the needs of young children with English as an additional language.* Abingdon: Routledge.

Murphy, E. (2011). *Welcoming linguistic diversity in early childhood classrooms: Learning from international schools* (Ser. Parents' and teachers' guides, [13]). Multilingual Matters.

Rogoff, B. (2003). *The cultural nature of human development.* Oxford: Oxford University Press.

Sammons, P., Sylva, K., Melhuish, E., Siraj-Blatchford, I., Taggart, B., Grabbe, Y., & Bareau, S. (2007). *Influences on children's attainment and progress in key stage 2: Cognitive outcomes in year 5.* Retrieved from: www.ioe.ac.uk/schools/ecpe/eppe/eppe3-11/eppe3-11pubs (Accessed 4th August 2022).

Smith, P. K., Cowie, H., & Blades, M. (2011). *Understanding children's development* (5th ed.) Chichester: Wiley.

Vygotsky, L. S. (1987). *The collected works of L.S. Vygotsky, volume 1.* New York, NY: Plenum Press.

Wang, X.-L. (2014). *Understanding language and literacy development: Diverse learners in the classroom.* London: Wiley-Blackwell.

8   CULTURAL APPROACHES TO PARENTING

HATTIE CAMPBELL

CHAPTER OBJECTIVES

By the end of this chapter, you will be able to:

- Reflect on the rich and diverse complexity of culture concerning parenting.
- Consider how early childhood practitioners can misrepresent parents' cultural context.
- Acknowledge the power residing in early childhood spaces and give some thought to how practitioners might work towards dismantling injustices in their settings.

KEY DEFINITIONS

Acculturation

Acculturation is the psychological, emotional and intellectual identification with a particular social group who may share values, beliefs and ideas.

Bias

Behaviours based on judgements or assumptions.

Culture

Culture involves the shared values, beliefs and ideas of a particular social group.

Homogeneous

Perceiving and treating individuals from a particular social group as being the same. This can be associated with stereotyping.

Parents

Any person who has parental responsibility or has care of a young child during early childhood (from conception to eight years of age).

Power

Power in which some groups have social, economic and political advantages over other social groups.

Practitioners

A person who is qualified to work with children (from conception to 8 years old) across health, education and social care.

Othering

The process of marginalising, dehumanising or excluding others.

Unconscious bias training

Intended to create awareness of an individual's implicit propensity for disliking others.

Introduction

The title of this chapter, *Cultural approaches to parenting*, is a turn towards the importance of culture, constructed through interaction with others and associated with social groups. However, no two individuals within a group share the same cultural characteristics. The chapter draws attention to the competing definitions of parenting culture. Forging meaningful relations with parents is the subject of much debate, with inclusion and diversity at the heart of early childhood practice.

While legislation and policy are solid indicators for inclusion and diversity, there is still confusion about how practitioners move beyond and into meaningful territory with parents. Indeed, while early childhood settings celebrate diversity, practitioners experience discomfort talking with **parents** about cultural differences, except in the context of shared events where early childhood professionals can unwittingly sweep individuality aside.

Although diversity in early childhood is an accepted discourse, its foundation balances notions of sameness with similarities that may be evident in various groups. By looking too rigidly at similarities in various groups, individuality can be overlooked. This can then result in tokenistic gestures from early childhood settings offering only minimal or superficial effort to the cultural context of children, parents and families in early childhood education. **Practitioners** should transition from the broad generalisations of inclusion and diversity and begin to move towards negotiating intersections such as race, gender, sexuality and other identity formations not as an abstraction but in human terms, with human rights and social justice in mind. Because this is by no means an easy transition, this chapter provides an opportunity to disrupt and motivate practitioners towards reflexive and trans-formational change. It is also for early childhood practitioners inspired to lead courageously with conviction.

One of the various definitions underpinning the discussion throughout this chapter is from Matsumoto (1996), who suggests that ideas about culture can mean different things to different people, even those whose identities are apparently within a shared cultural context. The chapter explores cultural approaches to parenting and the importance of acknowledging this in early childhood education (Paechter, 2001).

What is culture?

Understanding culture requires acknowledging individual and multiple repre-sentations of those realities (Briziarelli & Guillem, 2016). This explanation implies that culture conveys shared values, perspectives, behaviours and practices while being unique from one individual to the other (Pollard, 2008). Practitioners encounter parents through various cultural contexts, expanding opportunities to embody richer understandings of cultural norms and differences. Conversely, this also means that discounting cultural context from parenting underestimates the value of those lived and subjective experiences that may conceal 'abuses of power and processes of Othering' (Osgood, 2012, p. 85). **Othering** is a term used to communicate the idea of specific groups of people being marginalised, dehumanised or otherwise excluded. Conversely, otherness also reinforces 'normality and superiority' (Campbell, 1992, p. 8; cited in MacNaughton, 2005, p. 85).

Legislation and policy in early childhood education

The Equality Act 2010 guides early childhood practitioners in their understanding of equality, diversity and inclusion (EDI). *The United Nations Convention on the Rights of the Child* has fifty-four articles covering '…all aspects of a child's life and set out the … social and cultural rights that all children everywhere are entitled to' (UNCRC, 2022, para. 1). Additionally, the English statutory framework for the *Early Years Foundation Stage* (EYFS) refers to children under-standing the world around them and embracing difference (Department for Education DfE, 2021). Furthermore, the EYFS suggests the importance of culture as identity-forming, as well as building relationships with parents (DfE, 2021). Early childhood practitioners are governed by UK legislation to assist in under-standing these crucial issues. However, where guidance perhaps falls short is the government's tendency towards a universal one-size-fits-all approach. This approach may leave practitioners with less advice about the richness and indi-viduality of parenting cultures.

Nevertheless, some government directives do attempt to offer more nuanced guidance. Osgood draws our attention to early childhood policies that express respect for ethnic and cultural diversity becoming 'unwittingly homogenised and fixed' (Anthias & Yuval-Davis, 1992; Luke & Luke, 1999; cited in Osgood, 2012). **Homogeneous** means that people from shared cultural contexts are essentially perceived as sharing the same characteristics, ideas, experiences and beliefs. Osgood (2012) points out that early childhood practitioners deal with the inherent difficulties of difference through unquestioned dominant normalised discourses, often resulting in tokenism.

REFLECTION

As an early childhood practitioner, reflect on what the following statement might mean in terms of respecting the diversity of parenting cultures:

Firstly, ask yourself the question – how confident do I feel about diversity and difference? Then imagine yourself in unfamiliar surroundings with people who are speaking another language.

Now try this exercise again, this time imagine you are in a room with people who communicate using British sign language and lip reading. You are expected to communicate with at least half a dozen people in the room. How confident do you feel right now?

In this scenario, how would you demonstrate your interest in families? How would you generate a conversation about a person's job, specialist skill or heritage?

You may feel at ease with this exercise, reflect on and share why this is. Or you may know that you would be uncomfortable, again why is this?

Developing a reflective practice is about becoming aware of what you thought and felt in any given situation. It is also about being honest with yourself about those feelings. The important thing about reflective practice is to not feel guilty but simply to notice and ask important questions about how you might capitalise on what you felt was positive or what you would like to change and improve as an early childhood practitioner.

Unconscious bias and cultural approaches to parenting

Unconscious bias explores the notion of discrimination and social injustice implicit in individual behaviour. This section explores **power** residing in early childhood spaces, an essential criterion for understanding EDI. The basis for understanding the richness of parenting cultures is the sad truth that social injustice abides where there are differences. If this were not the case, unconscious bias training, which became mandatory in UK public and private institutions, would not exist. A definition provided by Murray (2016, p. 22) suggests theories underpinning unconscious bias presume that discrimination occurs because of learned behaviour 'which can therefore be unlearned'.

A report by the Behavioural Insights Team (BIT) (2020) in the government human resources department provides the rationale for unconscious bias training:

- Unconscious biases can influence a person's judgement without them being aware.

- Unconscious bias training in the workplace aims to make people aware of potentially harmful unconscious biases and to reduce the impact of those biases on their interaction with others.

Contested notions of unconscious bias training: Awareness of cultural approaches to parenting

A written ministerial statement by Parliamentary Secretary Julia Lopez highlighted concerns stating, 'given the evidence, now captured in the report accompanying this statement, an internal review decided in January 2020 that unconscious bias training would phase out from all government departments' (Lopez, 2020). It seems then that unconscious bias training is quietly departing. The report entitled *Unconscious Bias and Diversity Training – What the Evidence Says* states:

> *While some types of unconscious bias training may have some limited effects, including creating awareness of an individual's own implicit biases and wider diversity and discrimination issues in the very short-term, there is currently no evidence that this training changes behaviour or improves workplace equality in terms of representation of women, ethnic minorities, or other minority groups, in the position of leadership, or reducing pay inequalities.*

> *(BIT, 2020, p. 1)*

There is considerable research surrounding unconscious bias training, which attempts to tackle EDI in the workplace. Firstly, let us explore the idea behind unconscious bias, commonly understood as an attempt to raise awareness of suppressed unconscious tendencies whereby discrimination can occur. The purpose of unconscious bias training is to increase knowledge of the presence of one's own bias, thereby addressing discrimination at work (Osman, 2021). The connection is that if bias is present, stereotypical views about parenting styles might impact the practitioner's ability to develop meaningful relationships with families.

Various unconscious bias tests are used to raise awareness about workplace prejudice. One such test is the Harvard Implicit Association Test (IAT) (Osman, 2021). IAT is a psychological test intended to reveal unconscious bias in employees, designed to capture underlying positive and negative perceptions of others. Unlike self-reporting, employees cannot easily manipulate their responses to IAT assessments. There is no evidence to suggest that unconscious bias training is effective and was described by the IAT as 'pointless' because while the training can reveal existing bias, it cannot simply change workplace behaviour (Noon, 2018, p. 199). Noon (2018, p. 204) also points out that the emphasis on unconscious bias training tends to be on individuals rather than exploring systemic institutional failures. Other commentators argue that institutions should explore collective work experiences and recognise that the cultural context within institutions can influence attitudes of bias towards others (Brook, 2013; cited in Noon, 2018, p. 205; Fineman, 2008; cited in Noon, 2018, p. 205).

Robinson and Diaz (2006, p. 7) refer to anti-bias, a term derived from multicultural education in the 1970s and 1980s. They argue that multicultural education could fix biases with training. The idea was that by making intolerant individuals aware through training, they would become tolerant of others. However, instead of multicultural education creating tolerance in the workplace, it created a culture of 'superficial respect for cultural differences' (Robinson & Diaz, 2006, p. 7). This superficial behaviour became known as 'the tourist approach' (Denman-Sparks and the ABC Taskforce, 1989; cited in Robinson & Diaz, 2006, p. 7). Fast forward to the 21st century, and it is evident that anti-bias and unconscious bias share similarities to the tourist approach. Parents and children require more from early childhood practitioners than superficial respect for culturally nuanced approaches to parenting. For early childhood practitioners, responding appropriately in ways that demonstrate authentic and genuine concern for parents and their parenting styles is vital.

For practitioners to appreciate the varying cultural approaches to parenting, there should be thoughtful consideration of traditions, values, beliefs, gender, class and other identity formations inherited generationally yet changeable over time. As such, fixed ideas about cultural approaches to parenting are not only unhelpful but serve to reinforce discrimination and inequalities. One of the many ways to characterise culture is to understand that it is composed of various social groups constructed through social interaction with others, which influences behaviour. Therefore, it is essential for practitioners not to generalise but engage with the unique ways parents interpret their choice of parenting styles. There are various ways to achieve this, such as including parents in the life of the setting and creating spaces that give parents a voice. On the one hand, early childhood practitioners should develop an understanding of parenting across cultures. On the other hand, practitioners should recognise that parents from shared cultural groups 'may vary in modal patterns of personality, acculturation level, education, or socioeconomic status' (Bornstein et al., p. 214).

REFLECTION

Having explored unconscious bias above, let us consider potential connections between cultural approaches to parenting and unconscious bias training. Explore and reflect on one or more questions below:

- Why should we understand that culture and parenting are important?

- What is the intended purpose of unconscious bias training?

(Continued)

(Continued)

- Why has the UK government decided that unconscious bias training is ineffective?

- Considering that bias does indeed exist in all of us, what can we do to transform our practice and work meaningfully with parents?

- Why do you think a person's culture is important?

Parents, power and White Western ideologies

Parents often find themselves navigating the formalities of early childhood education and the uncomfortable reality that cultural approaches to parenting intersect with commonsense ideas privileging White Western parenting (Robinson & Diaz, 2006; Sian, 2019). This statement is not to suggest that White Western parenting is wrong. But it highlights that ideas about White Western notions of parenting tend to be afforded more value in education and society privileging one group over others. We have only to look at and use the #BlackLivesMatter or #Meetoo to appreciate the narrative of power in our community. These movements exist because of unexplained deaths of people of colour at the hands of the justice system and because women and girls experience sexual harassment often denied by men and disregarded by the justice system. These injustices are examples of legislation and education combining to reinforce narratives that disadvantage some groups while affording other groups privileges. These movements (#BlackLivesMatter and #Metoo) highlight that our society has less regard for people of colour and women. As such, political activists sought to change these injustices. Against this backdrop, we encourage early childhood practitioners to reflect on and challenge dominant Western assumptions about parenting. Why? Because parents are also people of colour and women.

Marginalised people are disadvantaged by these powerful, dominant narratives in which discrimination occurs as everyday norms. This chapter argues that while the change in individual practice is essential, collaborative change is more powerful. Early childhood practitioners should work alongside parents to understand the challenges experienced as such collaborations can be equally powerful in producing transformational change. Parents provide the best source of information about their cultural context and the nuanced ways that this influences their parenting. Approaches to parenting differ within communities, and they also differ in families, as well as between siblings. Practitioners should be purposeful in rebalancing positions of power to build meaningful relationships. They may be surprised at how open parents can be when they encounter a genuine interest in collaborating with them.

It can be argued that early childhood studies degrees refer overwhelmingly and are rooted in the importance of White male middle-class theorists. It is not that whiteness is explicitly referred to as privileging the content delivered – far from it.

But this sends a message to those studying (and future early childhood practitioners) that knowledge is meaningful only if it comes from these quarters. As such, the curriculum in further, and higher education can undermine the various and culturally diverse approaches to parenting while simultaneously encouraging students to challenge positions of power and inequality. These conflicting messages can be complex for early childhood practitioners to navigate. Additionally, as many early childhood practitioners are overwhelmingly women who are parents, working while studying, it would be helpful to share ideas about power and privilege in the safety of those learning spaces.

REFLECTION

Consider one or more of the points in either Section A or Section B.

Section A: Reflect on a particular incident in which you experienced discrimination in the workplace:

- Choose an incident that does not bring up trauma or cause you distress.

- Who did you tell when you experienced this incident (if anyone)?

- Was this an experience that may have been difficult to prove or communicate to others?

- Now picture in your mind parents of another cultural context to your own. What might encourage trust to develop between you and those parents?

Section B: If the questions above do not resonate with your lived experience:

- Consider whether you witnessed any form of discrimination towards other(s) that made you feel uncomfortable (i.e. work, school, socialising).

- Do not think about what you could have done at that moment or entertain notions of guilt or sadness; this is not the purpose of the exercise. Only use this time to unwrap your perception of what you believe took place.

CASE STUDY

The case study below is based on actual events. There are no right or wrong answers in your response. This exercise aims to explore your thoughts around the incident and discuss it with others. The case study will likely draw out varying perceptions. Start with the question below:

(Continued)

(Continued)

- Why do you think Jodie responded this way, and what were the biased assumptions about Edward?

- How do you think Edward felt?

- There is a lot of information in this case study. Discuss anything you believe may be relevant.

Jodie's cultural context is White British. Jodie's male partner is Black British of African-Caribbean descent. Jodie is an experienced early childhood practitioner of several years and believes she gets on well with parents from various cultural contexts. Jodie prides herself on forging positive partnerships with parents. She is White-identified and considers herself to be culturally open to difference. She is also confident in her practice as a key person.

Kai, an only child, is one of Jodie's key children. Kai's mother is Marie, and her father is Edward, both Black British of African-Caribbean heritage. Jodie discusses Kai's progress with her mother as Edward has never collected Kai. However, on one occasion, Jodie was approached by Kai's father, and although she met him when Kai first started at the nursery six months ago, she never saw him again. Hence, she usually discusses Kai's progress with Marie. On this occasion, Kai's father, Edward, came to collect Kai. He asks Jodie if she could update him on Kai's progress since starting six months ago. Jodie was a little unnerved since she usually discussed Kai's progress with her mother. Also, as Jodie had already held a meeting with Marie two weeks previously, she found it strange that Edward was unaware of Kai's progress. Jodie responded to Edward that she had updated Marie about Kai's progress two weeks earlier and so Kai was not yet due another report. Edward looked disappointed with her response but said nothing and left. Following this, Jodie was in the baby room and mentioned to a colleague that Edward 'waltzed into the nursery demanding to get an update about Kai when he hasn't even been seen for six months' and 'why could he not get this information from Marie – where has he been?'

Two days later, the nursery manager called Jodie into the office, who informed her that a parent had made a complaint and that it was Kai's father, Edward. Jodie was shocked by this and proceeded to explain to her manager that all she did was explain to Edward that she (Jodie) had already updated Marie about Kai's progress. Jodie's manager then explained that the complaint was not about that; it was that Edward overheard Jodie talking about him as he was outside the baby room while she was making disparaging comments about him. Jodie was utterly embarrassed and explained that Edward never usually came to the nursery. She wondered why he couldn't just ask Marie if he was so interested in Kai. The manager then explained that Edward never went to the nursery because he was a doctor who worked long, unsociable hours and even longer during the pandemic. He often could not return home as he was required to quarantine. His work also meant he was obligated to stay away from the nursery. The manager explained that Edward was not an absent father who hadn't bothered to investigate his daughter's progress. In fact, he was saving lives over the previous six months.

The role of the practitioner

When considering our motivations for careers as early childhood practitioners, we often highlight the desire to make a difference and forge lasting, life-enhancing experiences for children. Yet, the urgency of government directives can often at times overshadow these ambitions. Even the most experienced early childhood practitioners can reflect on a career that may or may not have achieved those early aspirations. Alternatively, those new to the profession may reflect on how to realise career goals in their journey towards professional practice.

Early childhood practitioners face competing demands and priorities. Reconciling those numerous requirements and conflicts may seem overwhelming. Becoming an early childhood practitioner involves facing some of the dilemmas and challenges involving professional skills, knowledge and positioning oneself within the large communities of practice. According to Ashwin et al. (2015, p. 42), this also involves 'managing emotional dimensions of personal development' and integrating those experiences of practice. Engaging with these dilemmas forces us to use our judgement and to 'assess the most appropriate course of action in any particular situation' (Ashwin et al., 2015, p. 43). Therefore, an essential aspect of the role is to develop as a reflective, receptive and responsive practitioner. Transforming into reflective practitioners helps develop a deeper awareness of our actions and honestly consider the rationale behind our practices (Brookfield, 1995; cited in Ashwin et al., 2015).

Ashwin et al. (2015, p. 45) identifies seven key characteristics of reflective practice as follows:

1 Reflective practice takes shape at a particular time and in a specific place.

2 Reflective practices are about making judgements at a particular time and place.

3 Reflective practices are sparked by dissatisfaction with existing arrangements and involve a cyclical process of questioning our everyday assumptions.

4 Who we are, emotionally and intellectually, is key to our reflective practices.

5 Contexts in which reflective practices take place play a critical role in shaping them.

6 Dialogue is essential in developing reflective practices.

7 Evidence is crucial in reflective practice.

Conclusion

In this chapter, we explored the importance of embracing the various cultural contexts of parents. It is argued that diversity provides opportunities for richer understandings of cultural norms and differences. Policy and legislation provide clear guidance for practice in early childhood education. However, policy and legislation can arguably seem prescriptive and thus influence practice and procedures within fixed and homogenised ideas.

This chapter raises important questions about unconscious bias training in early childhood education. The evidence suggests that unconscious bias training does not significantly affect changing behaviours and tackling discrimination. There appears to be a direct correlation between reducing the impact of discrimination through unconscious bias training and perpetuating tokenism. Moreover, no evidence supports the case that unconscious bias training as a management tool achieves its intended aim of raising awareness about implicit biases. To work meaningfully with the various cultural parenting styles, early childhood practitioners should have access to equally practical training.

The chapter also explored notions of power. There is a direct challenge to commonsense ideas that privilege White Western parenting concepts. Readers are challenged to evaluate these issues critically, to contemplate these contested views, as well as share, converse and debate in the safety of early childhood spaces.

This chapter contributes to developing a more profound understanding of cultural approaches to parenting by attempting to challenge biases, assumptions, discrimination and disadvantage. Before we can consider working with parents outside of our cultural context, we should first attempt to investigate the assumptions we make about difference. Although the chapter takes a contested view of unconscious bias, it does indeed have a place within the context of reflective practice. The questions raised in this chapter are born out of those critical social issues such as #BlackLivesMatter and #Metoo. The chapter highlights some wider social issues surrounding discrimination and encourages early childhood practitioners to recognise these insights as opportunities for forging powerful partnerships with parents.

Further reading

Sian, K. P. (2019). *Navigating institutional racism in british universities.* York: Palgrave MacMillan.

Warmington, P. (2014). *Black british intellectuals in education: Multiculturalism's hidden history.* London: Routledge Taylor & Francis.

Useful websites

Badshah, N. (2018). *GCSE textbook condemned for racist Caribbean stereotypes.* The Guardian. Retrieved from: https://www.theguardian.com/world/2018/oct/08/gcse-textbook-condemned-for-racist-caribbean-stereotypes (Accessed 01 April 22).

Department for Education DfE (22 September 2021). *Understanding the diverse world.* [Video]. YouTube. https://youtu.be/JQVWWjTFca8 (Accessed 03 August 22).

United Nation Convention on the Rights of the Child (UNICEF). (n.d.). *How do we protect children's rights with the UN convention on the rights of the child.* Retrieved from: https://www.unicef.org.uk/what-we-do/un-convention-child-rights/ (Accessed 28 June 22).

References

Anthias, F., & Yuval-Davis, N. (1992). *Radicalised boundaries: Race, gender, colour and class and the anti-racist struggle.* London: Routledge.

Ashwin, P., Boud, D., Coate, K., Hallett, F., Keane, K., Krause, K., Leibowitz, B., MacLaren, I., McArthur, J., McCune, V., & Tooher, M. (2015). *Reflective teaching in higher education.* London: Bloomsbury.

Behavioural Insights Team. (2020). *Unconscious bias and diversity training.* Retrieved from: https://www.bi.team/blogs/unconscious-bias-and-diversity-training-the-evidence/ (Accessed 12th December 2022).

Briziarelli, M., & Guillem, S. M. (2016). *Reviving Gramsci: Crisis, communication and change.* London: Routledge Taylor & Francis.

Department for Education. (2021). *Early years foundation stage (EYFS) statutory framework.* Crown copyright 2021.

Lopez, J. (15 December 2020). *Written ministerial statement on unconscious bias training.* Government UK. Cabinet Office. Retrieved from: https://questions-statements.parliament.uk/written-statements/detail/2020-12-15/hcws652 (Accessed 10 July 22).

MacNaughton, G. (2005). *Doing Foucault in early childhood studies: Applying post-structural ideas.* London: Routledge.

Matsumoto, D. (1996). *Culture and psychology.* California, CA: Brooks Cole Publishers.

Murray, B. (2016). The unconscious bias trap: How misconceptions about unconscious bias can trip up any business. *Effective Executive, 19*(4), 20–26. https://www.proquest.com/scholarlyjournals/unconscious-bias-trap-how-misconceptions-about/docview

Noon, M. (2018). Pointless diversity training: Unconscious bias, new racism and agency. *Work, Employment and Society, 32*(1), 198–209. doi: 10.1177/0950017017719841

Osman, M. (2021). UK public understanding of unconscious bias and unconscious bias training. *Psychology, 12*(7), 1058–1069. doi: 10.4236/psych.2021.127063

Osgood, J. (2012). *Narratives from the nursery: Negotiating professional identities in early childhood.* London: Routledge.

Paechter, C. (2001). Power, gender, and curriculum. In C. Paechter, M. Preedy, D. Scott, & J. Soler (Eds.), *Knowledge, power and learning* (pp. 1–17). London: Paul Chapman Publishing Ltd.

Pollard, A. (2008). *Reflective teaching – Evidence informed professional practice* (3rd edn). London: Continuum International Publishing Group.

Robinson, K. H., & Diaz, C. J. (2006). *Diversity and difference in early childhood education: Issues for theory and practice.* New York, NY: Open University Press.

UNCRC (2022). *The United Nations Convention on the Rights of the Child.* Retrieved from: https://www.unicef.org.uk/what-we-do/un-convention-child-rights/ (Accessed 12th December 2022).

9 SUPPORTING REFUGEE FAMILIES

DONNA GAYWOOD, TONY BERTRAM AND CHRIS PASCAL

CHAPTER OBJECTIVES

By the end of this chapter, you will be able to:

- Know the difference between a migrant, forced migrant, refugee or asylum seeker.
- Apply Bronfenbrenner's ecological systems theory to help understand about the life of people seeking refuge.
- Identify some of the hidden narratives about refugees and consider the implications.
- Have opportunity to consider your own beliefs and think about how these may impact your practice.

KEY DEFINITIONS

Parents

Any person who has parental responsibility or has care of a young child during early childhood (from conception to eight years of age).

Practitioner

A person who is qualified to work with children (from conception to 8 years old) across health, education and social care.

Alongsided

Alongsided is a term which was introduced by Dr Robyn Pound (2003) during her time as a health visitor. It describes how a practitioner positions themselves as a professional, in relation to the people they work with. Rather than adopting an expert model, which tends to lead to the professional holding more power and places them in a dominant position, alongsidedness requires the professional to adapt and consciously shift into a more equal power-sharing relationship.

ECEC

Early Childhood Education and Care.

Positionality

Positionality is a concept often used in qualitative research. To improve quality, trustworthiness and reduce bias, researchers openly identify their own values and backgrounds so that it is visible. By making it visible, they are able to interrogate any underlying assumptions and more able to identify potential blind spots, which may affect the research. For example, I am a White, cis, heterosexual, middle-class woman.

United Nations High Commissioner for Refugees (UNHCR)

The UNHCR was convened in 1950 in the aftermath of the World War II (1939–1945) to create legislative protection for people who needed to seek the protection of another country.

Vulnerable persons resettlement scheme

The UK government has committed to resettle refugees from other countries. To be eligible to come to the United Kingdom as part of these schemes, people have to already have their refugee status granted and must be either

- a victim of torture,

- a victim of rape or sexual exploitation or

- a child with SEND.

Introduction

Every year, thousands of people worldwide are displaced and forced to leave their homes for reasons which include war, climate change, natural disasters, political opposition and gender identity or sexual orientation. This is not a new phenomenon. Throughout history, different groups of people have been subject to persecution and oppression by their own governments, becoming victims of war, famine and repression. The increasing influence of the media has meant that people's experiences are being documented more often and the general public are becoming more aware of these stories of flight in search of safety. The United Nations High Commissioner for Refugees (UNHCR) suggests that by the end of 2021, 89.3 million people had been forcibly displaced worldwide. About 36.5 million of those were children under 18 years of age, 53.2 million were internally displaced within their own country, 4.6 million were asylum seekers and 27.1 million were refugees. From 2018 to 2021, 1.5 million children were born as refugees (UNHCR, 2022).

Working as an early childhood practitioner offers a unique opportunity to support young children and their families, but there is a paucity of research (Bove & Sharmahd, 2020) concerned with the lived experiences of refugee families, primarily because the lives of young children and their families are extremely complex due to the political nature of their situation. This chapter draws on a doctoral study (Gaywood, 2022), which investigated the post-migration lived experiences in Early Childhood Education and Care (ECEC) of four Syrian refugee children and their families. In this chapter, I have also drawn on many years of practice, working with very young children and their families who are facing significant life challenges.

Terms

The terms often used to describe forcibly displaced people can be confusing. It is important that early childhood practitioners are clear what the different terms mean but also understand that the use of words have political implications and impact the public's understanding (Kyriakides, 2017).

Refugee

The term refugee is defined in Article 1 of the Convention and Protocol relating to the Status of Refugees as set out by the United Nations in 1951. A refugee is described as a person with a

> *well-founded fear of being persecuted for reasons of race, religion, nationality, membership of a particular social group or political opinion, is outside the country of his nationality and is unable or, owing to such fear, is unwilling to avail himself of the protection of that country.*
>
> *(UNHCR Refugee Agency, 2019, p. 18)*

The British government has invested in a number of schemes which have granted refugee status to people on entry into the United Kingdom (the Vulnerable Persons Resettlement Schemes) (Home Office, 2017; Home Office, Department for International Development, Ministry of Housing, & Communities and Local Government, 2018). This has meant that they have not needed to go through the asylum-seeking process. Once refugee status has been approved, people then have access to universal credits.

Asylum seeker

An asylum seeker is a person who, on arrival in a 'safe' country, claims asylum. They declare to officials that they meet the criteria of a refugee (as outlined above). The process of asylum seeking then begins, and the asylum seeker is expected to prove that they cannot return to their own country due to a well-founded fear of persecution. The process can be long and protracted and is usually characterised by poverty as asylum seekers are not allowed to work and are not entitled to universal credit but can receive a payment currently of £40.85 per week (Asylum Support: gov.uk, 2022) They are often provided with insecure or poor housing, which may be subject to frequent moves with very little notice, and intense meetings with government officials in which people are required to re-live often traumatic events. Contrary to popular belief, these post-migration experiences can often lead to higher instances of poor mental health than the original pre- and peri-migration events (Hart, 2009; Measham et al., 2014).

Forced migrants

This term is used less often but is the correct term for people who have been displaced through natural disasters, which include famine, flood or fire. Although generally linked to the climate change emergency, it can also be used as an umbrella term to incorporate refugees and asylum seekers.

Migrant

A migrant is someone who has chosen to migrate, usually for economic purposes. Technically, a person who leaves their home country to 'work abroad' is a migrant, but currently in England, this term has negative connotations, so British people often prefer to refer to themselves as expats, rather than economic migrant, feeling more comfortable with a word which has its roots in colonialism. The word immigrant is also often used in an equally negative way with people being referred to as 'illegal immigrants'. A refugee or an asylum seeker should never be referred to in this way, as they have a legal right to seek out refuge. An undocumented immigrant is a person who has migrated for work or study, and their visa has expired.

Given the negativity around some of these terms, it is unsurprising that there are a number of unhelpful narratives about forcibly displaced people, which are often politically motivated, so it is common to find 'the terms "refugee", "asylum seeker", and "migrant" have been allowed to merge in public discourse into a single category of disapproval and disavowal' (Taylor, Debelle, & Modi, 2016, p. 1).

Host

The term *'host'* is used to describe the country which a refugee, migrant or asylum seeker chooses to settle. Children who have citizenship or who are born in the host country are referred to as *'host children'.*

Refugees in the United Kingdom today

Working with refugee children and their parents is complex, and understanding more about their lives is important. Bronfenbrenner's (1979) ecological systems model is a helpful frame to do this. The model is concerned with micro-, meso-,

Microsystem	Family
Mesosystem	Early Childhood Education and Care setting
Exosystem	The local authority
Macrosystem	Living in the United Kingdom and the impact of policy making
Chronosystem	International events

Figure 9.1   Application of Bronfenbrenner's ecological systems theory to the support understanding of refugee child's context

Source: Gaywood (2022).

exo-, macro- and chronosystems of a child and how this can impact their development (Figure 9.1). However, it is also useful for early childhood practitioners as not only does it highlight some of the challenges faced by refugee children and their parents but the model also offers an opportunity to reflect and consider how the wider narratives found within the child's macrosystem (living in the United Kingdom) may have influenced attitudes and practices which are then translated into everyday interactions (Figure 9.2).

Children from refugee backgrounds and their families' lives are often subject to changing policies, laws and the sway of public opinion. The current policies adopted by the British government (Home Office, 2022a: Home Office, 2022b; Home Office, 2022c) of requiring asylum seekers to gain a visa prior to entry into the United Kingdom, enforcing people to claim asylum in the first 'safe' country they arrive in, making arrival in small boats illegal and transporting asylum claimants to other countries for 'processing' all contravene international law regarding refugees, which protects the rights of individuals who are forced to seek asylum or refuge outside of their country of origin. It is difficult to know whether these repressive policies inform public opinion or are driven by public opinion.

There are several negative narratives about refugees, migrants and asylum seekers which form the backdrop to the lives of refugee families today and often have a more pernicious influence than would be expected.

The first narrative which appears to have been represented by the media and some politicians is that refugees pose a significant threat to the economic livelihoods of the host nation, and they are seen as being a drain on the country's already limited resources (The Guardian, 2016). Whereas in Germany refugees are seen as important contributors to the economy, in the United Kingdom, there is a less welcoming attitude. Piotrowski, Różycka-Tran, Baran, and Żemojtel-Piotrowska (2019) have helpfully applied a concept from games theory, which explains about zero-sum thinking. It is this way of thinking which leads people to believe

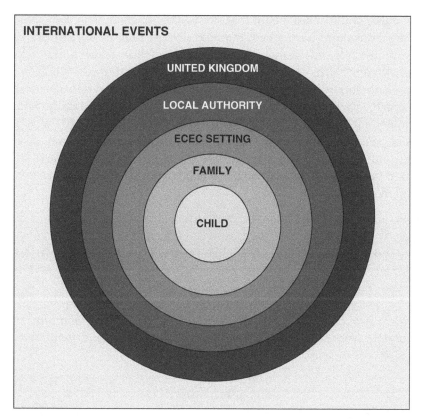

Figure 9.2   Adapted model representing a child's context
Source: Gaywood (2022).

that another person's gain is their loss, so when migrants, asylum seekers and refugees receive benefits, housing or employment, it is perceived to be at the expense of the host country citizens.

A second strong and equally negative narrative about refugees is 'the impression given . . . that the UK is experiencing a sustained surge of claimants' (Taylor et al., 2016, p. 1). This notion of being overwhelmed by refugees can lead to a fear-based response which Bauman (2016) describes as 'mixaphobia: fear of the unmanageable volume of the unknown' (Bauman, 2016, p. 9). However, although the United Kingdom is considered a high-income country, according to the World Bank categorisation (UNHCR, 2022), low- and middle-income countries tend to host the majority of displaced people, 83% of the total. Germany is the only high-income country which is within the top 10 countries accepting people seeking refuge, accommodating 1.3 million people (UNHRC, 2022). The number of refugees and asylum seekers accepted into United Kingdom is in reality significantly less.

It is likely that both national and international events have added to a fear-based response to people seeking refuge and asylum and have led to more and more securitised policies, with refugees being viewed suspiciously. The result of these shifts in policy and foci has meant that from 2014, **all** children in early, primary and secondary education have been required to be taught the British values of democracy, the rule of law, individual liberty and mutual respect and tolerance for those of different faiths or beliefs (Department for Education, 2014). Then in 2015, it became a safeguarding obligation to undertake the Prevent duty (Department for Education, 2015), where again all educators were expected to identify children who were 'vulnerable to radicalisation' (Department for Education, 2015, p. 5). These policies suggest an increased perceived threat to Britain and its way of life, from refugees and asylum seekers. Mayblin (2017) suggests that this move to a more securitised perspective, can also be explained from a post-colonial perspective and is rooted in racism.

A fourth and equally problematic discourse surrounding refugees is a trauma narrative about children and their parents. Whilst is it true that many refugee children and their families do experience mental health difficulties as a result of their displacement, these are not primarily located in pre- and peri-migration experiences, but

> *stresses experienced by young refugees during their exile and after their migration were more predictive of psychological problems than traumatic experiences before.*

> *(Measham et al., 2014, p. 208/9)*

This trauma narrative is potentially problematic because by focussing solely on trauma and its recovery, there is a subtle positioning of refugees as victims, which, if left unquestioned, perpetuates a power inequity between refugee families and host country. It also enables the country of refuge to adopt a saviour-like status, making it harder to identify and report difficult traumatic experiences post-migration. For early childhood practitioners living in a refugee-receiving country, the belief that children's trauma is solely experienced prior to arriving in a new 'safe' country can give rise to a less critical analysis of their current practices that are accepted as the norm, unwittingly re-creating a problematic narrative which positions them as saviour. Mavelli (2017) suggests that when a host country adopts a saviour status, it enhances positive feelings about the character of its citizens. He argues that this can be used by government 'as a way of promoting a self-understanding of Britain as just, moral and compassionate, and therefore, as a biopolitical way of promoting and enhancing the emotional life of its population' (Mavelli, 2017, p. 811).

Another consequence of the trauma narrative is an overly intrusive interest in people's pre- and peri-migration stories. It is inappropriate for early childhood practitioners to ask refugee parents to re-tell their stories and re-live difficult experiences unless they are working in a 1:1 capacity as a psychologist and offering professional support. Practitioners need to be wary of asking too many questions, as if parents have experienced trauma; heavy questioning may re-trigger memories and lead to periods of depression or anxiety.

However, it is important for early childhood practitioners to not only be aware of these varied narratives but also spend time reflecting on personal views, considering how they may unduly influence everyday practice.

REFLECTION

Lira, Muñoz-García, and Loncon (2019), from the suggested readings, chose to write letters to each other before they began their research with Indigenous people because they wanted to examine their own positionality and think about the lens they would be gazing through.

Spend some time writing a letter to a trusted fellow student. In the letter think about and explain:

1 What is your background and how this might have impacted your ideas and views of refugees.

2 How your lived experiences might have shaped what you believe.

3 If the current narratives from the government or the media have impacted your understanding about refugees.

Power

Within literature, there has been a clear movement away from the narrative of trauma and victimhood (Hart, 2014). This shift in focus is welcome as the 'trauma discourse and pathologization of refugees' not only dehumanises and is reductionist for refugees but also creates and reinforces a power inequity in any subsequent research which may claim to represent the refugee voice (Sigona, 2014, p. 372). Pace and Sen (2018) note the benefits of this change remarking that 'focusing on the vulnerabilities of refugee children can obfuscate the reality that minors are also future agents of progress and reform' (Pace & Sen, 2018, p. 1). Interestingly, as a result of their study in Canada investigating refugee post-migration lived experiences, Kyriakides, Bajjali, McLuhan, and Anderson (2018) have chosen to re-frame the refugee participants in their study as 'persons of self-rescue' who were successful in navigating a 'voyage of death' (Kyriakides et al., 2018, p. 65).

When working with parents who are refugees, it is vital to be aware of these subtle power interchanges if early childhood practitioners are going to develop authentic trusting relationships. Parents and children are very aware of the complexity of their position and often experience open racist hostility. They also sense unspoken attitudes.

The following case study is drawn from my doctoral study (Gaywood, 2022).

CASE STUDY

Rahima is mother of three children: Bilal, Amira and Yafiz. Bilal is 7 and is deaf. He attends a primary school which has a specialist deaf unit attached. Amira is 3 and attends a local church-run preschool, whilst Yafiz, who was born is England, is 12 months and Rahima cares for him at home. Rahima is married to Adeel who had a nut-selling business before the family left their home. They arrived in England on a Vulnerable Persons Resettlement Scheme. Rahima married young, so is still in her 20s. She does not like the label refugee and does not want people to know that her children are refugees. When the family arrived in England, Bilal was very withdrawn and it was hard for anyone to communicate with him. Amira was the first to learn sign language and was able to communicate with her brother. Rahima feels a lot of guilt about her son's deafness and worries a lot about him.

The family live in a modern two bedroom flat near to the city centre. Adeel works at a fruit market which he enjoys. His experiences in England have been more positive that Rahima, as his boss recognises that he is a good worker and Adeel has been trusted with more responsibility. Rahima has experienced racism which she feels might be because she wears a hijab. She worries about Amira and feels that Amira is too soft and maybe bullied in her preschool and her school. Rahima also wants Amira to do well educationally, but she does not want her to forget her culture and where she has come from. Rahima and Adeel have told Amira not to play with any of the boys at her preschool. Both Rahima and Adeel have attended English-speaking classes, and Rahima feels more confident than Adeel.

Rahima had a difficult relationship with her daughter Amira's nursery. She felt that the staff at the nursery were cold and standoffish and did not love Amira. Rahima thought this was why Amira was very quiet. The staff said that it was hard to make a relationship with Rahima because of the language barrier, but when asked about this, Rahima shared that the staff at Bilal's school were warm and friendly, and there was still a language barrier.

Rahima shared an incident during one research interview which seemed to encapsulate how she experienced the nursery. She talked of a non-verbal interaction with one staff member where the staff member smiled at her, but Rahima described it as a 'yellow smile', which is a smile only with the mouth and not the eyes. Rahima did not like it and felt the relationship was inauthentic. When asked about the incident, the team at the nursery shared that they were getting fed up with Rahima because she was often late picking Amira up. They tried to use body language to express their frustration.

Although Rahima did not like the preschool, Amira enjoyed her time there. She made friends with another child who was from a migrant family and grew in confidence speaking English. At first, Amira's keyperson reported that she was quiet and very reserved, but she noticed that although she was quiet, Amira was an unusually strong-minded person who was able to make her needs known.

Rahima managed to make a positive relationship with the manager of the pre-school, who Rahima referred to as the headteacher. However, due to the complexity of the relationships with some of the other staff, she decided that Yafiz would not attend the same nursery.

Questions to consider:

- Can you identify some of Rahima's feelings and circumstances which may have negatively impacted her relationship with the staff at Amira's preschool?

- As an early childhood practitioner, how would you begin to develop a trusting relationship with Rahima?

- In this case study, what resonated with you and what were you least able to identify with?

Unseen challenges faced by refugee parents and children

It is a commonly held belief that the most significant challenges that refugees face in a host country are a language barrier and cultural differences. However, there is a 'risk of invisibility' Bove and Sharmahd (2020, p. 3) particularly for very young refugee children. Entry into **ECEC** is often fraught with difficulties, and there are considerable barriers to access and inclusion (Lamb, 2020; Wolf, Broekhuizen, Moser, Ereky-Stevens, & Anders, 2020). Peleman, Vandenbroeck, and Van Avermaet (2020) and Lazzari et al. (2020) also conclude that ECEC can unknowingly perpetuate social exclusion through the processes and practice, which seems to favour children born within the host country. Zhang and Luo (2016) also note a subtlety of behaviour and attitude in operation, which appears to accompany this social exclusion of the children. They point to a hidden curriculum which they describe as 'the unspoken academic, social and cultural messages that are communicated to students through various indirect means' (Zhang & Luo, 2016, p. 218). Early childhood practitioners need to remain vigilant of a hidden curriculum or taken-for-granted norms which are unspoken and unseen, but often have a negative effect on both children and their parents.

Zhang and Luo (2016) also found that there was a tendency for practitioners to articulate the importance of treating all the children equally. Whilst this attitude may be well intentioned, to not show favouritism, the net result is that refugee children continue to remain invisible. Practitioners need to understand the difference between equality and equity:

> *Equity and inclusion require more than treating everyone the same. There is an important difference between equity and equality. Equality aims to provide*

fairness through treating everyone the same regardless of need, while equity achieves this through treating people differently dependent on need.

(Early Education, 2021)

Feelings of exclusion are common amongst refugees (Ukasoanya, 2014; Uptin, Wright, & Harwood, 2013) and Zhang and Luo (2016) suggest that this, alongside practitioners' (in this case teachers') attitudes, can perpetuate the inequality experienced by the children and families. Strekalova-Hughes (2017) picks up a similar point and notes that refugee children come from a variety of backgrounds so cannot be seen as a specific homogenous group in terms of their education and learning.

Alongside invisibility, refugee parents experience other significant challenges. Jacobsen (2014, p. 103) points out that although 'existing psychological research focuses on what can be done to help people recover from trauma', other elements of refugee suffering may be missed. Erdemir (2021, p. 548) also highlights the challenges for refugee parents and suggests that their experiences can lead to 'less warmth and more harshness toward their children'. Again, this foci on the terrible experiences of refugees or the resulting problem of the trauma is understandable as an emotional human response. When confronted by others' suffering, it is natural to care and want to promote healing.

It is a common experience that many have lost status through their forced migration experiences. People who have worked professionally as doctors or lawyers are often unable to practice in the United Kingdom, their qualifications may not be transferrable and they might have to pass a rigorous language examination. Alongside this loss of status, refugee parents may find themselves struggling with significant poverty which is exacerbated by their reduced capacity to earn. Due to the nature of being a refugee, it is likely that many parents have close relatives who have remained in their country of origin and continue to be impacted by the situation which forced their migration. The parents not only worry for their children growing up in an often-hostile environment, where they face ongoing negativity from host country citizens, but also experience a continual tension about the relatives and loved ones they have left behind. Refugee families also have experienced high levels of loss and grief because they have been forced to leave their own country, their culture, their homes and all they have known, out of significant fear for their lives.

REFLECTION

In small groups, think about and discuss the following:

- Identify taken-for-granted norms in operation in your practice or workspace.

- What does equity mean to you and how might this translate into your everyday practice?

- Has understanding about the significant challenges faced by refugee parents changed the way you might approach them? If so, what might you do differently?

The role of the practitioner

Given the complex nature of the lived experiences of refugee children and their parents, early childhood practitioners who want to work more effectively engaging with them need to exercise an ongoing commitment to change and self-reflective practice. They need to be aware of the shifting political landscape which impacts refugees' everyday lives and also can have an invisible influence on practitioners' own ideas and practices. To really address some of the issues around power inequity and exclusion, early childhood practitioners need to be brutally honest and willing to examine their own and their institutions' practices in order to enact deep level change. Practitioners should create opportunities to spend time thinking about how refugee parents and children are con-ceptualised, whether in terms of trauma, in need of rescue or as an homogenous group and consider the impact of these narratives on their practice or policies. Refugee parents inhabit precarious spaces, having experienced significant challenges, and so need practitioners to develop sensitive and generous ways to engage with them to develop trusting relationships. There also needs to be a re-calibration of narratives where families and children are conceptualised as enriching participants within communities of practice and bilingualism is no longer perceived as having the deficit connotation implied by the label 'English as an Additional Language'. Early childhood practitioners need to have a clear grasp of the difference between equality and equity and should think carefully about whether they are operating equitably, making changes, however small, where necessary. The children from refugee and migrant backgrounds bring a wealth of experience and have rich funds of knowledge. To ensure that they and their parents feel welcome, early childhood practitioners need to draw on this richness and celebrate their lives as part of a wider community rather than ignoring the issue and re-creating culturally vacuous spaces.

People seeking refuge and asylum arrive in the United Kingdom from countries across the world. Although they often tend to share similar experiences of exclusion, invisibility, loss of status, prejudice, high levels of grief and enforced poverty, it is wrong to essentialise the refugee experience. Each family is different, and their experiences, lives and culture are unique. There is no set way to interact with a parent who has experienced forced migration, but early childhood practitioners can develop new skills which are rooted in the domain of attitudes (Gaywood, Bertram, & Pascal, 2020), which include acceptance, openness, authenticity, honesty, being deeply interested and committed to giving refugees a voice by being trustworthy and operating an alongsided approach (Pound, 2003).

> **REFLECTION**
>
> - Consider your own positionality in relation to any refugee families you may be working with.
>
> - Look at the explanation of experiences and identify any experiences you may share.
>
> - Consider your own attitudes and think about to what extent these influence your current work.
>
> - What attitudes or practices are you able to develop, which might be helpful?

Conclusion

Working with refugee children and their parents requires more than just compassion and sympathy for their situation. Practitioners need to understand the complexity of the children's lives which is influenced heavily by the political status of being a refugee. They also need to be alert to the common narratives which often surround refugees, where refugees are homogenized, at times vilified or represented with less capacity to make decisions, all of which are unhelpful for the children they are working with. In addition, it is important for practitioners to really interrogate their own assumptions and beliefs about refugees, taking care to consider issues of power and positionality. To work most successfully and inclusively, practitioners should be mindful of the children's potential traumatic experiences but keep in mind their resilience and the richness refugee children and their families can bring to their ECEC settings.

Further reading

Bove, C., & Sharmahd, N. (2020). Beyond invisibility. Welcoming children and families with migrant and refugee background in ECEC settings. *European Early Childhood Education Research Journal, 28*(1), 1–9.

Kyriakides, C., Bajjali, L., McLuhan, A., & Anderson, K. (2018). Beyond refuge: Contested orientalism and persons of self-rescue. *Canadian Ethnic Studies, 50*(2), 59–78.

Useful websites

https://www.refugee-early-years.org

https://www.unhcr.org/uk/about-us.html

https://www.rescue.org/

https://www.redcross.org.uk/about-us/what-we-do/how-we-support-refugees/find-out-about-refugees

References

Bauman, Z. (2016). *Strangers at our door*. Cambridge. Policy Press.

Bove, C., & Sharmahd, N. (2020). Beyond invisibility. Welcoming children and families with migrant and refugee background in ECEC settings. *European Early Childhood Education Research Journal, 28*(1), 1–9.

Bronfenbrenner, U. (1979). *The ecology of human development experiments by nature and design*. Boston, MA: Harvard University Press.

Department for Education. (2014). *Promoting fundamental British values as part of SMSC in schools'. Departmental advice for maintained schools*. London: Crown Publishing.

Department for Education. (2015). *The prevent duty. Departmental advice for schools and childcare providers*. London: Crown Publishing.

Early Education. (2021). *Birth to 5 matters*. Retrieved from: https://birthto5matters.org.uk/ (Accessed 10th August 2022).

Erdemir, E. (2021). Transactional relations and reciprocity between refugee mothers and their children: Changes in child, parenting and concepts of child. *EECERJ, 29*(4), 547.

Gaywood, D. (2022). *The post migration lived experiences of refugee children in early childhood and education care in England: Four children's stories*. Unpublished thesis. BCU.

Gaywood, D., Bertram, T., & Pascal, C. (2020). Involving refugee children in research: Emerging ethical and positioning issues. *European Early Childhood Education Research Journal*. [Online] *28*(1), 149–162.

Hart, R. (2009). Child refugees, trauma and education: Interactionist considerations on social and emotional needs and development. *Educational Psychology in Practice, 25*(4), 351–368.

Hart, J. (2014). *Children and forced migration in Oxford handbook of refugee and forced migration studies*. London.

Home Office. (2017). *Syrian vulnerable persons resettlement scheme (VPRS) guidance for local authorities and partners*. London: Crown Publishing.

Home Office. (2022a). *Irregular migration to the UK, year ending December 2021*. London: Crown Publishing.

Home Office. (2022b). *Nationality and borders*. London: Bill Crown Publishing.

Home Office. (2022c). *Policy paper: Memorandum of understanding between the government of the United Kingdom of Great Britain and Northern Ireland and the government of the Republic of Rwanda for the provision of an asylum partnership arrangement*. London: Crown Publishing.

Home Office, Department for International Development, Ministry of Housing, Communities and Local Government. (2018). *Funding instruction for local authorities in the support of United Kingdom's resettlement programmes*. London: Crown Publishing.

Jacobsen, K. (2014). Livelihoods and forced migration. In E. Fiddian-Qasmiyeh, G. Loescher, K. Long, & N. Sigona (Eds.), *The Oxford handbook of refugee and forced migration studies* (1st ed.). Oxford: Oxford University Press.

Kyriakides, C. (2017). Words don't come easy: Al Jazeera's migrant–refugee distinction and the European culture of (mis)trust. *Current Sociology, 65*(7), 933–952.

Kyriakides, C., Bajjali, L., McLuhan, A., & Anderson, K. (2018). Beyond refuge: Contested orientalism and persons of self-rescue. *Canadian Ethnic Studies, 50*(2), 59–78.

Lamb, C. S. (2020). Constructing early childhood services as culturally credible trauma-recovery environments: Participatory barriers and enablers for refugee families. *European Early Childhood Education Research Journal, 28*(1), 129–148.

Lazzari, A., Balduzzi, L., Van Laere, K., Boudry, C., Rezek, M., & Prodger, A. (2020). Sustaining warm and inclusive transitions across the early years: Insights from the START project. *European Early Childhood Education Research Journal, 28*(1), 43–57.

Lira, A., Muñoz-García, A. L., & Loncon, E. (2019). Doing the work, considering the entanglements of the research team while undoing settler colonialism. *Gender and Education, 31*(4), 475–489.

Mavelli, L. (2017). Governing populations through the humanitarian government of refugees: Biopolitical care and racism in the European refugee crisis. *Review of International Studies, 43*(5), 809–832.

Mayblin, L. (2017). *Asylum after empire: Colonial legacies in the politics of asylum seeking.* London; New York, NY: Rowman & Littlefield International.

Measham, T., Guzder, J., Rousseau, C., Pacione, L., Blais-McPherson, M., & Nadeau, L. (2014). Refugee children and their families: Supporting psychological well-being and positive adaptation following migration. *Current Problems in Paediatric and Adolescent Health Care, 44*(7), 208–215.

Pace, M., & Sen, S. (2018). *Syrian refugee children in the Middle East and Europe: Integrating the young and exiled* (1st ed.). London; New York, NY: Routledge.

Peleman, B., Vandenbroeck, M., & Van Avermaet, P. (2020). Early learning opportunities for children at risk of social exclusion. Opening the black box of preschool practice. *European Early Childhood Education Research Journal, 28*(1), 21–42.

Piotrowski, J., Różycka-Tran, J., Baran, T., & Żemojtel-Piotrowska, M. (2019). Zero-sum thinking as mediator of the relationship of national attitudes with (un)willingness to host refugees in own country. *International Journal of Psychology: Journal International de Psychologie, 54*(6), 722.

Pound, R. (2003). How can I improve my health visiting support of parenting? *The creation of an alongsided epistemology through action enquiry,* Unpublished PhD. University of West of England. Retrieved from: http://www.actionresearch.net. Thesis section (Accessed 10th August 2022).

Sigona, N. (2014). The politics of refugee voices: Representations, narratives, and memories. In E. Fiddian-Qasmiyeh, G. Loescher, K. Long, & N. Sigona (Eds.), *The Oxford handbook of refugee and forced migration studies* (pp. 369–382). Oxford: Oxford University Press.

Strekalova-Hughes, E. S. (2017). Comparative analysis of intercultural sensitivity among teachers working with refugees. *Journal of Research in Childhood Education, 31*(4), 561–570.

Taylor, S., Debelle, G., & Modi, N. (2016). Child refugees: The right to compassion. *BMJ, 355*, i6100.

The Guardian. (27 January 2016). https://www.theguardian.com/uk-news/2016/jan/27/david-camerons-bunch-of-migrants-quip-is-latest-of-several-such-comments

Ukasoanya, G. (2014). Social adaptation of new immigrant students: Cultural scripts, roles, and symbolic interactionism. *International Journal for the Advancement of Counselling, 36*(2), 150–161.

UNHCR. (2019). *Handbook on procedures and criteria for determining refugee status under 1951 convention and the 1967 Protocol relating to the status of refugees.* Retrieved from: https://www.unhcr.org/publications/legal/5ddfcdc47/handbook-procedures-criteria-determining-refugee-status-under-1951-convention.html (Accessed 10th August 2022).

UNHCR. (2022). *Refugee data finder.* Retrieved from: https://www.unhcr.org/refugee-statistics/ (Accessed 12th December 2022).

Uptin, J., Wright, J., & Harwood, V. (2013). 'It felt like I was a black dot on white paper': Examining young former refugees' experience of entering Australian high schools. *The Australian Educational Researcher, 40*(1), 125–137.

Wolf, K. M., Broekhuizen, M. L., Moser, T., Ereky-Stevens, K., & Anders, Y. (2020). Determinants of early attendance of ECEC for families with a Turkish migration background in four European countries. *European Early Childhood Education Research Journal, 28*(1), 77–89.

Zhang, D., & Luo, Y. (2016). Social exclusion and the hidden curriculum: The schooling experiences of Chinese rural migrant children in an urban public school. *British Journal of Educational Studies, 64*(2), 215–234.

10 STUDENT MOTHERS IN HIGHER EDUCATION

KAY OWEN AND HELEN SIMMONS

CHAPTER OBJECTIVES

By the end of this chapter, you will be able to:

- Understand the challenges faced by student mothers.
- Recognise the impact that being a student mother can have on identity.
- Consider the reflections of student mothers regarding their experiences, support systems and recommendations.
- Consider the role of early childhood practitioner in working in partnership with student mothers.

KEY DEFINITIONS

Parents

Any person who has parental responsibility or has care of a young child during early childhood (from conception to eight years of age).

Practitioner

A person who is qualified to work with children (from conception to 8 years old) across health, education and social care.

Research participants

Enrolled, either full time or part-time, to a higher education degree. Participants in the research explored in this chapter were all enrolled onto childhood-related undergraduate or postgraduate degrees.

Student mothers

Mothers who are studying in higher education, with co-dependent child(ren), under the age of 18 years old.

Introduction

This chapter will explore the experiences of student mothers, shared through a research project conducted during the second wave of the coronavirus pandemic. **Participants** were drawn from undergraduate and postgraduate programmes within the discipline of education and childhood, in a UK university. The research was initiated in response to the strains and pressures academic staff noted during tutorials amongst **student mothers**. The study comprised a mixed open- and closed-question questionnaire, analysed through thematic analysis. Results suggested that student mothers face a range of issues resultant from their perceived need to excel in both roles, reflecting the internalisation of societal pressures that can be associated with intensive parenting ideologies. This chapter will explore the reflections of participants regarding pressures and sources of support, paying close attention to the role of the early childhood **practitioner**.

Living, learning and plate spinning

The very terms *working mother* or *student mother* reflect society's conflicting expectations of women. On the one hand, motherhood is still seen as an essential part of female identity and route to emotional fulfilment, yet on the other hand, society expects women to contribute financially and use their abilities and talents. This is reinforced through the 'cultural contradictions' (Hays, 1996) of ideologies that portray motherhood as natural and instinctive, whilst also promoting a culture of 'intensive motherhood' (Douglas & Michaels, 2005; Hays, 1996; Lynch, 2008), whereby motherhood and career success should be achievable for all.

Additionally, as Currie (2008) notes, motherhood brings a whole raft of challenges including changes to self-identity, a reduction in freedom and frequently an all-consuming tiredness. Furthermore, the dominant cultural assumptions regarding modern motherhood bring expectations of nurturing, compassion and the selfless gift of time and energy for the benefit of the children.

Over 70% of women in the United Kingdom are now in paid employment, and the proportion of working mothers with toddlers has increased from 55.8% to 65.1% over the past two decades (Office for National Statistics (ONS), 2021). Indeed, many of the student mothers interviewed during our research were part of the early childhood workforce and considered critical or 'key workers' (DfE, 2020) throughout the pandemic. Thus, many of the challenges faced by student mothers echoed the challenges and frustrations of the workforce during a time of extreme pressure.

Many mature women entering university are already juggling the competing demands of paid employment, childcare, children's education and their partners' work. Single mothers are particularly reliant on family and friends for practical and financial help. The general perception is that student mothers have emotional, financial and practical support from a partner and/or the children's grandparents.

However, Lyonette, Atfield, Behle, and Gambin (2015) discovered that this support is often patchy, with women generally retaining most of their previous childcare and domestic responsibilities.

For the reasons listed above, it may be more difficult for student mothers to realise higher education institutions' (HEIs') expectations regarding engagement, punctuality and commitment to study. Lyonette et al. (2015) discovered that universities generally lacked a cohesive policy and provided little in the way of facilities or adapted provision for student mothers. As a result, students were reliant upon ad hoc arrangements, sometimes having to miss lectures or sections of work if children were ill or if timetabling changed at short notice. For many, this lack of provision and apparent lack of awareness increased their sense of separation from other students, thus increasing their risk of dropping out.

The COVID-19 pandemic changed teaching and learning arrangements throughout education. In HEIs such as our own, virtual learning environments to support course management and delivery have been embedded for some time (Walker, Jenkins, & Voce, 2017), meaning we were able to adapt relatively quickly. However, for students, the change necessitated a marked increase in digital engagement and a level of digital competency that some found challenging. Many felt their learning suffered due to the loss of classroom learning environments, which are perceived to be highly personalised, and encouraging of active participation (Matsushita, 2018). The changes also occasioned the loss of many informal support mechanisms and, subsequently, the sense of belonging and motivation they provide (Vayre & Vonthron, 2017). Seventy-three percent of students reported a decline in their mental well-being during lockdown (Mind.org.uk, 2020), partially due to this sense of separation, isolation and loneliness. Furthermore, the demands created by partial closure of schools increased the difficulties faced by student mothers. The Office for National Statistics (2021) reported that a third of all women (as opposed to 20% of men) with school-aged children felt their mental health had suffered during lockdown.

Early research findings demonstrate that, when children were unable to attend school, it was women who assumed the majority of the childcare responsibilities, including homeschooling (ONS, 2021). Mothers of primary school-aged children spent an average of five hours per day on homeschooling, compared to father's two hours (Villadsen, Conti, & Fitzsimons, 2020). For many, this necessitated a reduction or withdrawal from employment in order to care for the family (ONS, 2021).

Whilst documenting the challenges, it is important to also recognise that engagement in higher education brings many opportunities. Most student mothers enter university to improve their career prospects and provide greater financial security for their children, then find that study also engenders personal growth through increasing self-confidence, self-esteem and pride. They thus rediscover a sense of personal identity outside motherhood (Winnicott, 1964) and feel able to provide positive role models for their offspring.

REFLECTION

With early childhood practitioners identified as fey workers (DfE, 2020) during the global pandemic:

- What challenges do you think student mothers who were also working as early childhood practitioners faced during the pandemic?

- What may have been the challenges for leaders and managers?

- What kind of support may have been needed for student mothers and their children at this time?

In the next section, we detail the findings of our research. We have divided this into the common themes mentioned by participants and included quotations from them regarding their experiences.

Student mothers and time

Challenges: time, time management, guilt, daily structure, balance, juggling and concentrating

When asked to reflect on their student mother experience, the overwhelming majority cited the challenges of time management associated with juggling so many aspects of home life and academia. Reflections on time constraints often carried associated feelings of guilt, guilt in relation to not spending 'enough' time with children and/or guilt in relation to not spending 'enough' time on their academic studies. Time pressures and guilt were linked to a perceived loss of control for participants, a feeling that they were unsuccessfully or inadequately juggling many activities was perceived as personal failure rather than a commendable attempt to dovetail a whole raft of demanding tasks.

- *Juggling everyone's needs and often feeling like a 'one man show' both emotionally and physically.*

- *Time management and having enough time to get into the right headspace, it has never been something I can jump into for half an hour or an hour.*

- *Guilt for increased attention on studying with decreased attention on the children. Trying to concentrate at home but constant noise/disruptions from the children.*

Von Benzon (2021) recognises this lack of control and acknowledges that mothers, and especially mothers of young children, are 'chronically "time poor", due to the time required to provide basic care of an infant' (Von Benzon, 2021, p. 481). This lack of time creates challenges not only in terms of academic performance but also in the development and maintenance of key relationships, including that with the early childhood practitioners of their children. With time constraints and managing many different aspects of life, 'partnerships with parents and caregivers' (ECSDN, 2018, p. 18) can encounter barriers.

Currie (2008) in her research into maternal mental health makes links between any loss of control as linked to 'coping' as a mother and is attributed to being 'good enough' in this role. Currie defines coping as including:

> *Efforts to manage stressful, challenging or difficult events, and is affected by lifestyle changes experienced since the birth of a child, the general difficulty of the mothering role and social pressures to succeed in that role.*

> *(Currie, 2008, p. 34)*

The societal pressures that Currie mentions here are echoed in the reflections of participants who clearly placed pressure on themselves to succeed as a mother whilst simultaneously succeeding in their academic life. The internalisation of social pressures is recognised by Beaupre Gillespie and Schwartz Temple (2011, p. 4) as resulting in a feeling that 'we are supposed to have it all'. This internalised pressure, it could be argued, places a heavy burden on the shoulders of women to succeed and results in the feeling that 'you can do anything' means 'you can do everything' (Beaupre Gillespie & Schwartz Temple, 2011, p. 4).

Student mothers and identity

Rewards: identity, future, role modelling and pride

Reflecting on the most rewarding aspects being a student mother, participants talked primarily about their hopes for future financial stability and a rewarding career. Overall, the importance of securing a strong sense of self-identity was clear.

The participants demonstrated a sense of pride in their accomplishments and spoke of the importance of being a positive role model, particularly mothers with daughters.

- *Feeling proud that I have achieved something for myself which will hopefully benefit my children in the long term.*

- *To hear my daughter say that she wants to do everything I have done, and to do 'school work' and be clever like me.*

It is acknowledged (Currie, 2008; Simmons, 2020; Winnicott, 1964) that motherhood often results in a major shift in identity. The transition into parenting brings changes, not only in daily routines and responsibilities but also related to the construct of self. The participants within this research identified life as a student mother as boosting their sense of their own identity. Reflections of life as a student mother went beyond the ambition to achieve a degree, into a reflexive construct of self with 'a greater sense of control in a life with glimpses, and sometimes more, of pre-baby self and life' (Miller, 2005, p. 113).

A sense of pride in reclaiming this identity was also linked to a need to be a positive role model for children and to 'do my little girl proud' (student mother). Linking back to the internalisation of societal pressures (Beaupre Gillespie & Schwartz Temple, 2011; Currie, 2008) and to ideologies of 'intensive mother-hood' (Douglas & Michaels, 2005; Hays, 1996; Lynch, 2008), participants reflected on the challenge of ensuring that they are both a 'good mother' and a 'good student'.

Student mothers, support networks and social mobility

Daily routines: panic, time and hurry

The participants provided insights into their daily routines as student mothers. Once again, time was cited frequently, with many reflections on the need for careful organisation and time management.

- *Breakfast, panic, join in group session fending off the child, lunch, play with daughter and forget all about Uni work, tea, panic, bedtime, catch up on recorded materials etc., attempt some reading – fall asleep.*

- *Get my child ready, have breakfast, take him [to] preschool, have my lecture, clean house, cook dinner, collect my child, spend time with him, put him to bed, then do reading from lecture.*

Along with the time pressures associated with studying, concerns regarding a lack of time with children were expressed by some participants. Concerns regarding how this impacts attachment are explored later in the chapter, together with consideration of the mediating role of early childhood practitioners. Ultimately though, strategies to support mothers to study are important for a positive sense of identity and for improved social mobility.

In their investigation into experience of higher education, Lyonette et al. (2015, p. 15) found that challenges regarding childcare related to financial concerns, coupled with tension regarding their own role and identity in finding suitable provision:

> *Many of the women relied upon other family members or spouses for childcare as a result (of financial concerns). Respondents devised certain strategies which included downplaying the maternal role in the academic realm ('maternal invisibility') as well as downplaying the student role outside of academia ('academic invisibility'). Many reinforced the cultural expectation that only mothers' care was good enough, with many excusing their male partners.*

REFLECTION

Lyonette et al. (2015, p. 13) found childcare to be a significant factor for student mothers during their experiences in higher education. They found the main barriers to success, in relation to childcare to be

- *Issues of flexibility, affordability, availability and suitability*

Taking each of the above in turn, consider what the main barriers may be.

What strategies would you suggest to reduce the barriers?

Are there any other barriers that you can think of?

Student mothers and the global pandemic

In common with previous studies, this research discovered that student mothers feel pressurised to perform each of their roles to an exacting standard. During the pandemic, their responsibilities further increased whilst the protective sources of support decreased. Subsequently, student mothers experienced even greater pressures.

Isolation/loss of self: no help from family or friends; partners working

Due to government regulations and changes, participants saw an expediential increase in their responsibilities during the pandemic, coupled with a reduction in childcare and informal support mechanisms during lockdown. In combination, this meant that the student mothers had more to fit into their already busy days, and less help to enable them to successfully meet the requirements of university, home educating, household responsibilities and work. As a result, the positive sense of self that had been engendered by their studies began to falter and diminish.

- *I had to juggle my degree and 4 children at home. It is such hard work.*
- *Balancing being a mom, referee, home teacher and a student was near impossible at times.*
- *My carefully organised timetable went completely to pot.*

Homeschooling

Many participants reflected on the demands of homeschooling and lockdown. Participants reported on the challenges of sharing technology with their children and of maintaining a balance when faced with the additional responsibilities of supporting children with their schoolwork.

- *I put everything on the back burner to give up most [sic] importance to (my child's) home-schooling. This resulted in so much stress and anxiety building up about assignments and deadlines.*

- *Routines slowly went out the window and we took each day as it came. Sometimes I knew I would get no work done and I had to make myself OK with that.*

- *I felt guilty that the children spent so much time on iPads, but after talking to other people most felt the same. Looking back, we have fit [sic] a lot in and we did play and go on walks so technology probably didn't dominate other things.*

Pandemic positives

The student mothers reported not only on challenges they faced during the global pandemic but on surprising opportunities too. Positive reflections related to increased quality time with their children and an opportunity to connect and develop a deeper understanding of their child's education. Participants also reflected on academic opportunities that were developed during the pandemic including increased agency in relation to study skills, the development of their technological skills and how they used time more productively once relieved of the need to commute to university.

- *Spending lots of wonderful time with my children, being able to be included in their education. My husband now works more flexibly, rather than in the office all of the time, this has really helped our family balance. A slower paced life, appreciating the smaller things in life more.*

- *I became more confident in learning in a different style as to how I would on campus and team meetings were really helpful.*

- *I got to see more of what the children in education were doing in lessons and understand the subject matter and their strengths and weaknesses. I could get my washing done during coffee breaks! I have had to navigate technology more, which can only be a good thing for me.*

For some participants, the release of rigid daily structures and routines provided a welcome opportunity. As highlighted in the previous section, student mothers reflected on a feeling of increased support from personal academic tutors during the pandemic and increased value placed upon this relationship through a shared human experience.

In addition to reflections regarding quality relationships, participants considered that having the chance to step off the hamster wheel of daily life including childcare, commuting and responsibility for everyone's timetables created space for quality time. Recent research conducted by Von Benzon (2021, p. 487) regarding home-schooling agrees that this provides a 'time gain' opportunity whereby mothers:

> *Are ostensibly able to shrug off schedules and routines, without specific responsibilities to be in particular locations at particular times. Their daily routines, the rhythm of their lives and therefore their habitus, is not controlled by external structures or state agency.*

Reflections and the future

The future: Pride, identity and empowerment

As participants considered the future, reflections related again to the importance of identity, their sense of self and pride in their accomplishments. Reflections also related to the post-pandemic future and a returning sense of normality.

- *Graduation, that sense of achievement and proving to myself I DID it!*

- *Being able to go into a profession that I am passionate about and do my little girl proud.*

- *Embarking on a career – making a difference, not just clock watching... feeling I wasn't fulfilling my potential.*

Reflections: Pride, support, challenge

Final comments from participants reflected a sense of emerging pride and an awareness of the importance of motherhood, supportive networks and how these contributes to their determination to succeed.

- *Life has been challenging and stressful, but my four children are amazing my oldest has just got into university and is starting her journey to become a doctor. I am so proud of them all.*

- *I have found other parent peers on the course to be supportive as we can all share tips on keeping motivated with both studies and family.*

- *I would say that giving yourself a challenge that pulls you out of your comfort zone is quite empowering and builds self-efficacy.*

CASE STUDY

Supporting student mothers – Becky, BA (Hons) in Early Childhood Studies with Graduate Practitioner Competencies.

As a practitioner who has recently completed my own studies, I saw firsthand how struggles with childcare impacted the workload of friends who were not only practitioners but also student mothers. Instead of being able to stay and study in the library, they had to leave in order to collect their child from school or nursery. The workload and childcare balance became stressful and often meant they had to request extensions in order to meet deadlines.

Having witnessed the impacts childcare difficulties have on student mothers or working mothers has helped me to reflect on my practice and now I always check in with them to make sure everything is okay and see if there is any support I can offer.

Mums who are returning to education may have to juggle time in placement and childcare hours whilst having to deal with being away from the baby for the first time. I have also seen **parents** reluctantly deciding to take their baby to day care because juggling studying and having a baby or toddler at home is just impossible.

If the mother is alone, having support from practitioners is extremely important, as we can fill the gaps, explaining what the child has done and achieved while they had to work or study. It is a responsibility that practitioners take on daily without question. We understand that people need to work and want to study to improve their lives not just for themselves but their child too.

Building relationships with the child's mother is vital in making them feel less stressed and worried about leaving their child. I feel a lot more help could be given for student mothers in terms of childcare and having the freedom to leave work or university at appropriate times to allow them to spend that much needed time with their child.

1 Using Becky's account above, consider what the issues student mothers face in terms of childcare

2 Consider the support strategies Becky has recommended, from the setting and the University.

Parental relationships

Over the years, much consideration has been given to which factors influence children's well-being. Key theorists such as Ginsburg (2011) and Goleman (1995) stressed the role of primary carers in enabling children to develop the skills and attitudes that underpin emotional intelligence and resilience. Many years of research led the Harvard Centre on the Developing Child (2015) to suggest that the single most important factor in establishing emotional well-being is the existence of a stable, supportive adult in the child's life. This is further endorsed by Barnardo's Arch Project (2003) which concluded that secure early attachments and confidence of being loved and valued are pivotal. Secure attachment, as defined and initially explained in Bowlby's (1958) classic theory, regards the role of the mother as crucial. Having access to a secure base and haven gives the child confidence to explore and experiment as they know their attachment figure is available and will provide protection and security if necessary (Ainsworth, 1982).

In combination, these factors may appear to suggest that any lapses in maternal attention or engagement are damaging to the child. However, over the years, Bowlby came to realise that children can form secure and meaningful attachments with a range of individuals irrespective of whether they are related to the child. Similarly, Ginsberg suggests that, whilst ideally practitioners and teachers perform a supportive role that is secondary to that of the parents, when necessary, they can assume primary responsibility for supporting children's emotional well-being.

We have noted that attempts to combine the academic demands of student life with motherhood (and possibly also with work) are stress inducing. However, the extent to which this impacts the woman, and subsequently her children, will vary according to a range of internal and external factors. Belsky's determinants of parenting (1984) suggest that the key factors, in order of importance, are

- The personal psychological resources of the parent (this includes her mental health, her perception of the quality of her relationships and her own developmental history)

- Contextual sources of support (Are her partner, relatives, friends, employer and/ or tutors supportive? Can she manage financially?)

- The characteristics of the child (the individual child's temperament influences parental expectations and behaviours)

Thus, whilst some will successfully navigate the multiple demands of being a student mother, the majority will experience dips in their ability to parent normally, and it is at these times that practitioners need to increase their personalised responsiveness in order to buffer children from developmental disruption.

The role of the practitioner

As identified throughout this chapter, student mothers feel the challenges of not only juggling the demands of their degree, often whilst working as early childhood practitioner themselves, but also retaining a sense of their own identity (Miller, 2005; Winnicott, 1964) whilst also ensuring secure attachments and positive experiences for their children.

The pressures of meeting the societal expectations of being 'good enough', according to Dalli (1999, p. 92 in Page, 2013, p. 548), stem from media representations that suggest that 'good mothers want to look after their child at all times'. The cultural contradictions (Hays, 1996) of motherhood position women who strive to build a career, through higher education, as role models and simultaneously position them as placing their children at risk due to unfamiliar environments and insecure attachments. This results in confusion for women and adds to the guilt and doubt demonstrated in the responses from the student mothers who participated in our research.

It is therefore more important than ever to ensure that true partnerships with parents are established and that support systems around student mothers, including family, university and childcare, are consistent and of high quality. An important aspect of the role of the early childhood practitioner is to establish a strong relationship with young children in the setting; the work of Page (2013, p. 548) is particularly pertinent here, as she explored how a close relationship in the context of childcare provision, or 'professional love', can provide a safe and secure attachment for young children, whilst also bringing reassurance of support for parents.

The early childhood practitioner can support student mothers through the development of relationships, strong communication and sharing of information. 'Partnership with parents and caregivers' is identified as Competency 7 in the Early Childhood Graduate Practitioner Competencies (ECSDN, 2018, p. 18), with 'respectful partnerships' highlighted as a key attribute here. The role of the early childhood practitioners, along with establishing strong relationships with children, is also to 'apply knowledge to practice, about the diversity of family, life and society'.

A well-qualified, critically reflective practitioner can also support parents who are navigating any confusing societal messages, which may be fuelled through the misrepresentations of attachment theory. These representations and the impact of them will be all too familiar to student mothers who are also early childhood practitioners themselves and they may, at times, need the support from children's providers. As stated by Page, Clare and Nutbrown (2013, p. 37):

> Attachment theory has a troubled past, and (as is the danger that findings
> from neuroscience will also be misunderstood and misused) so
> Attachment Theory has, at times, been used and manipulated throughout
> its history for economic and political ends.

Page's work demonstrates the complexities that mothers face as they navigate contradictory messages about what being a 'good mother' looks like. Ultimately though, Page (2013, p. 560) stresses the 'significance mothers place on close loving attachment relationships between carers and babies'. High-quality, trusting relationships between parents and early childhood practitioners play a huge role in the experiences of student mothers.

REFLECTION

- Why is a trusting relationship between a student mother and their child's early childhood practitioner so important?

- How has attachment theory been 'manipulated throughout history for economic and political ends' (Page et al., 2013, p. 37)?

- What other strategies could the early childhood setting and practitioner implement to support student mothers?

Conclusion

The aim of this chapter was to explore the experiences of student mothers undertaking undergraduate and postgraduate childhood-related courses at a UK

University. Reflections from participants provided insight into some of the challenges that were experienced as a student mother. It is clear that a combination of being 'chronically time poor' (Von Benzon, 2021, p. 481) and feeling pressure in the meeting of societal expectations to be both a 'good mother' and 'good student' resulted in an internalised guilt in participants, heighted during the global pandemic. Participants also reflected upon the opportunities that life as a student mother presented, including a feeling of being a positive role model for children along with rising feelings of self-esteem, identity and pride.

Some important messages regarding the need for additional support systems were also clear. Participants reflected that they would benefit from networks and opportunities to share experiences with other student mothers. It was clear from participants that support strategies play a fundamental role in the road to success and that they are ready and willing to share their experiences with other student mothers, build networks and work collaboratively to support one another. Wider support systems are essential, including high-quality early childhood support and strong relationships with early childhood practitioners.

Overall, this study provided a useful insight into the experiences of student mothers, the pressures and support systems they have and their fundamental resolve. In the words of one of the participants:

> *Mums should not be underestimated – what we may lack in time and youth, we make up for in sheer determination (student mother).*

Further reading

Lyonette, C., Atfield, G., Behle, H., & Gambin, L. (2015). *Tracking student mothers' higher education participation and early career outcomes over time: Initial choices and aspirations, HE experiences and career destinations.* Institute for Employment Research, University of Warwick.

Owen, K., & Barnes, C. (2023). *Family relationships in the early years.* London: SAGE.

Von Benzon, N. (2021). Unschooling motherhood: Caring and belonging in mothers' time-space. *Gender, Place & Culture, 28*(8), 476–497. https://doi.org/10.1080/0966369X.2020.1784100

Useful websites

Early Childhood Studies Degrees Network (ECSDN). (2022). *Competencies.* https://www.ecsdn.org/competencies/ (Accessed 12th July 2022).

Mind. (2022). *Student mental health hub.* https://www.mind.org.uk/information-support/tips-for-everyday-living/student-life/ (Accessed 25th July 2022).

References

Ainsworth, M. (1982). Attachment: Retrospect and prospect. In **C. M. Parkes & J. Stevenson-Hinde** (Eds.), *The place of attachment in human behaviour.* New York, NY: Basic Books.

Beaupre Gillespie, B., & Schwartz Temple, H. (2011). *Good enough is the new perfect.* Toronto: Harlequin.

Belsky, J. (1984). The determinants of parenting: Process model. *Child Development, 55,* 83–96.

Bowlby, J. (1958). The nature of the child's tie to his mother. *International Journal of Psych-Analysis, 39,* 350–373.

Center on the Developing Child. (2015). *The science of resilience.* Harvard University. Retrieved from: www.developingchild.harvard.edu (Accessed 10th July 2022).

Currie, J. (2008). Conditions affecting perceived coping for new mothers, analysis of a pilot study, Sydney, Australia. *International Journal of Mental Health Promotion, 10*(3), 34–41.

Dalli, C. (1999). Learning to be in childcare: Mothers' stories of their child's 'Settling-In'. *European Early Childhood Education Research Journal, 7*(2), 53–67.

Department for Education. (2020). *Critical workers and vulnerable children who can access schools or educational settings.* Retrieved from: https://www.gov.uk/government/publications/coronavirus-covid-19-maintaining-educational-provision (Accessed 12th July 2022).

Douglas, S. J., & Michaels, M. M. (2005). *The mommy myth: The idealization of motherhood and how it has undermined all women.* New York, NY: Free Press.

Early Childhood Studies Degrees Network. (2018). *Early childhood graduate practitioner Competencies.* ECSDN.

Ginsburg, K. R. (2011). *Building resilience in children and teens: Giving kids roots and wings.* Washington: American Academy of Pediatrics.

Goleman, D. (1995). *Emotional intelligence: Why it can matter more than IQ.* London: Bloomsbury Publishing.

Hays, S. (1996). *The cultural contradictions of motherhood.* New Haven, CN: Yale University Press.

Lynch, K. D. (2008). Gender roles and the American academe: A case study of graduate student mothers. *Gender and Education, 20*(6), 585–605.

Lyonette, C., Atfield, G., Behle, H., & Gambin, L. (2015). *Tracking student mothers' higher education participation and early career outcomes over time: Initial choices and aspirations, HE experiences and career destinations.* Institute for Employment Research, University of Warwick.

Matsushita, K. (2018). *Deep active learning: Toward greater depth in university education.* Singapore: Springer.

Miller, T. (2005). *Making sense of motherhood: A narrative approach.* Cambridge: Cambridge University Press.

Mind. (2020). *The mental health emergency: How has the coronavirus pandemic impacted our mental health?* London: Mind. Retrieved from: mind.org.uk (Accessed 14th July 2022).

Office for National Statistics (ONS). (2021). *Dataset available from coronavirus and home-schooling in Great Britain.* Retrieved from: https://www.ons.gov.uk/peoplepopulationandcommunity/educationandchildcare/datasets/coronavirusandhomeschoolingingreatbritain (Accessed 19th August 2021).

Page, J. (2013). Will the 'good' [working] mother please stand up? Professional and maternal concerns about education, care and love. *Gender and Education, 25*(5), 548–563.

Page, J., Clare, A., & Nutbrown, C. (2013). *Working with babies and young children: From birth to three* (2nd ed.). London: SAGE.

Simmons, H. (2020). *Surveillance of modern motherhood: Experiences of universal parenting courses.* Basingstoke: Palgrave Macmillan.

Vayre, E., & Vonthron, A.-M. (2017). Psychological engagement of students in distance and online learning: Effects of self-efficacy and psychosocial processes. *Journal of Educational Computing Research, 55*(2), 197–218.

Villadsen, A., Conti, G., & Fitzsimons, E. (2020). *Parental involvement in home schooling and developmental play during lockdown – initial findings from the COVID-19 survey in five national longitudinal studies.* London: UCL Centre for Longitudinal Studies.

Von Benzon, N. (2021). Unschooling motherhood: Caring and belonging in mothers' time-space. *Gender, Place & Culture, 28*(8), 476–497. doi: 10.1080/0966369X.2020.1784100

Walker, R., Jenkins, M., & Voce, J. (2017). The rhetoric and reality of technology-enhance learning development in UK higher education: Reflections on recent UCISA research findings (2012–2016). *Interactive Learning Environments*, 3 October 2018, *26*(7), 858–868.

Winnicott, D. (1964). *The child, the family, and the outside world.* London: Penguin Books.

11 PRACTICE PERSPECTIVE: PARENTS AS EXPERTS

WENDY KETTLEBOROUGH

CHAPTER OBJECTIVES

By the end of this chapter, you will be able to:

- Consider that parents are experts in relation to their children and that 'perception' and 'mindset' drive actions, reactions and interactions with others.
- Reflect upon how being seen, heard and valued impacts on the self-efficacy and emotional well-being of all practitioners, parents and children.
- Acknowledge that although the rhetoric and reality surrounding the inclusion of the voice of the parent is incongruent, sources and strategies are available to correct this.
- Recognise and practice the role of the practitioner as an advocate in capturing the voice of all parents.

KEY DEFINITIONS

Parents

Any person who has parental responsibility or has care of a young child during early childhood (from conception to eight years of age).

Practitioners

A person who is qualified to work with children (from conception to 8 years old) across health, education and social care.

Life map

A personal viewpoint which has been constructed by our 'interactions, circumstances, observations and expectations' (Borland, 2019, p. 39), where single words have different connotations for each individual.

(Continued)

(Continued)

Unconscious bias

Unconscious bias is a term that describes the associations we hold, outside our conscious awareness and control. Unconscious bias affects everyone.

Introduction

The Best Start for Life: A Vision for the 1,001 Critical Days (Department for Health and Social Care, 2021) may be one of the most recent acknowledgements that parents are the single most important factor in the development and educational achievement and well-being of their children. However, it is not the first. Over the last 55 years, since the Plowden Report (Department of Education and Science, 1967) advocated parental involvement, successive reports and research papers have all stated the importance of parental engagement. Unfortunately, although there has been sustained recognition of the value of parental engagement and involvement (DfES, 2003; The James Report, 1972; The Rumbold Report, 1990; The Warnock Report, 1978), investment as a result of these reports, with the exception of Sure Start, has been limited. The disappearance of many Sure Start centres from 2010 onwards is testimony to this.

The brain is designed for survival. It is experience expectant and is built as a result of the interactions we encounter.

> *Neuroscience has highlighted the fundamental importance of early experiences on the developing brain and the associated risks of poor-quality experiences and environments. During the early years, particularly, the first three years it provides a scientific argument for the nurturing that most parents are able to provide for their young children.*
>
> *Ministerial Council for Education, Early Childhood Development and Youth Affairs (MCEECDYA) (2010, p 10)*

These interactions begin during pregnancy, well before birth. From 18 weeks, an unborn baby will start to not only hear sounds, like the heartbeat of the mother, but also 'feel' the emotions the mother experiences. These initial sensory interactions start to construct the architecture of the brain, which becomes the basis for future perception. From the earliest of times, our reality and our beliefs are shaped from our personal perception of the experiences we have encountered within our own world.

In essence, two people could experience the exact same event, yet recall totally different experiences. This is due to their personalised perception of the incident.

Many things impact on our personal perspective. Our focus, mindset, likes, dislikes and expectations will play a huge part in how things are perceived, so will the strengths, weaknesses, gender, culture, sexual orientation and current mental health status of any individual. Even the position of a person in the family and the expectations of others will contribute to their frame of reference. The perspective of all individuals is constructed and refined through ongoing interactions, interactions that a practitioner may not be aware of.

Children and adults absorb what they believe to be the salient points from their immediate physical, social and emotional surroundings. The single most important factor is the relationships we have with the people we consider most significant. These relationships and interactions construct and impact on our self-image, self-efficacy and belief in ourselves (Harris & Orth, 2019). New ideas will also be viewed as threatening depending on our current position. Often, new ways of being are rejected due to the fear of being displaced. Ideas are also dismissed due to an individual having a limited perspective. Individuals may believe they have a wider, more holistic perspective than they actually do, unaware of the gaps in their knowledge or limited perception. Knowing yourself is vital to being able to know others. Understanding your motivation and preferences is helpful when uncovering **unconscious bias**.

Recognising the vast amount of knowledge parents hold in relation to their child should be a prerequisite to working within the early childhood sector. Practitioners who acknowledge parents have much to offer are more effective and engaging than those who subscribe to the deficit approach that is quite often the accepted norm. Working in respectful partnership with parents improves outcomes for all, the parent, the child and the practitioner (Einarsdottir & Jónsdóttir, 2019).

Partnership and respectful engagement are needed if practitioners are to enrich professional relationships and enhance outcomes for all, the parent, the child and the practitioner. Hearing what parents have to say about a specific issue and looking at a situation holistically often unearths an alternative perspective to the initial interpretation. Only when we had the full picture can we offer appropriate support, guidance or information. Acknowledging where your own perceptions originate can be insightful and enlightening. Respectful dialogue leaves no room for presumptions and assumptions.

Parents as experts

If we examine the title used in this chapter in greater detail, we find the value attributed to the role of parents is an issue here too. The word 'Are' as in Parents Are Experts implies a fact. A definitive declaration. Something that is undeniable. Whereas the word 'As' indicates something could be a possibility. A mere transient proposition or an attempt to be something more than is currently recognised.

The reluctance to recognise parents really are experts could be due to a perceived threat by those who currently hold the power. Does the word 'Are' threaten the position or power of the practitioner, undermining their perceived generosity of seeing parents 'as experts' rather than stating they 'are' experts? Could the choice of word be an example of unconscious bias? Alternatively, it could be acknowledged that the use of the word 'as' is an indication of the early stages of learning.

When it comes to our bodies and our minds, we as individuals are the definitive experts. We know how we feel, and we know what we think. The knowledge attuned parents and practitioners hold in relation to the children in their care is similar. Their knowledge is central to understanding each unique child. This is especially true for preverbal children, those with a limited vocabulary or those lacking in confidence. Parents and practitioners know their children. They know their routines, their idiosyncrasies and their motivation. Or at least they have their own perception of these things.

Parents and practitioners know their child's story and their own story too. Being able to share the expertise they hold is fundamental to feeling like they have a voice. When working with practitioners, parents need to feel validated and know what they contribute holds value. All too often if the voice of the parent is not heard or when individuals feel they are not seen or not valued, their behaviour becomes their voice. This leads to missed opportunities. Change is strongly influenced by mindset. Dweck (2012, p. 245) suggests people have either a fixed or growth mindset. These differing approaches influence our predisposition to believe either our intelligence or abilities are static or can be developed. Individuals with a fixed mindset go through life believing that their innate skills, talents and mental capacity cannot be changed or expanded upon. Alternatively, those with a growth mindset are open to experiencing the constant evolution of life, believing intelligence is something that grows and develop (Table 11.1).

Fixed	Growth
Inability to hear or accept negative feedback or criticism	An open-minded approach to negative feedback and criticism
A strong drive to prove their intelligence by avoiding failure	The ability to see failure as an opportunity to learn
A tendency to avoid challenges and tasks that require extra effort	The desire to seek out challenge in order to grow
The inclination to give up when things do not go as planned	The perseverance and determination to overcome setbacks
Feeling threatened by the success of others	Finding inspiration in the achievements of others

Table 11.1   Fixed or growth mindset

Source: Adapted from Dweck (2012, p. 245).

REFLECTI●N

Considering the qualities listed above that identify the fixed and growth mindsets.

Do you identify with one particular mindset over another?

Do you find that you ever alternate between the two?

Try to identify the areas of your life where you feel you are utilising a fixed mindset and any occasions you feel you may utilise a growth mindset.

Growth mindset	Fixed mindset
....	....
....	....
....	....

'Parents <u>Are</u> Experts': A new way of working in practice

As practitioners working with expectant, new, experienced or established parents, the responsibility is on us to find ways to connect and hear their voice, to acknowledge their perspective and to see their unique set of circumstances. Identifying ways to ensure parents feel seen, heard and valued is imperative to the successful construction of a reciprocal relationship (Torronen, Munn Giddings, & Tarkianinen, 2017) Trust, acceptance and authenticity are all key components of this connection. All are essential for the flow of honest dialogue, which is needed if parents are to feel accepted and affirmed. Creating a safe space, free of judgement, is central to the success of interactions Kline (2009).

Manor and Castle Development Trust (2022), based in Sheffield, is a community development organisation that place voice and lived experience at the centre of their vision, values and practice. Designed to be a catalyst for economic and social change in the community, they take an enabling role towards empowering local people to take control over their own lives. They have led the design, delivery and development of 'Parents Are Experts', a series of self-awareness sessions designed for parents and carers. These sessions ensure parents have a voice, feel affirmed and promote a sense of belonging. 'Parents Are Experts' holds parents in the highest esteem and validate the individual skills, knowledge and insight parents hold in relation to their own children.

Building the self-efficacy of parents, these sessions ensure parents start to accept and believe that they are vital to the success of their children. Parents access the most recent research and information in an accessible format. The practical activities are relatable and easy to understand. This is imperative as it is not the information provided, but *how* the information is presented, dissected and interpreted that creates an impact. Affirmation and scaffolding by people who value parents and children as individuals has proved to be the best way to make a positive impact on resilience and self-efficacy.

The concepts and activities shared during the 'Parents Are Experts' sessions include perception, the Enneagram, mindset, the signals of deep level learning, schemas and adult strategies. The reflective approach utilised helps these concepts resonate on an individual level and they therefore provide a catalyst for change. This approach is grounded in positivity and promotes a proactive stance which encourages growth. The emphasis during the course is on the strengths and positive attributes of the children and parents. Throughout 'Parents Are Experts', the concept of **attachment** is strengthened, and peer support networks form organically.

CASE STUDY: 'PARENTS ARE EXPERTS' PARTICIPANT, 2021

*Because I had a history of depression, when I was given information about post-natal depression with the rest of the group at the ante natal classes, it was like … this is what it **will** be like to have PND, not how I could prevent it occurring in the first place or any coping strategies.*

Having completed 'Parents Are Experts' I think that although it may not have fully prevented the PND it *This word was used by the participant it is authentic so I included it gave me the coping strategies that I was missing and the confidence to know that what I was doing as a parent was the best I could do.

My mindset, and the mindset of the professionals as I went into parenthood, was that post-natal depression was inevitable for me. Through 'Parents Are Experts' I learned that nothing is fixed and that with the right support and a new perspective you can become more tolerant of yourself, accepting of your flaws, and more tolerant of others and their flaws. It's about learning everyone is just trying to survive in their own way, the best that they can.

This has had a huge impact on my life and the quality of my interactions. The information and discussion around Mindset and The Enneagram challenged my perception as I initially thought I had a growth mindset. Realising that I had a fixed mindset on some issues challenged my idealistic view of myself and of others. I can now see that although my ideals and theirs may be different the tolerance and understanding I acquired means it does not bother me as it did before.

Basically, 'Parents Are Experts' brought the written word to life. Applying the written examples to my lived experience made me understand their relevance and I changed my behaviour as a result.

The evaluations collected at the end of 'Parents Are Experts' sessions provide evidence that through engagement and observation of play, exploration, discussion, acceptance and awareness, children and their parents can gain a growth mindset. This impacts directly on their self-esteem, self-efficacy and self-compassion for years to come. The language utilised throughout 'Parents Are Experts' is linked to 'The Power of Yet' (Dweck, 2014), a concept that promotes the idea that by facilitating time, space and patience to allow for mastery, children and parents will be helped to develop skills and understanding at their own pace.

The word 'failed' is replaced by 'not yet' which in Dweck's words provides 'a pathway into the future ... instead of 'luxuriating in the power of yet, you are gripped in the tyranny of now' (Dweck, 2014). The idea that 'being present' and allowing time to think and try again helps to form strong attachments and build reciprocal relationships, fostering a culture of reflection, discussion, improvement and success. It provides hope.

'Parents Are Experts': The sessions

Participants, both men and women, consider the concepts of perception first utilising optical illusions and using memory games. This creates a supportive environment and helps them to view things differently. The sessions also identify their dominant learning style which informs the delivery of future sessions. The value placed on them as parents is highlighted, and the idea that they should acknowledge the important role they play in laying down the foundations for their child's brain is introduced. The term conceptual engineers is explored as a new term initially created for the sessions and is used in relation to parents and practitioners. It challenges their dismissive personal perception that they are 'just a parent'.

The Enneagram (Riso & Hudson, 1999) is explored in the second session. This insightful personality portrait system is a tool for identifying personality types. Feedback confirms parents often feel this is the most enlightening and fun element of the sessions. An online quiz is undertaken, and the answers determine the feedback. Other personality tests are available such as Myers-Briggs (1943), but the Enneagram is extremely accurate and relatable. Participants generally request access to additional quizzes for significant adults in their lives, as the level of insight and understanding reached in a short space of time is phenomenal.

The third and fourth sessions combine the signals of well-being and involvement (Laevers, 1994) and explain how these signals relate to the concept of deep level learning. Parents watch videos and assess the signals. Familiarising themselves with these strategies helps them assess their own children and many parents apply the signals to themselves. Parents often find carrying out the assessment affirming, especially as they are using videos of local children that parents have recorded in previous sessions. Mindset is also revisited with practical application and discussions of their children and their actions.

Schemas (Atherton & Nutbrown, 2013; England, 2018; Meade & Cubey, 2008; Whalley et al., 2007) or patterns in children's play is another topic that is examined.

Many children are fascinated by repetitive actions as they make sense of the world. Allowing children to explore materials in the manner that are drawn too as they construct their understanding of the world is beneficial to their problem-solving skills. Turning a car upside down and spinning the wheels is typical behaviour associated with a rotation schema. This can be frustrating for parents and practitioners as many feel there is a 'proper' way to play with a car. Other common schemas such as trajectory, enclosure envelopment and going through a boundary are also explored as it is not what children are playing with but how they are playing that is key to understanding what they are learning. Once parents understand these patterns are evidence of learning, rather than dysfunctional behaviour, they see their children in a new light. 'As daft as it seems him spinning round and rolling them balls down that banking is teaching him a lot about gravity', Parent A (2019). Allowing children to lead their own leaning and explore schemas in their own way is central to the construction of a positive self-image and self-efficacy (Bandura, 1997). Using the past successes and failures, of ourselves, of our peers and of other relatable figures, including those we see on social media, helps us to understand ourselves. Parents also state that understanding why children do what they do 'helps melt- frustration', Parent B.

The 'Little Schema Series' Kettleborough (2019) have proved invaluable. These books, written at the request of Parents Are Experts participants, help challenge the perception of parents that children need to be 'taught'; they begin to accept and believe that their children are strong, capable and intelligent. This is reiterated throughout Parents Are Experts and reflects the beliefs of Edwards, Gandini, and Forman (2011) and the Reggio Emilia approach. Parents also start to look at themselves in a different, more respectful light too. Nurturing a love of learning is central. The transformational approach utilised guarantees a positive impact. This is reflected in the evaluations received from participants of all genders.

The philosophy of the approach is that the tacit knowledge parents hold about their children and themselves can be deeper and more detailed to that of the specialised professional. Parents focus on a holistic and rounded approach when given information and the tools of reflection. Working together in a respectful manner has proven to be transformational. It benefits the child, the parent and wider society and provides confirmation and reassurance that parents are indeed the experts. A positive outcome from the Parents Are Experts sessions is that there are improvements in the parent's confidence and their self-efficacy. Practitioners report improvements in children's self-efficacy, behaviour and their self-esteem. Parents also spoke of how the number of positive interventions increased within the home learning environment, alongside more purposeful conversations and an increase in the incidence of compliance.

The final session relates to the role of the adult. Peer support is key. Parents bring their lived experience and discuss strategies that have worked well and those that have not. Utilising the ideas of De Bono (1985), we again reflect using his world-renowned Six Thinking Hats method of thinking.

Following the sessions, many parents progress into further or higher education, volunteer work or make changes in their employment status. Most importantly though, parents reported that they enjoy being parents. All because we value parents as the experts they are. Recognising the importance of building reciprocal relationships, talking with, rather than to, parents explaining the latest research and listening to their ideas and concerns.

The role of the practitioner

Staying up to date in the professional sphere is key. Seeking to understand developments in all areas and identify ways to apply them for optimum impact is part of the role of the practitioner. The developments in neuroscience, for example, are relatively new, and although they are beginning to trickle down to practitioners, many practitioners who have been trained for some time may not be aware of their value. Utilising the recent information is vital to improve outcomes for parents and children across society.

The recent high-profile survey carried out by Ipsos MORI (2021) in conjunction with the Royal Foundation found 'parents tend to underestimate the importance of the early years' (p. 22).

Seeking to understand your why, your purpose and the purpose of others are paramount to understanding how to support others. Putting learning into practice is essential. Working with others, in collaboration, is also an enormous part of a practitioner's role. This will diversify perspective, making practitioners aware of the varying viewpoints previously not considered and being able to cascade this information.

The role of the early childhood practitioner is to create meaningful relationships which support learning and development, while facilitating reflective practice (Whalley et al., 2007). The ability to provide respectful challenge which may facilitate change and extend understanding is pivotal to being a successful practitioner. This means listening.

If you are genuinely interested in someone, they will know. Listening to understand is a skill that needs regular practice. Once practitioners have mastered the skill, they will be able to quickly establish rapport and ask at least 'one good question'. The question asked should resonate with the individual concerned and inspire them to think in a way that challenges, helping them make choices and become confident in their decision-making ability.

Generally, people listen while waiting for their turn to speak. The desire to contribute to a conversation often leads to interruptions. Practitioners presume their perspective and opinions are vital. What most people need, however, is the space and time to think (Ephgrave, 2017; Fisher, 2016; Kline, 1999). Practitioners may have an idea of what choices they think a parent, child or colleague may have, but this presumption can be unfounded. It is based on their own view of the world, their own life map (Borland, 2019). Learning to lay a personal perspective of the world, or a specific situation to one side when involved in active and effective listening, is a complex skill. What works for one parent will not always work for another.

When a practitioner is driven to help to solve a problem on behalf of a child, parent or colleague without providing the time for all those involved to think, there is a limited purpose attached to the solution. It places the recipient of that solution as a passive participant, rather than the protagonist. It disregards the intrinsic motivation needed to change behaviour or a perspective. Allowing sufficient time to think can result in them identifying their own solution.

By listening to understand and gain clarity about the circumstances of an individual, practitioners provide time for that individual to reflect on their position and perspective. Parents generally have their own solutions and answers to complex issues but need information before they can verbalise their solutions. Speaking our thoughts out loud without being interrupted is invaluable. When parents are seen as experts and explore solutions collaboratively, they are more invested in the strategies or learning that occurs.

REFLECTION

Listen to a parent, child or colleague without interrupting in an attempt to learn something new.

Ask them one good question and give them the opportunity to answer. This means leaving them with enough time to think a minimum of up to 60 seconds, ideally 2–3 minutes. Do not attempt to fill the perceived void. Record the response.

Reflect on your own **'life map'** and how this may have an impact on effective listening.

Ensuring adequate time to think, without polarising options, is crucial. Given a specific situation, people often believe their options are limited. The idea they have to do one thing or another is generally accepted, that is, I don't like my job – put up with it or leave. The reality is different. As practitioners, it is important to encourage people to explore the middle ground. Learning to leave our life map under our chairs while listening to others helps in our quest to listen to understand. Effective listening is central to the role of a good practitioner (Kline, 1999).

Conclusion

The rhetoric surrounding the value of parents is both audible and visible. It is reflected in the current language of politicians and professionals. But the reality is far different. The term *Parents Are Experts* appears within the non-statutory guidance relating to the progress check for two-year-olds provided by the Department of Education.

While practitioners and other professionals can support children's development and wellbeing individually, they can achieve so much more by working together.

(DfE, 2022, p. 2)

Yet collaboration with parents is still limited. The 2-year-old progress check (DfE, 2022) has a small section reserved for parents to complete. True partnership dictates this should be completed **with** the parent in collaboration throughout its entirety. This would provide a holistic view in relation to the child and ensures the parents' voice is heard and acknowledged. The fact that within the United Kingdom this document is only currently available in English speaks volumes.

Over half a million people in the United Kingdom recently took part in the largest public study that has ever been undertaken on the early years (Royal Foundation, 2020). The findings within the study back up the personal experiences shared by parents who have accessed the Parents Are Experts sessions over a 15-year period. The inescapable fact is that parents have and still feel undervalued, undermined or dismissed by many professionals and society. This needs to change.

A high number of parents, 70% admitted to feeling judged by others, with 48% saying this had taken an emotional toll. We want society to feel involved in the collective nurturing of the next generation but it is important that we make this a positive mission, giving parents encouragement in place of critique.

(Royal Foundation, 2020, p. 2)

Support and an inclusive approach needs to be more forthcoming from professionals and practitioners. It needs to be the norm rather than the exception. It would benefit society as a whole if all professionals collaborated and consulted with parents in relation to their children. Information relating to developmental science, specifically brain development in the early years, needs to be available, considered and actively promoted.

Understanding the varied circumstances parents encounter is a start. The subsequent chapters within this book aim to provide an additional perspective for all readers. Information is vital if we are to make a difference in the lives of others. Listening is our superpower. Allowing people and children to feel seen, heard and valued is the key to transforming our work environments and society as a whole.

Further reading

Bandura, A. (1997). *Self-efficacy: The exercise of control.* New York: W.H Freeman.

Conkbayir, M. (2017). *Early childhood and neuroscience: Theory, research and implications for practice.* London: Bloomsbury.

Department for Health and Social Care (DHSC). (2021). *The best start for life, a vision for the first 1001 critical days: The early years healthy development review report.* Retrieved from: https://assets.publishing. service.gov.uk/government/uploads/system/uploads/attachment_data/file/973112/The_best_start_for_ life_a_vision_for_the_1_001_critical_days.pdf (Accessed 9th August 2022).

Useful websites

www.manorandcastle.org.uk/little-schema-shop/

www.enneagraminstitute.com

References

Atherton, F., & Nutbrown, C. (2013). *Understanding schemas and young children.* London: From Birth to Three SAGE Publications.

Bandura, A. (1977). Self efficacy: Toward a unifying theory of behaviour change. *Psychological Review. Stanford University, 84,* 191–215.

Borland, J. (2019). *Coaching in the great unknown: Why not knowing matters more than you know.* Independent Publishing Network.

DeBono, E. (1985). *Six thinking hats.* New York, NY: Little Brown Company.

Department of Education and Science. (1967). *The Plowden report: Children and their primary schools.* London: HMSO.

DfES (Department for Education and Skills). (2003). *Every child matters.* Green paper, Cm. 5860. London: The Stationery Office (TSO).

Department for Health and Social Care (DHSC). (2021). *The best start for life, a vision for the first 1001 critical days: The early years healthy development review report.* Retrieved from: https://assets.publishing. service.gov.uk/government/uploads/system/uploads/attachment_data/file/973112/The_best_start_for_life_a_ vision_for_the_1_001_critical_days.pdf (Accessed 9th August 2022).

DfE. (2022). *Progress check at two-non statutory guidance for the early years foundation stage.* Crown Copyright.

Dweck, C. S. (2012). *Mindset – how you can fulfil your potential.* London: Robinson.

Dweck, C. (2014). *The power of yet.* TED Talk. Retrieved from: https://www.youtube.com/watch?v=J-swZaKN2Ic (Accessed 14th September 2022).

Edwards, C., Gandini, L., & Forman, G. (2011). *The hundred languages of children. The Reggio Emilia l experience* (3rd ed.). Connecticut: Praeger, ABC-CLIO.

Einarsdottir, J., & Jónsdóttir, A. H. (2019). Parent-preschool partnership: Many levels of power. *Early Years, 39*(2), 175–189. doi:10.1080/09575146.2017.1358700

Ephgrave, A. (2017). Planning in the moment with young children. In *A practical guide for early years practitioners.* London: Routledge.

England, L. (2018). *Schemas: A practical handbook.* Bloomsbury Publishing.

Fisher, J. (2016). *Interacting or interfering improving interactions in the early years.* Berkshire: Mc Graw Hill Education. Open University Press.

Harris, M. A., & Orth, U. (2019). The link between self-esteem and social relationships: A meta-analysis of longitudinal studies. *Journal of Personality and Social Psychology,* 2020 Dec, *119*(6), 1459–1477.

HMSO. (1972). *The James Report: Teacher education and training.* London: HMSO.

Kettleborough, W. J. (2019). *Matthew lines things up.* Sheffield: Northend Print.

Kline, N. (1999). *Time to think: Listening to the human mind.* London: Cassell.

Kline, N. (2009). *Time to think: Listening to ignite the human mind.* London: Octopus.

Laevers, F. (1994). *The Leuven involvement scale for young children, LIS-YC manual and video tape, experiential educational series no. 1.* Leuven: Centre of Experiential Education.

Manor and Castle Development Trust. (2022). *Who we are.* Retrieved from: https://manorandcastle.org.uk/ (Accessed 9th August 2022).

Meade, A., & Cubey, P. (2008). *Thinking children, learning about schemas.* Berkshire: Open University Press.

Riso, D., & Hudson, R. (1999). *The wisdom of the enneagram. The complete guide to psychological and spiritual growth.* London: Bantam.

The Royal Foundation. (2020). *State of the nation: Understanding public attitudes to the early years.* Ipsos MORI.

The Rumbold Report. (1990). *Starting with quality the report of the committee of inquiry into the quality of the educational experience offered to 3 and 4 year olds, chaired by Mrs Angela Rumbold CBE MP london: Her Majesty's stationery office 1990.*

Torronen, M., Munn Giddings, C., & Tarkianinen, L. (2017). *Reciprocal relationships and wellbeing: Implications for social work and social policy.* London: Routledge.

Warnock Report. (1978). *Special educational needs. Report of the committee of enquiry into the education of handicapped children and young people.* London: Her Majesty's Stationery Office.

Winter, P., Ministerial Council for Education, Early Childhood Development and Youth Affairs (Australia), & Early Childhood Services Ltd. (2010). *Engaging families in the early childhood development story: Neuroscience and early childhood development: Summary of selected literature and key messages for parenting.*

Whalley, M. (Ed.), & Pen Green Team. (2007). *Involving parents in their children's learning.* London: SAGE.

12 PRACTICE PERSPECTIVE: LEARNING FROM TANZANIA

MWAJUMA KIBWANA, DAVIS GISUKA AND PHILIPPA THOMPSON

CHAPTER OBJECTIVES

By the end of this chapter, you will be able to:

- Reflect on the influence of parental engagement on learning at home and in school environments.
- Consider the role of parents in the child school feeding programme in Tanzania.
- Review parental engagement mechanisms and approaches in Tanzania.
- Consider the importance of engaging parents in the early years of children's learning using a range of methods.

KEY DEFINITIONS

Parents

Any person who has parental responsibility or has care of a young child during early childhood (from conception to eight years of age).

Practitioner

A person who is qualified to work with children (from conception to 8 years old) across health, education and social care.

BRAC Maendeleo

This is an international organisation, a subsidiary of Stichting BRAC International (BRAC), a global non-government working in Asia and Africa. In Tanzania, BRAC Maendeleo is focussing on thematic areas of early childhood development, education, youth and women empowerment, agriculture, food security and livelihood, water and sanitation. Their focus is to reduce poverty and empower marginalised people to realise their potential.

CiC

Children in Crossfire – an international organisation working on early childhood development, particularly offering early stimulation opportunities through pre-primary education as well as promotion of quality access of early childhood development services in Tanzania.

CRS

Catholic Relief Services – an official international humanitarian agency of the Catholic community in the United States founded in 1943 by the US Conference of Catholic Bishops.

EGPAF

An international organisation working to prevent, care and optimise both HIV treatment and early childhood development alongside strengthening government systems.

Maarifa ni Ufunguo (MnU)

A non-government and non-profit organisation with a vision of advocating for equity and accessible and affordable good quality education for marginalised and impoverished communities.

PPE

Pre-primary education.

TAHEA

A national professional non-government organisation of nutritionist, agriculture, home economics and other related social sciences.

TECDEN

Tanzania Early Childhood Development Network – a national NGO mandated to coordinate non-state actors in supporting the government to promote early childhood development in Tanzania.

Introduction

This chapter explores how the United Republic of Tanzania early childhood services responded to children and families during the recent COVID-19 pandemic. The key to the success of the work, which was spread over a wide geographical space, was the partnership with parents and the community leaders. The chapter explores the development of the project and how by responding quickly, utilising a range of services, all parents, children and practitioners were involved in a successful scheme that has had far-reaching and unexpected positive outcomes. This global perspective enables practitioners and students to consider their own local and possibly national practice during this time and beyond. Understanding how and why this project developed enables us to question how we support and work in partnership with vulnerable families in times of continuing crises.

United Republic of Tanzania is an East African country made up of the union of Tanganyika and Zanzibar Island. It has an estimate population of 60 million, out of which 50% is estimated to be below the age of 18 years, while more than 30% are 0–9 years (National Bureau of Statistics, 2013). The country has formalised pre-primary schooling, whilst early childhood development (ECD) programmes remain for 0–8 years. Tanzania is like many other African countries where parenting work has been left to the mothers with the belief that they are sole primary caregivers. This cultural perspective has made all the burden of nurturing to be left to the mother alone, for example, playing with a child, feeding and caring for sick child; hence, there is very minimal interaction between father and young children.

The UNICEF Child Care Development (CCD) package has catalysed father's engagement in child rearing. Examples taken from Elizabeth Glaser Pediatric AIDS Foundation (EGPAF) in the Tabora Region and Catholic Relief Services (CRS) in the Mbeya Region have generated evidence on parenting transformation following the implementation of CCD programmes. Children in Crossfire (CiC) has engaged parents in their ECD programmes through parent groups that are vested with responsibilities to contribute to the development of low-cost/no-cost learning materials for their children to use them in schools and at home. This good practice in parental engagement is considered in the recently launched National Multi-sectoral ECD Programme (NM-ECDP 2021/2022-2025/2026) as an effective model in improving children's learning outcomes.

Working collaboratively with the government, ECD stakeholders worked to innovate solutions to mitigate COVID-19 effects, related to early learning. This chapter explores how *Maarifa ni Ufunguo* presents parental engagement is supporting child learning both at school and in the home environment.

National pre-primary education curriculum

In 1995, the government of Tanzania reviewed their Education and Training Policy and, in this year, pre-primary education (PPE) was recognised as part of the primary education in Tanzania. However, it was not emphasised that it was necessary to be considered as part of the education system. There was no curriculum which was prepared to support the implementation of the PPE.

A further Education and Training Policy review was completed in 2014, resulting in a new education policy. This Education and Training Policy of 2014 (ETP, 2014) made it clear that PPE was obligatory and that each primary school would need to allocate a pre-primary class. Tanzania Institute of Education (TIE) had the mandate to develop the first pre-primary curriculum ever in Tanzania. This first pre-primary curriculum was developed in 2016 and introduced in 2017 following a curriculum orientation for all pre-primary teachers across the country. TIE also developed textbooks for the children, which focussed on a play-based approach with a shift from knowledge-based curriculum to a competence-based curriculum.

The education policy allowed children aged 3–5 years to be enrolled in PPE, who will then spend one year of PPE before being enrolled into Standard One. The policy has said that 'the government will ensure that PPE is mandatory for children between 3 and 5 years for a period of not less than one year' (ETP, 2014, p. 24). However, the curriculum has made it clear that its focus is on 5-year-old children (PPE Curriculum, 2016, p. 4). It has provided an opportunity for 3- and 4-year-olds to be enrolled if pre-assessment is done and found that they have criteria which have been set.

In Tanzania, there is a large scarcity of the pre-primary professionals despite the policy and curriculum focus on the pre-primary practitioners. Pre-primary practitioners are responsible for implementing this curriculum. The pre-primary practitioner must have a minimum of a certificate in teaching though the major focus for a qualified teacher is a diploma holder and above. As explained in the previous paragraph, each primary school must allocate a classroom for the pre-primary school children. All pre-primary settings are found within the school compound and this involves both public and private schools.

The PPE curriculum has a section describing the importance of involving parents and the community into the implementation of curriculum. It also states that parents and community engagement in the PPE is extremely important in early stimulation for children 'so as to prepare a child ready for learning and entering into Standard One' (PPE Curriculum, 2016, p. 15).

This section in the PPE curriculum has listed some of the responsibilities of parents and community members in relation to the implementation of the curriculum. It has listed five roles as seen below:

1 Making decisions about the establishment and implementation of the pre-school at their locality

2 Contributions from parents, practitioners and other professionals for school development

3 Following up child learning progress at both school and home

4 Participating in the learning and teaching via various ways such as developing and providing learning materials, telling stories and preparing positive, enabling learning environments that consider inclusive education

5 Assessing children's learning progress.

Other major activities which parents have been highly involved in are the provision of a feeding programme at school as well as constructing and renovating classrooms for the pre-primary children. Clear involvement and engagement of parents has helped children access good infrastructure and nutrition. Through parent meetings, teachers and parents discuss about many challenges which need to be addressed so as to have smooth implementation of the PPE. Therefore, as part of the agreement, parents normally contribute some money for renovation of the classrooms. Organisations like CiC provide funding for classroom construction, whilst parents contribute people power and some construction materials like sand and stones depending on the need.

In the past two years, CiC, in collaboration with parents and school management committees, has managed to construct about 30 new classrooms for pre-primary children across Mwanza and Dodoma Regions. Moreover, about 200+ classrooms were renovated through the efforts put together among CiC and parents of pre-primary children. At some schools, age-appropriate toilets were constructed. Interestingly, at one school called Bukindo in Ukerewe Island in Mwanza, parents of the children who were in pre-primary in 2018 contributed money and managed to construct a new classroom for their children. CiC together with the district council was able to construct age-appropriate toilets to support young children. Similar to the contributions on construction of school infrastructures, parents are also contributing food for their children (mainly porridge). Parents through their meetings with teachers at school form a parent committee which is vested with responsibilities to collect parental contributions (money) as well as agreeing the schedule for them to prepare porridge throughout the school calendar.

It is a requirement for all government and private schools/settings in Tanzania to use the PPE curriculum to teach children. The Ministry of Education, Science and Technology (MoEST) has a quality assurance department that is responsible to follow up on how the curriculum is using the national school quality assurance framework. They monitor how the curriculum is implemented as well as all other issues that are relevant for making positive and inclusive learning environments such as infrastructure. They do this using a mentorship approach to help education practitioners improve their work. Therefore, all schools are monitored to ensure that the PPE curriculum is implemented as per the required standard.

REFLECTION

Consider the website (https://www.tie.go.tz) in conjunction with the section you have just read about the Tanzanian PPE curriculum above. Reflect on the following activity:

- Find the section on pre-primary curriculum and look at page 17 (4.12). Whilst a short section, it is powerful. How does this compare with wording about parent partnership in the Early Years Foundation Stage statutory framework (Department for Education, 2021) and Birth to 5 Matters (Early Years Coalition, 2021)?

Using distance learning during the COVID-19 pandemic in Tanzania

Following the first confirmed case of COVID-19 in March 2020, Tanzania banned all public gatherings and closed all educational institutions. This included pre-primary,

primary and secondary schools; technical and vocational education; training institutions and universities (International Labour Organization (ILO), 2021). The use of information and communication technology provided alternative learning to the majority, although this was not equally accessible to all children as some of the villages (2,384 out of 12,884) still did not have access to electricity. Schools remained closed until June 2020 when Tanzania became the first among East African countries to re-open the schools.

The MoEST has the department for the quality assurance from the ministry level to the ward level. Their main role is to monitor the quality provision of education at all schools. So, this body looks at the quality of provision of education using the National School Quality Assurance Framework. They monitor how the curriculum is implemented as well as all other issues that are relevant for making positive and inclusive learning environments such as infrastructure. They do this using a mentorship approach to help education practitioners improve in their work.

To respond to the COVID-19 onset and nationwide school closures, CiC conducted a rapid assessment pointing to the majority of rural young children missing out on digital broadcast remote learning programmes given lack of access to television, radio and smartphones. CiC worked with the Tanzania MoEST and other ECD stakeholders including **BRAC Maendeleo** and **Tanzania Early Childhood Development Network (TECDEN)** to develop a print-based PPE activity workbook aligned to the national PPE curriculum, providing simple guidance on play-based learning activities that parents could facilitate with their young children at home using locally available no-cost resources.

The printed workbook was chosen versus the online resources due to poor access to technological devices such as smartphones; unavailability of electricity in some rural areas as well as poor purchasing power of Internet bundle to give access to the online resources. Moreover, 80% of Tanzania citizens live in rural areas and with no capacity to own smartphone. Therefore, the printed workbook could reach everyone regardless of their socioeconomic status.

Constructing the workbook

The idea of developing this workbook came from CiC following the closure of the schools due to the COVID-19 impact. The schools were closed for undisclosed periods and children would miss out learning opportunities as they had no access to school.

Initiatives began with delegates from CiC communicating to the sector ministries. The MoEST which is responsible for developing policy and guidelines and the President's Office, Regional Administration and Local Government (PO-RALG) were contacted as those with responsibility for monitoring implementation of education activities. After holding discussions between these agencies, it was agreed that the virtual meeting which would involve other stakeholders could be organised. Therefore, this initiative involved pre-primary teachers, TIE, CiC, sector ministries, regional education officials, district education officials, ward education officers, education development partners and CiC's implementing partners.

The idea of developing a workbook was to support children to have access to learning while they were at home waiting for when the schools would re-open. As has been discussed previously, most children live in rural areas where many parents have no access to technology. It was not possible there-fore, to support the children with learning activities like those in private schools. There were no health practitioners involved as this was an initiative heavily focussed on the education curriculum. This has potential to be considered in future work.

The role of the participants in this meeting was to think how the workbook should be designed and what activities should be included in the workbook. Pre-primary teachers and the ECD and education technical specialist from CiC were assigned to develop and design activities. These activities were shared in the large group for review and decision. It was agreed that a small technical team from CiC and TIE would meet for two days to fine-tune the contents, and finally the contents were taken to the designer who could draw pictures before being taken to the printers for printing. A large number of activities were extracted from the existing PPE curriculum.

CASE STUDY: PARENTS SUPPORTING CHILDREN LEARNING AT HOME

At the meeting, participants decided that all activities that would feature in the workbook would reflect the PPE curriculum. It was then decided that pre-primary teachers and an education specialist from CiC would take part in the designing and developing activities. Therefore, activities came from the 1026 PPE curriculum by making them simple and user friendly for the parents to be able to support their children at home.

Despite a willingness to engage with parents, this proved almost impossible for a variety of reasons. One of the key reasons was that the meetings were conducted virtually and needed strong Internet as well as the participant having a smart-phone or computer. Due to COVID-19, there was no opportunity to have physical meeting and by that time the government had banned all public physical meetings.

It took two months from the start to finish for the workbook to be ready for use. After two months, CiC in collaboration with the sector ministries and the TIE went to the field for practitioner orientation. This included how to use the workbook. This was done by taking all precautions towards COVID-19. Practitioners then took the role of orienting parents on how to use the book. They also distributed the books to parents. In order to fund this initiative, CiC wrote a proposal to UK Aid to request funding for support in responding to the COVID-19 pandemic so as to continue to support the learning activities for children. This was approved and the entire project was funded by UK Aid.

REFLECTION

This family workbook was constructed in a collaborative way with engagement from a range of services and for specific families. Whilst the country may have differing needs, there will also be similarities. In the United Kingdom, schools and settings remained open during the pandemic for key worker and vulnerable families. At the same time, there was an expectation for children of school age that learning should not be interrupted and teachers and early childhood practitioners were expected to adapt online systems to provide online learning at home. This had mixed results and for many families caused extra strain. Those without access to the Internet or without laptops were disadvantaged despite government introducing a laptop scheme. In Tanzania, the starting point was accessibility for all as is discussed in this chapter. The following reflective questions support thinking about how we can learn about parental engagement from a global perspective and to be inclusive in our practice.

1   What can we learn from this approach in Tanzania that could improve parental engagement across the United Kingdom?

2   How do you think the workbook experience benefitted families in a different way to online?

3   Why is it important to reflect on this approach within early childhood settings in the four nations of the United Kingdom?

Working with other agencies

The workbook was endorsed by government, and 14,000 copies printed to reach all PPE children enrolled in 142 PPE streams across Dodoma, Morogoro and Mwanza regions where CiC programming is implemented. The workbook development involved various education stakeholders and this happened after the schools were closed due to corona pandemic. Children needed continuing learning and as they had no access to school, the only way was to develop the activity workbook and support children to continue learning at home. National and local government oversaw the dissemination and orientation of PPE teachers and parents of PPE children across all schools to ensure adequate risk mitigation procedures in COVID-19 context. The workbooks were distributed to all parents alongside a basic learning kit. This learning kit included stationery items such as erasers, sharpeners, pencils, colour pencils, crayons and exercise books. This was decided by pre-primary practitioners with the knowledge of their children and families. The books were taken to the Department of Education at the district level and were received by the district education officer's office. It was then distributed to each school by the district education officer's office in collaboration with the chief quality assurance officer's office.

Once the workbooks were received by the parents, they started using them with their children. The project team and the government official made a follow-up visit to receive feedback from parents on how the books were used. From the feedback received from the parents, the workbooks proved very popular, with parents confirming the activities were practical for them to lead with their children and stimulated playful learning experiences at home using materials locally sourced. National and local government conducted field visits to observe use and receive feedback. With minor modifications, the workbook is currently being certified as a curricular resource.

CASE STUDY: HOME LEARNING ENVIRONMENT IMPROVED TO SUPPORT CHILDREN LEARNING

Matilda Mnyambugi a mother of Branslav and residence of Songambele village in Kongwa District in Dodoma Region was quoted by CiC when conducting field visit to assess impact of the family workbook. She said: *'When schools were closed because of COVID 19 it was a challenge for parents on how to help their children learn at home. We wanted to help our children but how? This family book has provided us with a guideline on how to help our children learn including drawing, identifying various pictures in the book and names of fruits in the book. For parents who were reached by this book has helped children to have continuation of learning while schools were closed contrary to those not reached by this book. There was a big different between those with access to this book and those who didn't have access of family workbook'.*

A joint visit which involved the national government officials, local government officials and the project team was organised and conducted with the aim of getting an insight of how the book was used by the parents. The feedback was collected by having a discussion with family members representatives, practitioners (pre-primary teachers and head teachers) and village leaders. This was done by asking questions whereby respondents responded by answering questions and sharing their experience.

The joint visit team comprised of the Assistant Director of Education and Administration for Pre- and Primary School, Pre-Primary Coordinator from PO-RALG, Quality Assurance Officers from both regional and district level, Regional Education Officer, District Education Officer, Ward Education Officers, CiC technical staff and CiC implementing partners-aarifa ni Ufunguo Tanzania Home Economic Association (TAHEA) and Childhood Development Organization staff.

The joint visit team met the Schools Management Committee representatives, village leaders, parents' representatives, school management, pre-primary teachers and children. Some of the questions which were asked involved but not limited to:

1 How has the activity workbook been successful?

2 How has it been beneficial to children?

3 Do you see it as part of the important curriculum resource? If yes, why?

4 Apart from being beneficial to children, do you see any other benefit of this book to you?

5 Who is involved in supporting young children learn at home using this book?

Through the discussion between the government, the book beneficiaries and CiC, the workbook was found to be a good curriculum resource which could benefit more children across the country, and government decided that it should be approved by TIE and used across all pre-primary unit in the country. Moreover, it has been adapted into large font, tactile and braille formats for children with visual impairments. Production and dissemination of this book was very important because it supported children with special needs to learn, especially those with visual impairment.

Post pandemic

Importantly, with the re-opening of schools, parents and PPE teachers continue to embrace the workbook, bringing closer together both teachers/parents and schools/homes in supporting a PPE child's learning. An additional 16,000 work-books have since been printed and distributed to PPE families in the Dodoma Region (located in central Tanzania) to support young children's learning. Dodoma is located at the middle of Tanzania geographically and is the capital city of the country. More than 14,000 workbooks have been distributed to the other two project regions, reaching a total of 30,000 workbooks distributed across all three regions.

After the re-opening of schools, practitioners are using the workbooks to assign homework to the children and parents are responsible for supporting children do their homework. Practitioners ensure that parents support their children by asking them to sign into the exercise book of the child to show that they have seen the homework.

The workbook has been submitted to the TIE for verification and approval so that it becomes a PPE resource for the PPE in all schools in Tanzania. It is still used by parents and other family members to help their young children learn at home. This has raised the parents' motivation and responsibilities to support their children through a meaningful and playful activities with children. Other neighbouring districts have been requesting to also be provided with the activity workbook so that their children can participate in activities at home.

The formation of parent learning groups

During the field visit to collect data on how the workbook has been successful or not, some area parents and village leaders declared that the workbook has helped them very much. At one village, a village chairperson said that this workbook has not only helped their children but had also helped parents to learn how to read and write.

When he was asked a question to explore more about how the workbook has helped parents, he stated that parents who were not able to read and write did not feel confident enough to seek support from a neighbour. To address this challenge, they decided to form village learning groups and asked teachers to start teaching them.

They started using evening time after they have completed their daily activities and met at a local learning centre. Through the dedicated support from the practitioners, they have managed to learn how to read and write. They are now able to support their children to take on learning activities at home. The parents stated that if it was not for this workbook, they would not have developed this motivation that has led them to be eager to learn how to read and write. This was one of the unexpected outcomes of the workbook. The project team and the government knew that there were parents who were not able to read and write, but nobody expected that parents of this group would think and decide to form learning groups. However, this motivation was also catalysed by the fact that there were good relationships between parents and practitioners. Parents were free to explain their wish and decision to practitioners because there was a good relationship. They did not feel shame to express their personal issues and practitioners were able to address this challenge. This now no longer exists within the group of parents who had children in pre-primary class at that time.

This is a good lesson to be taken to other areas which are experiencing a similar situation. It is planned that practitioners and community can work to establish good working relationships and seek out other parents who also would like to develop their literacy skills. Through working with local village communities and their young children, parents can also form small groups, start learning how to read and write and therefore support their own children whilst learning themselves.

REFLECTION

- How have you experienced partnership with parents that develops such strong relationships that enables parents to ask for further support?

- Parents are often very skilled at hiding their own literacy and mathematical needs. Can you think about how a setting could be inclusive for parents who are unable to read and write?

- Can you think of any unexpected benefits of family learning that you have been involved with or read about?

The role of the practitioner

The role of the early childhood practitioner is crucial in supporting children's learning at home. This is universal and is widely researched in both Tanzania and the United Kingdom (Russell et al., 2022; Sylva, Melhuish, Sammons, Siraj-Blatchford, & Taggart, 2004). Developing relationships where parents feel comfortable to engage with practitioners both in the setting and at home is crucial in early childhood. During the pandemic, many early childhood settings in the United Kingdom stayed open but struggled with a staffing crisis due to illness. In Tanzania, settings were closed and the knowledge of practitioners was valued as services came together in support of children and families.

For those children who were at school in the United Kingdom during the pandemic, and who were not children of key workers, many were at home being home schooled by parents. The issue here was that many of the parents were also trying to work from home. This caused high stress levels with parents trying to combine working and teaching (see Chapter 10 for links to the United Kingdom). The other rapid change was the move to instant online learning without a significant understanding of how many families did not have Internet access or access to laptops or computers. Whilst there was an emphasis to provide laptops through schools, demand outstripped supply so again the most vulnerable were excluded despite the best efforts of practitioners.

The role of the practitioner in Tanzania appears to be thoughtfully coordinated across government departments and practitioners with a strong understanding of the needs of families. This is perhaps a model for local authorities to consider in the future. Local practitioners understand local need, and in emergency situations such as a world pandemic, this local knowledge is vital, as Tanzania has demonstrated.

The regular communication between practitioners and parents to continue discussions around the workbook use was an important part of the process. Considering how we work together for outcomes that benefit all should be part of all team discussions. Practitioners in Tanzania were supported with communication bundles (including phones and sim cards) to support them to follow up with parents. The infrastructure was simple but thoughtful and supported by the wider community. Post pandemic, the practitioners continue to visit parents and encourage parents to visit the settings to share their experience. The emphasis on parental voice and inclusive partnerships have been key elements enabling this project to be successful.

The success of the project relied on the following:

- Conducting field visits for collecting feedback from the parents and other family members who support their children.
- Regular communication with parents on how the book was being used.
- Parents visiting practitioners and discussing various areas that they felt looked challenging.
- Strong understanding of the PPE curriculum and child development.

- Practitioners need to know the needs of children in terms of learning aspect.

- They need to know how best children of this age learn – play-based learning.

- They need to have teaching skills that focus on the activity/play-based knowledge.

There are also some excellent examples of parent partnerships in the United Kingdom, but it is important to remind ourselves that going back to basics and remembering that knowledge, communication and contact are the most vital aspects. It is often difficult for practitioners in the United Kingdom to prioritise outreach and home visit work whilst knowing that it really makes a difference. Perhaps it is time to reassess post pandemic how those relationships can be developed in a new era.

Conclusion

Through this workbook, parents have formed firm partnerships with practitioners regarding the PPE curriculum implementation. There were parents who were not able to read and write and the workbook has motivated them to form groups and use practitioners in their locality to teach them how to read and write. They are now able to read and write, and as a result, they are now able to support their children to engage with learning activities. They are no longer seeking for support from neighbours to come and support their children.

Since the activity book success with both parents and children, the TIE approval department has taken it to the commissioner for education for sign up so that it can be used by PPE implementation in Tanzania. Moreover, many parents across this project implementation have established a habit of visiting schools to talk to practitioners on how best they can continue supporting their children. Through regular visit of parents to school and parents' meetings, many parents are now approving and supporting a feeding programme and engaging in the development of learning and teaching materials.

Early childhood practitioners have declared that through this workbook, there has been a huge increase in positive engagement and participation of parents in various activities of PPE curriculum implementation. This emphasises that practitioner–parent partnership has been strengthened because of the development of this workbook. Even when meetings are scheduled by practitioners, a large number of parents attend and their participation has been positive. Despite the pandemic providing many challenges, the situation has enabled practitioners to come together with the local government and national government to work together to improve the life chances of both parents and young children.

Further reading

Mtahabwa, L., & Rao, N. (2010). Pre-primary education in Tanzania: Observations from urban and rural classrooms. *International Journal of Educational Development, 30*(3), 227–235.

Ndijuye, L. G. (2022). Developing conflict resolution skills among pre-primary children: Views and practices of naturalized refugee parents and teachers in Tanzania. *Global Studies of Childhood, 12*(2), 159–169.

Pence, A., & Shafer, J. (2006). Indigenous knowledge and early childhood development in Africa: The early childhood development virtual university. *Journal for Education in International Development, 2*(3).

Useful websites

https://www.worldbank.org/en/news/press-release/2021/12/17/tanzania-more-than-12-million-children-to-benefit-from-improved-preprimary-and-primary-education

http://www.tzonline.org/pdf/childdevelopmentpolicy.pdf

https://www.akdn.org/where-we-work/eastern-africa/tanzania/early-childhood-development-tanzania

https://m.youtube.com/watch?v=9Eb_RBulkOc&feature=youtu.be

https://www.moe.go.tz/sw (Education & Training Policy 2014)

https://www.tie.go.tz (The PPE Curriculum and related tools)

References

Department for Education. (2021). *Early years foundation stage: Statutory framework.* Retrieved from: https://www.gov.uk/government/publications/early-years-foundation-stage-framework–2 (Accessed 8th December 2022).

Early Years Coalition. (2021). *Birth to 5 Matters: Guidance for the Sector by the Sector.* Retrieved from: https://birthto5matters.org.uk/ (Accessed 8th December 2022).

National Bureau of Statistics, Ministry of Finance, Office of Chief Government Statistician President's Office, Finance, Economy and Development Planning Zanzibar. (2013). *Population distribution by age and sex. 2012 population and housing census.*

Russell, A. L., Hentschel, E., Fulcher, I., Ravà, M. S., Abdulkarim, G., Abdalla, O., & Wilson, K. (2022). Caregiver parenting practices, dietary diversity knowledge, and association with early childhood development outcomes among children aged 18-29 months in Zanzibar, Tanzania: A cross-sectional survey. *BMC Public Health, 22*(1), 1–14.

Sylva, K., Melhuish, E., Sammons, P., Siraj-Blatchford, I., & Taggart, B. (2004). The effective provision of pre-school education (EPPE) project: Final report. In *A longitudinal study funded by the DfES 1997–2004.* London: Department for Education and Skills/Institute of Education, University of London.

United Republic of Tanzania. (2012). *Basic statistics in education.* Dar es Salaam: Ministry of Education and Vocational Training.

United Republic of Tanzania. (2014). *Education and training policy.* Dar es Salaam: Tanzania Institute of Education, Ministry of Education and Vocational Training.

United Republic of Tanzania. (2016). *Pre-primary education curriculum, Tanzania Institute of education (TIE).* Dar es Salaam: Ministry of Education and Vocational Training.

United Republic of Tanzania. (2020). *Pre-primary, primary, secondary, adult, and non-formal education.* Dodoma: President's office, Regional Administration and Local government.

INDEX